THE DIVORCE
OF NATIONS

THE DIVORCE OF NATIONS

A DIPLOMAT'S INSIDE VIEW AS THE GLOBAL ORDER COLLAPSES

JOÃO VALE DE ALMEIDA

FL◈NT

To Miana

First published 2025

FLINT is an imprint of The History Press
97 St George's Place, Cheltenham,
Gloucestershire, GL50 3QB
www.flintbooks.co.uk

British Library Cataloguing in Publication Data.
A catalogue record for this book is available from the British
Library.

ISBN 978 1 80399 767 4

Typesetting and origination by The History Press
Printed and bound in Great Britain by TJ Books Limited, Padstow,
Cornwall

MIX
Paper | Supporting
responsible forestry
FSC
www.fsc.org   FSC® C013056

Proudly supporting

Trees for Life

Contents

Author's Note

This book reflects my own personal views and does not commit in any way other persons or institutions, and certainly not those with and for whom I worked. It is made from memory and notes, including personal recollections of single facts and events, and is an attempt to contextualise them in their contemporary reality and to put them in perspective against the current global landscape. It comprises my personal impressions of events at the time and my personal reflections today, acknowledging that what has happened in the meantime might have had an impact on the assessment I make of past situations. For all these reasons I appeal to the indulgence of my readers and those who are directly or indirectly mentioned or quoted in the book for any involuntary misrepresentation of facts, dates or statements.

Regardless of how they react to my own opinions and comments, I hope readers will find here ingredients for a better understanding of the current global context and an urgent reflection on how it could evolve, in the light of what has happened in the first quarter of the twenty-first century. The relative weight of each of the issues covered reflects their relevance in my professional experience and not necessarily their historic importance.

This book was written in different periods in 2023 and 2024 in Brussels, New York, Cambridge and Vilamoura. With the exception of the afterword, the drafting was concluded on 21 July 2024, the day US President Joe Biden announced his decision no longer to seek re-election – a significant date, among many, in a highly eventful first quarter of the century.

Introduction

No Century for the Old Order

As children, learn good manners. As young men, learn to control
the passions. In middle age, be just. In old age, give good advice.
Then die, without regret.

> Greek inscription from 300 BC at Ai-Khanoum,
> an ancient city in Afghanistan

These are alarming and puzzling times for each of our countries
and for the world as a whole. As the first quarter of the twenty-first
century wraps up, we have a clear sense of disruption and often
feel in despair. It is hard to understand how and why we got here.
And even more difficult to predict what to expect.

What we know for sure is that when the world needed convergence and joined-up efforts to shape a new century and address
global challenges, the international order did not help – it broke
down. We also realise that in our countries public opinion is more
polarised and extreme views are gaining ground. There is tension
in the air. And sometimes even politically motivated violence.

Historians will one day accurately describe and interpret the
last eventful twenty-five years, with the benefit of hindsight, critical distance and full access to documents. While we wait for their
assessment, first-hand accounts and personal, fresh memories –
even if necessarily subjective and partial – are useful contributions
to the full grasp of events and can provide inspiration for action.

As a European diplomat, I have had the opportunity to hold a
front-row seat for some significant geopolitical moments in recent
decades. As a citizen, I have lived through unique changes in our
societies, on both sides of the Atlantic and beyond. Now is the time

to follow the old Greek inscription and to try to 'be just' and 'give good advice'. It is time to revisit events and share my contemporary impressions as the European Commission president's chief of staff in Brussels and as the European Union (EU) Ambassador to the USA, to the United Nations (UN) and to the post-Brexit UK, and to reflect, from an assumed Euro-Atlantic perspective, upon what the future might bring.

This personal testimony of how nations – and indeed the world – have been sleepwalking towards what could become an 'Age of Divorce' is my contribution to raising awareness and urging action to prevent it.

• • •

Rather than following a rigorous chronological order, the lens of the book's narrative often zooms in, then out, bringing together single events and big-picture analysis, as well as mixing anecdote with more elaborate reflection, with the purpose of making it easier to identify the roots of the challenges facing our societies and the world today. Chapters can be read in isolation if so wished, as each of them attempts to put comments into a wider perspective, although collectively they aim to provide a comprehensive overview of the period.

The initial chapter provides a snapshot of the first quarter of the century and how it differs from the last one of its predecessor. I then go 'behind the scenes' to share an inside view of relevant events I attended and key personalities I met or closely observed, which somehow shaped the period, before looking at curious calendar coincidences and the main landmarks of four significant years in this period. Brexit, as the 'mother of all divorces', deserves both a personal and colourful recollection of the first 1,000 days and an analysis of the reasons behind it and its consequences. The EU's accomplishments as well as its underperformances at home and abroad and some of its most relevant actors are observed against the background of the evolving geopolitical and geoeconomic realities, with a sympathetic but also critical eye, considering the EU's global relevance and untapped potential. The last chapter before the afterword looks at the future with concern – but also with hope – and provides recommendations for what the EU and the West in general can and should do to avoid a global divorce. The afterword provides an assessment of the most recent, and worrying, events against the backdrop of the book's main assertions.

•••

As its first quarter winds down, how has the 'young' twenty-first century governed the world so far? How did it manage to 'control the passions'?

On balance, not well. Particularly in recent years. So far, the century's record is not flattering.

On the global front:

- Russia unlawfully invaded Ukraine and war returned to the European continent and to its political lexicon.
- The Middle East peace process and the Arab Spring frustrated the hopes they had raised, and open conflict and violence returned to the region with unpredictable consequences.
- China and the USA deepened their great-power rivalry.
- The Group of Seven (G7) and its challengers (China, Russia, Iran and others) grew as antagonising blocs, while countries in the South were tempted by a transactional approach, hedging their bets between rival axes.
- Jihad-inspired terrorism marked the beginning of the century and introduced non-state actors to the international relations landscape.
- Brexit proved to be more of a self-inflicted wound than a liberating act for the UK and weakened the EU and the West's collective global clout.
- Nuclear proliferation was given a freer ride, again risking international security.

- Globalisation thrived before it stalled, while new threats of de-coupling, protectionism and trade wars appeared on the horizon.
- The Covid-19 pandemic revealed the fragility of global responses to shared threats within an interconnected and interdependent world.
- The multilateral liberal order entered stress territory and the UN dangerously approached irrelevance, precisely when both were needed most.

At national level:

- Populism increasingly ravaged the USA, the EU countries and other liberal democracies, and promoted domestic polarisation, undermining governments' willingness and capacity to act on the global stage and damaging the overall reputation of democratic systems.
- Levels of inequality blamed on free trade and unfair sharing of wealth became intolerable for many and triggered anti-globalisation sentiment.
- Culture wars boosted by often manipulated social media exacerbated tensions, prejudice and violence in our societies.
- Sustainable development and climate action became top global priorities but began losing public support as their immediate cost became more visible than their long-term benefit.
- Breakthrough technological innovations promised new solutions for old problems but threatened existing jobs and skills, and could defy human control.

This is only some of the most recent evidence of the unfolding of a process of national and global fragmentation, which is unlikely to stop here. Today, all signs point in the wrong direction: if not corrected, the current trajectory will lead to a divorce both within and among nations and between humankind and planet Earth.

How and why did this happen? Where did we go so wrong?

The deep underlying trends that explain today's global context have been building up in recent decades, reflecting widening gaps in the way countries and populations perceive the world and would like to see it moving forward.

From the 2001 attacks in downtown Manhattan to the 2022 attacks in downtown Kyiv, throughout the deepest ever process of globalisation and technological revolution and an accelerated redistribution and dispersion of power among and within nations, the tensions that resulted in the current volatile context can be traced back at least to the dawn of the twenty-first century.

Brexit was the clearest illustration of how the convergence of exogenous and domestic factors can produce unexpected radical separations. The UK is not, however, an isolated case – far from it. The truth is that in each of our countries, distance and mistrust have grown – and are still growing – between globally minded liberal elites and those who feel left behind, shocked by the evidence of inequality and the emergence of new moral values, and anxious about what the future will bring. Populists take advantage of uncertainty and fear, and impose their simplistic and divisive narrative, without providing any feasible solutions. Short-term domestic priorities and national political polarisation increasingly determine foreign policy options and limit the margin of manoeuvre of leaders and their effectiveness on the global stage.

Divorce literature is consistent in identifying the warning signs of trouble in personal relations: breakdowns in communication, negative feelings associated with the partner, constant financial disagreements, lack of respect, loss of happiness, loss of intimacy, loss of trust, poor conflict resolution. Defensiveness, criticism and contempt are considered critical predictors. Applying this analytical tool to diagnose relations within nations and among nations could seem inadequate. Surprisingly, it is not. Parallelism is striking. Maybe because, after all – be it politicians or anonymous citizens – we are all human beings, even if some carry more responsibility than others.

That is precisely why we should not totally despair. It is impossible not to admire human inventiveness, creativity and ingenuity, and the range of technological innovations that have materialised during these last few decades or are announced for the coming ones. One cannot ignore the extent to which the international community has come closer together thanks to the 'digital, mobile and remote' technological revolution, to new infrastructures of all kinds, and to the opening of markets and the sophistication of supply chains. It is impossible not to recognise and rejoice in the fact that millions of people have been taken out of poverty, have gained easier access to sources of information and education, and have been blessed with new economic opportunities and better living standards. The world has become narrower, flatter and wealthier.

Ten years ago, the UN adopted seventeen far- and wide-reaching Sustainable Development Goals (SDGs) and a platform to fight climate change was agreed upon in Paris, proving that it is possible to establish a common agenda for humankind. It took scientists and industry less than two years to conceive and produce a vaccine for the most devastating virus of this century. In Europe, we made enormous progress in integrating the continent through the deepening of the EU and its enlargement to more than a dozen new member states, mostly coming from behind the former Iron Curtain. The EU and what it has accomplished, against all historical odds, is the most comprehensive peace, security and prosperity-building operation in recent history.

We should be – and I certainly am – extremely proud of all these global and European achievements of recent decades. The question remains, however, whether all these positive developments and our collective political will are capable of halting the current slide towards fragmentation and confrontation. It is too soon to answer this with certitude but high time to start working on it. What we can say for now is that underestimating the seriousness of the current challenges would be suicidal and that collective awareness and resolute action are mandatory.

What should we do now? The first task is to try to understand better this polarisation, otherwise we will not be able to overcome it – and prevent the unpredictable consequences of a global divorce. The next is to set out a vision and a plan to adjust the international order, preserving the essence of what we built in the last century while adapting it to the realities of the new one. Countries in the 'Western world' will need to do this with modesty and without naivety or arrogance, in frank dialogue with the emerged and emerging powers and with the 'South', but also with confidence in our values and determination to protect our interests. The new powers and the emerging ones have a particular role to play, assuming the responsibility that comes from having access to the 'high table' – and with full awareness of how much an integrated global landscape, as opposed to a de-coupled one, is indispensable for their own economic and social upgrading. All should provide common sense, moderation and a constructive attitude at home and abroad. All should try to be adults in the room. All should engage in a serious conversation. The planet Earth and all who live in it would thank them.

1

Rebel Without a Cause

At the age of 25, and with a flare of belated juvenile rebellion, the new century is actively challenging the patterns of international behaviour it inherited from its predecessor. Worryingly, it has not yet been able to design a credible, better alternative.

THE END OF THE END

The nature and pace of events have been surprising. How many times in recent years have we not said to ourselves: I never expected this to happen! And how often have we not concluded: nothing should be taken for granted!

One by one, several consensuses on how nations should engage with each other, and on how governments and citizens should interact, have gradually been eroded. Since the beginning of this century, we have been witnessing a continuous process of deconstruction of conventions that had been established in the 1990s, in the wake of the end of the Cold War.

Even earlier elements of the organisation of global governance, agreed upon immediately after the Second World War, are being challenged: the principles, values and operational tools of the multilateral institutions, the vital role of the UN and its Security Council and the system they oversee, as well as the sanctity of international law and of the territorial integrity of states.

Some of these consensuses were more 'consensual' than others, but they all reflected a build-up of patterns of behaviour that, for better or worse, have contributed to a period of relative peace and growing prosperity, which compares positively with the bloody first part of the twentieth century. Whether we call it Pax Americana or prefer to describe it as a bipolar world turned into a unipolar one, the fact remains that the output of the post-Second World War order, consolidated by the fall of the Berlin Wall and of the Soviet Union, was better for humankind than any available alternative. Not perfect, but certainly better. And that is what we should not forget in times of doubt.

The most obvious and consequential victims of this erosion have been the patterns of behaviour among major players established after the end of the Cold War. Some of those patterns were codified, others not, at a time when we all thought we were starting a new era, a new age of security, prosperity and democracy, after the fall of the Soviet Union. Idealistic expectations, first articulated by Francis Fukuyama,[1] that a solid and consensual international rules-based order, combined with a sound and unchallenged model of liberal representative democracies, would become the default operating system for humankind, have faded.

We have almost forgotten how encouraged we were by the fall of the Berlin Wall and the advent of democracy behind what had been known as the Iron Curtain or, more recently, by the Paris agreement on climate change and Agenda 2030, which provided welcome co-operative platforms to set SDGs and address some of the most pressing global challenges. The international agreement to prevent Iran from acquiring nuclear weapons capability, the 2015 Joint Comprehensive Plan of Action (JCPOA)[2], was a rare example of close and effective co-operation between Western powers and China and Russia for the sake of preventing nuclear proliferation.

Geopolitical calm and mutual respect of norms and conventions – and of international law – allowed open trade and technological innovation to usher in a new global middle class and to 'narrow' and 'flatten'[3] our planet. Creatively paraphrasing Winston Churchill, never had the world changed so much for the better in such a brief period of time, positively affecting such a large segment of humanity.

And yet, unfortunately, the reality is that, today, the conditions that allowed that to happen – call it international liberal order if you like – are being seriously threatened. Its opponents – and those who felt that it had not been designed by them and for them – abandoned earlier discretion and tacit acceptance. They no longer hesitate to criticise it and feel strong enough to push back. Worryingly, even some of its proponents seem tempted to disrespect it. We are now witnessing a dramatic challenge to a global order that we once took for granted.

Today, the positive trends in global governance risk being reversed (be it on climate action or SDGs) or are already being reversed (nuclear proliferation is again a real threat and democracy and respect for human rights are in retreat), and the negative ones have regained strength (the challenging of territorial integrity, the claiming of zones of influence and the surge in authoritarianism, not to mention the global rise of populism and nationalism).

The 2022 invasion of Ukraine and the war that followed came after similar earlier violations of those consensuses by Russia elsewhere in the country (Crimea) and before that in Georgia. A permanent member of the Security Council has thus been actively and openly violating the letter and the spirit of the Charter of the United Nations, with the assumed purpose of erasing from the map another member of the same UN. Unthinkable just a few years ago.

China has moved from a process of gradual and remarkable internal economic change, combined with discretion and strategic patience, to an assertive discourse increasingly perceived as a means to modify the assumptions of the current order, with the goal of gaining global leadership. From Deng Xiaoping's 'hide our strength and bide our time' to Xi Jinping's 'dare to fight', there is a sea change.

Extending the metaphor literally, the South China Sea has returned to the front pages. Given Beijing's growing self-confidence and assertiveness, it could well be the theatre of an escalation in the great-power rivalry that now dominates the political narrative in Washington and Beijing and has a huge impact on global security and prosperity.

Russia aims at creating a zone of influence and dictating the rules of the game in its close environment, but it has no sophisticated vision for an alternative global order, apart from the protection of a narrow concept of national sovereignty and an obsession with reducing the USA's and the West's clout. China's is a power project, not of a colonial, territorial nature (apart from the issue of Taiwan), but one that fundamentally challenges American hegemony and the universal values behind the international order that the UN has upheld – and that is what has turned these two 'frenemies' into tactical allies.

In order to reinforce its credibility and more effectively fight back against these revisionist efforts, the so called 'West' could use some retrospective self-criticism. Individual or collective action by Western countries, not wholly supported by international law, in Iraq, Afghanistan, Kosovo and Libya – as justifiable or indispensable as it may have been judged, in order to safeguard human rights and prevent human suffering or to protect national security – has had a negative impact on how others view our consistency and coherence with the principles and values we uphold. In contrast to our inaction in other crisis theatres, some of our foreign interventions have dented the perception of our moral leadership and weakened our capacity to influence and convince, and ultimately to act further when needed. Bearing in mind that nothing will ever justify Putin's actions, that he should be held fully to account, and that our focus should be on ensuring Ukraine's sovereignty and territorial integrity, when the context is more appropriate we could retrospectively ask ourselves whether we have exhausted all opportunities to prevent Russia from drifting away.

Some of the critics of the West are eager to conclude that a degree of hubris after the fall of communism may have clouded our judgement. That is a disproportionate accusation, but the sad fact is that we are today less willing and less capable of coming to the rescue of those who need us, or confronting those who oppress others, because our past record often haunts us.

New and old conflicts have irrupted or resurfaced with a particular degree of intensity and violence in the Middle East and parts of Africa, for example, and the international community appears today largely incapable and sometimes even unwilling to help reach solutions. Conflict prevention and conflict management are dramatically underperforming. We are living through times of uncertainty, volatility and change, while our planet is confronted with existential challenges requiring – more than ever – international co-operation. Divorce comes at the worst possible moment for planet Earth.

Some may think that I am too obsessed with 'divorce', having had direct contact with the traumatic Brexit as EU Ambassador to London, or that I may be overlooking the fact that divorce is sometimes the best solution for strained relationships. To that I reply that it is exactly because I witnessed how it was possible for nations to approach the cliff edge without preventing the fall that I am so worried and suspicious of divorces with global implications. In international relations, divorce can only exacerbate tensions, not relieve them, and the chances are that divorce creates the bedrock for a further stage of acrimony and possibly hard confrontation. We should not take that chance.

Polarisation and fragmentation are not limited to geopolitics. They also, unavoidably, impact the economy.

The turn of the century has witnessed the amazing deepening of globalisation and the emergence of unprecedented technological advances. Their combined effect gave new hope to hundreds of millions of people – and this is a tremendous success that cannot be underestimated. The problem is that it also threw millions into despair and identity loss. We created new middle classes but also new poor. In too many parts of industrialised countries we were not able to find new jobs for those whose skills were no longer needed because others, elsewhere, were more competitive. We were blessed with breathtaking technological innovation and created jobs that had never existed before, but we came to realise that technology, and the capital investment associated with it, did not necessarily create new jobs in the places where they had previously destroyed them. Regrettably, in line with the contemporary dominant economic thinking, governments did not do enough, and did not act early enough, to fill the gaps where needed.

Global wealth grew and the gap between the developed and the developing world narrowed. However, revenue disparity also grew in many parts of the globe and people blamed trade or imports, foreign powers or simply 'the rich' for it. Particularly important in our information age is the fact that inequality became much more visible. You cannot hide inequality any more, or its effect on less privileged citizens who feel even more left behind. This affects the public perception of open markets and open borders.

Demographic asymmetry between North and South created increasing migratory tensions, but international efforts to deal with them consensually fell flat. Migration flows are necessary and justifiable from a human and economic perspective, but they are extremely difficult to manage politically. They risk becoming a lose–lose phenomenon if not adequately governed.

On the ground, we made enormous gains in the efficiency of supply chains and in productivity, but some of our nations allowed external dependency to reach dangerous levels, to the point where trade started to be seen as a threat to national security. Protectionism, closed borders, localism, onshoring, reshoring, friendshoring and other old and new concepts have penetrated the policy and political lexicon. 'Economic security' became an intrinsic element of 'security'. The jury is still out on whether it will bring more wealth and less inequality than what it wants to replace, but it is definitely the 'flavour of the month'.

The combined effect of all of these developments is that globalisation as an economic model has lost the reputation battle (public opposition started already back in 1999 with the protests in the streets of Seattle, in the margins of a World Trade Organization ministerial meeting, as people of my generation will remember), and it now needs revamping.

More politically, we used to expect that trade, open markets, technology, increased economic interdependence and the emergence of a new global middle class would change the paradigm of relations among nations and particularly between the 'new kids on the block' and the 'old hands' of the neighbourhood. Regrettably, all that looks naive today, as we witness the return of old reflexes and 'basic instincts' to international relations, amidst a war of narratives and renewed competition between value systems and models of national and global governance. Geopolitics trumps geoeconomics. This time 'It's politics, stupid!'

Then there is a critical factor, often underestimated: culture. Not in the strict sense of the word, but in a wider one that connects to civilisation, identity and more. Politics and economics are not enough to understand this century's context. Gaps in values and beliefs have widened. Fast-evolving concepts of family, gender and ethnicity are liberating but also anxiogenic. Echo chambers exacerbate apprehension and animosity, and enhance tribal reflexes. Tolerance is becoming a rare commodity in public space; a dialogue of the deaf is spreading. And so is politically motivated violence. 'The world I knew is disappearing', many citizens complain – but their default comfort reflex is not to try to understand and adjust, nor to open up and reach out; it is too often to close down. Radical political forces capitalise on all this.

The first quarter of the twenty-first century tells an eloquent story of the end of the 'end of History'. We need to acknowledge it if we want to launch a new beginning.

2001 AND 2022: THE BOOKENDS

Life is made of moments we will always remember, for good and bad reasons. Like many, I know exactly where I was on 11 September 2001, when the terrorist attack on the Twin Towers signalled the delayed beginning of the twenty-first century. For more benign reasons, the same goes for the day, in April 1974, when my country, Portugal, regained democracy and freedom. The first time I met my wife, when I became a father and grandfather, and the day I lost my own father, are of course at the top of my hierarchy of memories, but they are only relevant for me and a reduced number of people. In contrast, the latest addition to the list of moments I am unable to forget is as universally meaningful as the 2001 attack on downtown Manhattan: Vladimir Putin's invasion of Ukraine on 24 February 2022.

In an unexplainable coincidence, I woke up in the middle of the night at my London apartment only ten minutes after the public announcement of the beginning of the invasion. In the early hours of that fateful day, I was still unaware of what was happening not too far away on continental Europe. As I checked my iPhone and Twitter feed – an inescapable part of my regular middle of the night practice – the news I read shocked me even more than I could have expected. After all, there was a relatively high probability that Putin would take that fatal step and I should not have been too surprised. But the confirmation on screen really struck me. There it was, blunt and dramatic: we had war in our near neighbourhood, triggered by a permanent member of the UN Security Council that happens to hold one of the world's biggest nuclear arsenals.

So much for the 'end of History', I said to myself, then already watching the BBC. Still half asleep, my mind tried to focus on the magnitude of the unfolding events: this was the end of a reality – a post-Cold War 'order' – that we had maybe taken too much for granted. This was the beginning of a chapter of our history yet to be written but which looked far from promising – a multipolar 'disorder'?

A few days later, I scribbled down in my notebook a message, obviously never sent, that reflected well, in assumed innocent and even naive terms, my deep personal feelings:

Vladimir Vladimirovich,

I address you in this colloquial Russian way not because I want to sound friendly, far from that, but because I want to send a message to you as a man who was born five years before me, a man of my generation.

This is actually more than a personal message. I am addressing it on behalf of the generations after ours, those of my sons and of my grandchildren. In their homes, offices, schools and even in their kindergartens, the thunder of your bombings and the suffering you are imposing on the streets of Kyiv and Kharkiv reverberate as a threat on their own future. And they wonder: why? And I wonder what to reply to them.

Wasn't this the generation that had learned the lessons from two world wars that devastated Europe, which killed millions of Europeans and, yes, sacrificed many courageous Russian soldiers and civilians? Wasn't this the generation that committed to security and co-operation in Europe through organised dialogue and confidence-building structures, that promised never again to violate the rule of law, to respect human rights and jointly agreed conventions and to uphold international order? Wasn't this the generation that solemnly voted in New York to implement the UN agenda for Sustainable Development Goals?

How come that you are now inflicting on innocent Ukrainians the exact same pain that others inflicted on our parents and grandparents for exactly the same unjustified reasons, in total disrespect for commitments made? How come you are now triggering instability, insecurity and economic pain upon your people, our peoples and peoples around the world when what we all need now is to recover from the worst pandemic in our lifetime, build back better and save the planet from the devastation of climate change? How come you have learned nothing from the generations before us? And what lessons do you expect us to convey to the generations ahead of us?

Vladimir Vladimirovich, stop now.

Today things are clear: 24 February is the opposite bookend to 11 September. They uphold and contain the first quarter of a new century that gradually annihilated the consensus inherited from its predecessor on how nations should treat one another. Between these bookends we have seen an incredible sequence of events, resulting from the interaction of domestic and external factors, the weight of historical grievances and unresolved disputes, the prevalence of an immutable geography, the unbalanced impact of economic globalisation and climate change, the disruption of technological advances, and the rise of populism favoured by the behaviour of both strong and weak leaders. Some call it the revenge of history. Others the revenge of geography. I choose to call it the 'divorce of nations'.

All this has produced a sharp acceleration of events. Unfortunately, not one that has consolidated the benign post-Cold War balance but rather one that risks destroying it without yet being capable of replacing it with any workable global operating system.

I see in this cycle, spanning at least twenty-five years, a sort of 'long adolescence' of the century, heavily loaded with contradictory impulses, anxieties, dreams and nightmares. All exploited and magnified in our countries by the internal enemy of democracy: populism.[4]

At 25 years old, the new century is still a rebel without a cause.

2

Behind the Scenes

Before making more elaborate comments about this 'global divorce', it is useful to identify precursive and warning signs – and detect trends. Private and semi-public moments among global actors can tell us a lot about how the divorce of nations has been building up. Putin, Russia and the West; the financial crisis and global capitalism; Bush, Obama, Trump and the USA's place in the world; Hu, Xi and China's new assertiveness; the pandemic and the blurring of lines between domestic and foreign policies and the overall global role of the European Union – these are some of the stages of this short personal journey behind the scenes.

PUTIN, THE RED THREAD

Konni saluted us even before her master did, and more effusively. She reminded me of our own family dog at the time, also a black Labrador retriever, like Vladimir Vladimirovich's favourite pet. President Putin came right behind his dog and shook hands with José Manuel Barroso, then President of the European Commission, and me. He then introduced my counterpart, his EU adviser, Sergey Yastrzemski. Konni stayed in the room until something more interesting happened in the kitchen, where dinner was being prepared. A Russian interpreter joined us as we sat down around a small table.

There was no one else in the room on that dark afternoon of 17 March 2006, at one of Putin's residences in the outskirts of Moscow. Of all the close to fifteen times I have met Vladimir

Putin, in bilateral meetings with the President of the European Commission and in EU/Russia, Group of Eight (G8) and Group of Twenty (G20) summits, this intimate gathering at Novo-Ogaryovo was to be the most revealing one.

Putin's words and body language conveyed his deep feelings of humiliation and non-recognition by the West and his desire to set things straight. In the early hours of 24 February 2022, sixteen years later almost to the day, what he said and what he hinted at in Novo-Ogaryovo came back to my mind as a tragic premonition. But I also felt that Putin's personality had become darker with time.

During almost four hours of uninterrupted conversation, Putin outlined in detail his grievances, his obsessions and his frustrations with the West as well as the difficulties of governing such a large and multifaceted country as the Russian Federation. He used our criticism of recent arbitrary, top-down changes of governors in the provinces of the Federation to justify Moscow's iron fist:

> You must bear in mind that in Russia we have more than 130 ethnic groups. We need ten hours' flight to reach the Pacific coast but only eight hours to get to New York. Also: we have 254 million ethnic Russians living abroad. This is a total catastrophe, and nobody seems to care or consider its implications for us. In Ukraine only we have 17 million ethnic Russians.[1]

And he added: 'We do not want to maintain an empire. We want to keep the state in place. You do not understand our domestic political scene. The changes we are making are as good as those in democratic countries.' He was growing in impatience. 'And still, everybody wants to teach us something!'

He certainly did not refrain from 'teaching' his interlocutors when talking about energy, and gas in particular. We were in the middle of several serious crises regarding the supply of Russian gas to and via Ukraine. On that evening in 2006 and on every other occasion when the issue was discussed, Putin was incredibly detailed about the respective contractual obligations of parties and even about the technical specifications of the pipelines. At one point I had trouble understanding his extremely technical comments about the different diameters of the pipelines and the reverse flows of gas. His deep knowledge of the gas file struck me at the time. I noted down: 'Putin speaks as if he is the CEO of Gazprom ...'

José Manuel Barroso emphatically rejected any insinuations of hostile treatment by the West and instead laid out a forward-looking agenda centred on common interests, founded on a shared geography and economic complementarity, and reflecting Russia and the EU's role in Europe and in the world. The Russian leader seemed, however, more obsessed with the past than interested in the future, more deeply focused on the way his country had been and still was being treated and perceived by the West than on what it could do to contribute to good neighbourhood relations or global wellbeing.

Putin had kicked off with his usual ironic, sometimes cynical and in any case always dismissive remarks about the state of the EU. Faithful to well-known Kremlin tactics, he sought (unsuccessfully) to destabilise his interlocutors from the very start. A year earlier, we had given him good reason to doubt the EU's health when French and Dutch voters rejected a draft Constitution, but Barroso fought back and highlighted our bold steps in preparing a new treaty (which would be signed a year and a half later in my hometown, Lisbon) and the fact that the EU had moved on from that setback.

This time the criticism of internal EU matters did not last long as Putin clearly wanted to speak more generally about Russia's relationship with the West. And he was bold and blunt: Russia is Christianity's bridge to Asia and the Pacific, but the West refuses to recognise it. Looking straight and intensely into his interlocutors' eyes, he said:

> Russia has European culture, historical power, and the capacity to prolong European radiation until the Pacific Coast. We are natural allies with the EU and the USA in an unpredictable world. The Christian ideology is common to all of us; this is even

obvious for atheists (it runs deep, for centuries). We should be natural partners with a long historic perspective.

He continued:

The problem is that we have changed drastically but the West has not changed: it keeps a block-type mindset. The USA wants to maintain a block-type discipline in the West. I told it to Bush. As the world is restructuring, we are ready to play with natural partners a common game with common rules, but with respect for national interests.

Putin mentioned Chechnya and the role of Al-Qaeda there, and the lack of understanding by the West. Then, even more upbeat, he asserted: 'I don't like us to be seen as big and ugly, but neither as idiots!'

We now know that Putin was particularly upset with the way the USA had reacted to the Beslan massacre in 2004. Following a Chechen terrorist attack on a school in northern Ossetia, and Russia's particularly robust intervention thereafter, more than 300 people, including many children, had died. The reaction of the West was not as supportive as Putin had expected and he felt that he could no longer trust Bush, accusing him of cynically supporting the terrorists in order to weaken Russia. In the same year, the election of Viktor Yuschenko as President of Ukraine, replacing Putin's ally Viktor Yanukovitch, would represent a major addition to his grievances against Europeans and Americans. At the time, in 2006, the expansion of the North Atlantic Treaty Organization (NATO) was still being tolerated and was not yet a cause for complaint. The fact that Ukraine was getting closer to the EU through a trade and association agreement that reflected the wishes of large parts of the Ukrainian population was Putin's main concern.

The restricted meeting at Novo-Ogaryovo was only the first of several encounters with Putin scheduled in 2006. It was followed by the first of the twice-yearly EU/Russia summits, which took place at Sochi, Putin's favourite Black Sea resort.[2] A few weeks

1486 Bexleyheath
89 The Broadway
Postcode DA6 7JN
Tel: 020 8301 0802 Vat: 493 6076 60
www.tgjonesonline.co.uk

NEW INTERNATIONALIST (M)	8 45
PRACTICAL WIRELESS (M)	5 99
Total	£14.44
Cash	20.00
Cash Change	£5.56

2 item(s) sold
0 item(s) returned
Thank you. Please retain your receipt
as proof of purchase.

0148606108571618082 5

18/08/2025 15:47:45 01486 0061 085716 FL

later, in mid-July, we would meet again in St Petersburg, where an annual G8 summit provided him with a moment of global recognition as host of the most important gathering of world leaders.

In all honesty, the atmosphere in the Sochi villas or at the Constantine Palace in St Petersburg did not fully anticipate the total breakdown of relations between Putin and the Western leaders that would happen in the years to come. As they prepared to check in at the individual dachas reserved for them at the compound around the G8 summit building, Bush, Merkel, Blair, Chirac, Koizumi, the Canadian PM Harper, Prodi, the Finnish PM Vanhanen (rotating President of the European Council) and Barroso were genuinely giving Putin a chance to show he deserved to sit at the 'high table' of global governance.

None of them had any doubts about what separated them from the former Committee for State Security (KGB) agent or about the quality of Russian democracy, but they saw the need at least to try to have Putin share the terms of engagement that bonded the group and behave accordingly. Over dinner among only the leaders, the conversation became looser – and tougher. Putin introduced the discussion of Russian democracy and Barroso, as was often the case with the subject of human rights, took the lead for the European camp. He used his own personal experience as a Portuguese young man growing up under a dictatorship to emphasise the importance of freedom:

> The problem is not having a strong Russia. What is relevant is to have not only a strong state but a strong and stable country. And for that you need mechanisms of control and the freedom to express different views. For instance, a free press is the best way to fight corruption and fighting corruption is a necessary tool to have a strong and stable country.

Putin defended his alleged 'democratic' credentials. 'If I wanted, I could be president for life but I respect the Russian Constitution', he said, according to a participant, before criticising Western non-governmental organisations (NGOs) for their interference in

Russian internal affairs. As the meal went on, and Russian food and drink flowed, the levels of sincerity went up and at least one national European leader could not hide his own misgivings about some NGOs in the West.

The Europeans in the room were all also aware of how much Russian oil and gas had been – and still were – critical for the EU economies, and all leaders had in mind the relevance of current and future Western investments in Russia. We knew how much longer our border with Russia had become after the latest enlargements of the EU and how much our overall security depended upon the quality of relations with our big eastern neighbour. We knew that geography could not be changed. Our economies complemented each other quite significantly, and changing that paradigm – and particularly our energy dependence – was hard to do, certainly without huge costs. Some of us may have overlooked the fact that Putin also knew all that. Some of us may have underestimated how serious he was about using it to his advantage. However, in all honesty, no one predicted how radically Putin's personality would change, for the worse, in the next decade and a half.

The Russian president played his role as G8 host efficiently, capitalising domestically on the international recognition it had given him, but deep in his soul – despite what George W. Bush may have seen in his eyes the first time they met[3] – Putin was not ready to change gear. A few months later, at the Munich Security Conference, he would translate his grievances into an overly aggressive speech 'pre-announcing' the invasions of Georgia in 2008 and Crimea in 2014, not to mention his move of February 2022. The Atlantic alliance was now the main problem: 'NATO has put its front-line forces on our borders. We have the right to ask: against whom is this expansion intended?'

To be historically correct, Putin's grievances have their source a long way back, well before his ascent to power. They originate in the events of the 1990s, following the fall of the Berlin Wall in 1989 and of the Soviet Union in 1991. As brilliantly described and explained by Professor Mary Esther Sorotte in *Not One Inch*,[4] it was about the management of the moving tectonic plates liberated by the seismic end of the Cold War. It is no exaggeration to say that the brief experience with democracy in Russia in the last years of the twentieth century, because of its chaotic nature and the traumatising effects it had on the Russian economy and on Russian citizens themselves, may well have curbed the enthusiasm for further opening up of the country. It is also fair to conclude that it renewed an aspiration for strong leaders, a crucial feature of Russian history. Putin capitalised on the Russian people's disappointment with democracy and their nostalgia for authority.

In 2006, in St Petersburg, the West 'proposed' to Russia. In 2007, in Munich, Putin set a high price for the 'marriage settlement'. In 2008, the US-inspired open offer of Ukraine's NATO accession, even if without a roadmap, and the Russian invasion of Georgia made the Euro-Atlantic–Russian 'break-up' ultimately unavoidable. The invasion of Crimea in 2014 led to Russia's expulsion from the G8. 'Divorce' had started. The rest is history. And not a good one.

Vladimir Putin has been in power in different iterations at the top of the Russian Federation since 2000. No other leader present at the 2006 G8 summit in St Petersburg, let alone those on duty when Putin started, is in power anymore and some have even passed away. Putin is the only major global leader who has survived since the dawn of the millennium. He is the red thread of the first quarter of the twenty-first century.

'W' AND THE CRACK IN THE CEILING

At least one other G8 leader hosted by Putin at the Constantine Palace owned a dear pet dog. Barney stood for Bernard, Bernard Bush. Not a member of George W. Bush's family as such, obviously, but a particularly important element of his entourage. Barney, one of the presidential Scottish Terrier dogs together with Miss Beazley, was not around at Camp David on Saturday, 18 October 2008, but we knew how fond 'W' was of him. In any case, it did not really matter because the mood on that bright autumn afternoon was not for 'dog talk'.

We arrived at the Virginia country residence of the President of the United States in the early stages of what was to become the Great Recession, a defining moment of the early twenty-first century. The rotating President of the European Council, French president Nicolas Sarkozy, and the President of the European Commission, José Manuel Barroso, had only one issue in mind that they wanted to discuss with Bush: Lehman Brothers had dramatically imploded on 15 September, a month earlier almost to the day, and action was urgently needed to address its global consequences.

Since then, European capitals, already active on their own turf in defining a counter-strategy to avoid a painful recession, had been pressing Washington for a more global response to what increasingly looked like an acute worldwide financial crisis. They did not meet with immense success at the beginning. Bush was at the very end of his mandate, tired by what had been an excruciating experience, and his successor would be elected on 4 November. He was not necessarily eager to assume new responsibilities so close to the end of his term, and some in his entourage tended to diminish the gravity of the situation, while others resisted drawing too much attention to the American financial system's role in triggering the crisis.

Inside the EU, we were adamant that the USA and its president had to rise to the occasion. If not for more noble reasons, the fact that the crisis originated in California's subprime mortgage market should have been enough to justify it. We could not ignore either that Bush's Treasury Secretary, Hank Paulson, also present at Camp David, had basically let Lehman fall, ignoring the systemic impact of that decision. However, what was even more important now was that the potential magnitude of the crisis required a forceful global response and that could not be achieved without strong US–European leadership.

Bush finally came to realise that he had to act. Stepping out of the 'Marine One' helicopters that had taken us from Andrews Air Force Base, Sarkozy and Barroso lined up on the Camp David tarmac side by side with George W. Bush for a short press call. Before taking the wheel of a golf buggy to drive his invitees to his log cabin, Bush announced to the media that he was ready to call an international leaders' gathering to tackle the crisis. He mentioned no date and no location. Sarkozy wanted it to be held symbolically in New York, at the centre of American capitalism, and he said so publicly, to the astonishment of many. Barroso recalled recent EU decisions but insisted that the crisis required 'global solutions', to be agreed upon at an urgent international summit.

Camp David is a countryside setting and Bush, the Texan, was particularly happy and at home there. His two immediate successors – Barack Obama and Donald Trump – as different as they are, never enjoyed it as much. George Bush's informal style and friendly attitude – which should not be taken as a sign of lesser rigour and knowledge – melded perfectly with the log cabins and narrow pathways among the tall trees, made even more pleasant by the beautiful autumn colours. The whole atmosphere was very informal and relaxed. And so was dinner, starting at the very early time of 6.30 p.m. that was typical in the USA. We had a home-made country buffet of fried chicken, mashed potatoes, sautéed green beans and carrots, fresh dinner rolls and the unavoidable American standard of home-style gravy. We finished off with a double coconut layer cake.

Before and during the family-style meal, however, the conversation could not avoid the reason why we had flown directly from Quebec, where we had just held an EU–Canada summit and participated at the 'Francophonie' leaders' gathering. It was about the financial crisis and how to respond to it, but also about whom to involve in the process. Sarkozy was on the offensive, as he always was, Bush on the defensive, for obvious reasons, and Barroso opted for a conciliatory, results-oriented mode, as his hands-on role advised. We wanted a clear American commitment to act. And soon. The situation was serious and required swift action. The future would prove us right.

Since the fall of Lehman there had been different schools of thought regarding both the degree of structural relevance of the crisis and the format of any event that should trigger an international response to it. The analysis of the origins and magnitude of the crisis was still in its early stages and those present at Camp David did not go too deeply into it, all sharing the feeling that, whatever the diagnosis, the perception of the markets and the level of distress were such that something had to be done about it. In our view, there were two major dimensions to consider: the direct impact on the financial system, with a serious risk of implosion and meltdown; and the overall economic effects of the crisis, namely the potential for a global recession.

During the two-hour working meeting, in spite of the different starting points, there was nonetheless a clear consensus on the need for a strategy and a process, involving a series of international summits and adequate technical preparation in between, as well as the involvement of Russia, China and India, at least, in order to make sure they were part of the action and would share responsibility for its success or failure. In fact, Russia, China and India had no real options: if they came, they would be on board; if they didn't, they would be isolated in the middle of a storm.

'The risk is doing nothing', Sarkozy said, but Bush, aware and suspicious of the French president's well-known hyperactivity, advised caution in the management of expectations in order not to frustrate the markets.

On the format of an international kick-off meeting and its location, some suggested an enlarged G8, to include some emerging economies and obviously China (mention was made of a 'G13'), while others wanted even more ad hoc formulas. In earlier intra-EU consultations, the British prime minister, Gordon Brown, and his experienced 'sherpa' – my good friend Jon Cunliffe, future deputy governor of the Bank of England – were particularly adamant about a G20 format, which according to them had proved right during a recent Asian financial crisis at finance ministers' level and could easily be duplicated at leaders' level. Barroso said the most important goal was to have a sort of 'foundation act' followed by a sequence of meetings, regardless of the national leaders' gathering format but guaranteeing appropriate EU representation. Everyone agreed that it was crucial to ensure that the responsibility and the burden of finding a way out was widely shared, so the final consensus, weeks later, was to reflect the G20 composition without calling it as such.

On where to hold a first global summit about the financial crisis, Sarkozy half-jokingly suggested having it in Wall Street itself, but this was flatly rejected by Bush, who saw it for the provocation it actually was. The French president insisted on New York and even mentioned the UN (also immediately rejected by Bush), but the American president eventually agreed to hold it on American soil in Washington DC, on 14/15 November 2008, a few days after Barack Obama was elected, but still under Bush's chairmanship (when we went to Washington for the summit, a few of us met Madeleine Albright in her private consultancy office to brief the incoming Obama team).

The meeting held in Washington was officially called the 'Summit on Financial Markets and the World Economy'. History will record it as the first G20 leaders' summit to tackle the impact of the biggest financial crisis in many decades and the major recession it triggered. Our Camp David meeting turned out to be a successful one, as it effectively launched the process that would ultimately drive the international response to the Great Recession.

All those seated around the long table inside the presidential Camp David log cabin understood that we were embarking on a serious crisis, but I am sure that no one imagined the repercussions of what had just been unleashed.

• • •

The 2008 financial crisis and the recession that followed – the most serious since the Great Depression of the 1920 and '30s – would indelibly mark the first quarter of the century. It stunned the world, signalled the end of the sanctity of financial markets and their respective operators, and revealed the vulnerability of regulatory and supervision systems – at both national and global levels – when confronted with the superior level of sophistication of the 'markets'. It also revealed the extent of interlinkage and interdependency among all the economies of the globe, resulting from decades of accelerated globalisation. The crisis produced reputational hazard that would have direct and indirect political implications in the short and long run – the image of financial capitalism, of the USA as the hegemonic financial power and of the West in general would be tarnished.

A number of citizens now share a negative perception of banks, bankers and anything 'financial and global' – including globalisation itself – and see them as the reflection of reckless behaviour and the source of a blatant inequality. The financial crisis and the Great Recession it triggered in the first half of the quarter-century became a fertile ground for populism of both right- and left-wing inclinations and thus a major source of 'divorce within nations'.

Leonard Cohen, my favourite singer-poet, put it correctly when he said that everything has a crack through which the light gets in.[5] I guess he meant that nothing is perfect but everything can be restored, provided light allows us to detect and redress imperfection. The 2008 financial crisis was the first major crack in the ceiling of globalised capitalism and had serious financial, economic, social and political consequences, particularly in the Western world and even more acutely in Europe with its subsequent sovereign debt crisis. In 2008 and following years, a serious effort was deployed to limit the damage. Today, an additional effort – more light – is needed to limit the chances of its repetition.

• • •

Back to Camp David: as I boarded the after-dinner flight to Europe, I had no suspicion that less than two years later I would fly back in as the first EU Ambassador to the United States, after the entry into force of the Treaty of Lisbon had enhanced the powers of what was formerly a European Commission representative. Apart from working with the Obama administration to strengthen EU–US relations, despite the administration's focus on the 'pivot to Asia', my other main task would be to deal with the fallout of the financial crisis. I would be on the front line deflecting criticism, incredulity and outright cynicism towards one of the major collateral victims of the financial crisis: the European economic and monetary union, or the euro area as the Americans preferred to call it, which was confronted with the enormous challenge of a sovereign debt crisis. It was a challenge we eventually overcame.

The 'euro crisis', as the media stubbornly insisted on calling what was not really a currency crisis, but rather a debt crisis triggered by budgetary imbalances in a number of euro area countries, was a daily feature of my diplomatic life in the USA. A day, a press meeting or a diplomatic dinner would not go by without a more or less polite enquiry about the future of the EU and the euro, and without my repeated reassurance that (a) we would take all necessary measures to protect and safeguard them, (b) it was my firm belief that no country would leave the euro and (c) the euro would survive as the second most important currency in the world.

Reality proved me right even beyond my expectations: twenty EU member states are now in the euro area, four more than at the beginning of the crisis, and no member opted out or was forced to leave. In spite of similar assurances given earlier by the EU heads of state and government, the perception started to change fundamentally only after the then President of the European Central Bank (ECB), Mario Draghi, made a now historic statement on 26 July 2012: 'Within our mandate, the ECB is ready to do whatever it takes to preserve the euro. And believe me, it will be enough.'[6] It was.

Draghi's assertive words would not, however, have had real effect if national and EU authorities had not stood their ground and applied 'fiscal rectitude', before and after his speech. Against the background of a financial crisis that soon became economic and social, against the combined campaigns from opponents of the EU and the euro – and certainly in spite of the unconfessed undue influence of outside adversaries – we painstakingly managed to extract ourselves from some of the worst moments of European integration. We did this with blood, sweat and tears, but also with some significant progress in equipping the EU and the euro area with the tools to avoid, if not all future crises, at least one as serious as this one.

More globally, the response to the crisis that kicked off at Camp David, thanks to European and American leadership, proved to be effective in avoiding a total financial meltdown and in strengthening mechanisms of dialogue, co-ordination, supervision and crisis management at international level. During the most intensive crisis management phase, successive summits between 2008 and 2010 in Washington, London (the most impactful one, thanks largely to the efforts of Gordon Brown, who chaired it), Pittsburgh (with Obama already at the helm) and Toronto consolidated what we had started in Virginia.

Regrettably, the ensuing G20 leaders' process failed to address some underlying structural weaknesses of international financial markets and respective governance. It provided emergency assistance and treatment, and revealed a level of resilience and adaptability that was remarkable, but it was not able to eradicate some highly resistant systemic viruses and imbalances. As EU G8 and G20 sherpa, I witnessed the highs and lows of this critical period of international governance.

G8 sherpas are the personal representatives of leaders who spend several months preparing their summit deliberations, and are the only officials allowed in the meeting room, sitting behind their political masters. As EU sherpa, I found a co-operative working relationship with other personal representatives of the four EU member states' leaders also present (France, Germany, the UK and Italy). Similar tasks were performed in the G20 setting, with even more EU member states represented, as Spain and the Netherlands had obtained G20 seats as guests. However, contrary to what happened in the G8, where our only non-like-minded partner was the Russian Federation, in the G20 we were faced with a plethora of countries and leaders who were definitely not in sync with us (or with each other, for that matter!). This was a price we were ready to pay for the benefit of having virtually all relevant actors around the same table.

The fact remains that from China and India to Argentina, Brazil and Saudi Arabia, either nuances or real differences with the 'West' were visible, even if everyone tried to compromise for the sake of avoiding making things worse than they were. It gradually became clear that, sooner or later, the issue of the relative weight and role sharing among countries in the Bretton Woods institutions, and other pillars of the global 'liberal order' that the West had shaped, would be frontally challenged. Once the most acute moments of the financial crisis were behind us, I started hearing dismissive noise coming from non-Western colleagues. 'After all, this is your crisis, not ours', an Indian colleague told me in 2010.

Camp David and the process it started nevertheless demonstrated why, in an interconnected and interdependent world, a global crisis requires global responses through co-operation among a great number of stakeholders, even if they do not share the same values, do not have the same degree of responsibility and have different strategic interests. This being said, if a similar crisis occurred now or in the near future, would the G20 or other leaders' formats still be successful? Has the G20 itself maintained its capacity to act in unison? Do we need other settings? Would Europeans and Americans still have enough clout to steer a similar process now? Or will the growing divorce make the next financial crisis one too many?

In the case of divorced couples, I am told, the real test of their capacity still to act together in spite of the separation comes when children require their joint support. When things get tougher again on the financial and economic front, let's hope that nations will be able to show the same degree of altruism and dedication that we expect from parents towards their offspring, even after divorce.

WHEN OBAMA BLINKED

Talking of dogs again ... it came as a pleasant surprise to me that Barack Obama chose a Portuguese Water Dog as his first 'presidential pet'. Low allergenic levels – and cuteness – had led to the choice of breed and of 'Bo', the first of two. The Portuguese dimension was very welcome to me, as I was about to start my tenure as EU Ambassador to the United States in August 2010. Diplomats are always searching for ice-breaking conversational topics ...

In all fairness, I had not heard much about this breed before, even if it originally came from the Algarve, the southernmost region of my country, where our family had spent holidays for several years. I compensated with some background reading in case the issue came up in conversation. When it eventually did, I chose to quote former US President Harry Truman, who famously said about the antagonistic atmosphere he found in DC: 'If you want a friend in Washington, get a dog!' None better than a Portuguese ...

Bo was most likely jumping around his master when President Obama invited his Chief of Staff, Denis McDonough, for a walk in the Rose Garden, in the summer of 2013. This would turn out to be a most significant stroll. Their conversation was formally about redlines and chemical weapons and Syrian President Assad's behaviour and what to do about it. Events would ultimately prove that it was in fact about the perception of the USA's place in the world.

A year before, in August 2012, when asked about the Syria regime's behaviour and the American response to Assad's war against the opposition, President Obama said that 'a red line for us is we start seeing a whole bunch of chemical weapons moving around or being utilised. That would change my calculus.'[7] That was understood as a clear warning to President Assad of potential American military action if Assad chose to use chemical weapons against his people. The red line started to materialise at the end of the year, and by April 2013, as Ben Rhodes, former speechwriter and deputy national security adviser to Barack Obama, wrote in *The Atlantic*, 'the Assad regime had in fact used chemical weapons. The question then became what we were going to do about it.'[8]

A few months later, on 21 August, news came in of a sarin gas attack that had killed thousands of people in a suburb of Damascus. Obama was advised to order a military strike, even if McDonough and others expressed serious doubts about its legal basis and consequences. In the following days, the spectre of the Iraq invasion and the flawed intelligence that had triggered it haunted the Oval Office. Congress became nervous and some allies of the USA, such as Angela Merkel, advised caution, having Iraq in mind. That did not, however, stop Rhodes from starting to prepare a public announcement of the strike or the military from preparing a plan.

In the meantime, in London, a major setback happened: the Commons voted 285–272 against joining an American strike. Rhodes recalls:

> A shell-shocked David Cameron called Obama to apologise, explaining that he could no longer offer his support. The hangover from the Iraq war had left us staggering toward military intervention with next to no international support, and a Congress demanding that we go through the same divisive process of seeking authorisation that had just failed in London.

What followed was a parallel escalation with, on one hand, an active preparation for a strike, whose justification was announced by the National Security Council and by Secretary of State John Kerry himself, and, on the other, an active campaign against it. The escalation only stopped, or deflated, when Obama decided, allegedly during his walk in the park with his Chief of Staff, that he would not act without congressional approval. That critically wounded the chances of a strike. Obama eventually reached agreement with Putin to force Assad no longer to use chemical weapons, but the fact is that Obama never followed through on his red-line threat.

Barack Obama's decision not to strike Syria, despite Assad's proven use of chemical weapons against his own people and in contradiction with his own threat, shocked Washington and many capitals around the world. As I sat in my office on the corner of K Street with Washington Circle, a few blocks away from both the White House and the State Department, I thought of John Kerry and François Hollande. The Secretary of State had just issued a complete set of arguments to sustain and justify the attack and, in contrast to others, the French president had kept his promise to join the American initiative and French planes were said to be ready to take off. Even if David Cameron had just lost a vote in the House of Commons and could no longer join the operation, and Merkel was extra cautious, Kerry and Hollande, like many others, were gearing up for an attack on Assad when Obama pulled the rug from under their feet.

The diplomatic community in Washington was surprised by the move because we had overlooked how much the president was unconvinced about his country's role as the alleged 'policeman of the world', how traumatic it had been for him to watch the invasion of Iraq and its outcome, how suspicious he was of 'forever wars' – and also, of how much he wanted to be 'different from Bush'. He preferred the predictable reputational costs of inaction or withdrawal to the unpredictable damage of careless adventures in foreign lands.

In addition to the actual impact of Obama's decision on the situation on the ground in Syria and the immense suffering of its people, my other main concern had to do with the 'big picture': I was wondering how much the president's back-pedalling would harm the USA's credibility as the feared hegemon and how much it would impact the Western world's stance vis-à-vis its partners. Independently of the rational arguments that the president put forward to justify not acting as he had threatened to, in international relations – as much as in politics generally – perception is often more relevant than reality. Sometimes it *is* the reality.

Obama's Syrian gesture has been the object of many academic and diplomatic assessments and discussions, as it was undoubtedly a major diplomatic milestone of the first quarter of the century in terms of the balance of power in the Middle East and the wider world. One may even conclude that it was the right call. What history will record, however – and what those leaders around the world who are less sympathetic to the West have carefully taken note of – is that an American red line is not, after all, that red anymore ...

TRUMP'S HAZARDOUS WASTE

Donald Trump could not have been more different from his predecessor in numerous respects (including regarding dogs, which he is apparently not too fond of), and I regretted the departure of the two 'Bos' as much as I was worried about the arrival of the new White House tenant, in early 2017.

I had great memories of my attendance at an American presidential inauguration, Obama's second, in January 2013. The day was extremely cold and ambassadors and spouses were asked to take their seats, in open air like everybody else, well ahead of the beginning of the ceremony. The winter wind coming straight from the Potomac river was almost freezing in the upper rows of the West Terrace amphitheatre, where ambassadors were seated (spouses were luckier, as they gathered at ground level and were better protected), but the long waiting time proved to be well worth it. Obama's speech was captivating, as always, and the whole ceremony reflected the symbolism of the occasion: the expression of the democratic will of the American people in full alignment with the principles and values of the US Constitution and reflecting the global relevance and credibility of the President of the United States.

Those memories came to mind when watching on television, in New York, Donald Trump's inauguration, four years later. He had won the election by a narrow margin but was, of course, fully legitimate as the expression of the democratic will of the American people. However, his speech and his demeanour were the polar opposite of Obama's inauguration. They pre-announced an awkward mandate. For sixteen minutes, Trump spoke of the need to 'make America great again'. He promised to put 'America first' as a pillar of his foreign policy. 'The American carnage stops right here, right now. From this day forward, a new vision will govern our land. From this day forward, it's going to be only America first. America first.' The rest is well known.

Recollecting my times in the USA during Trump's presidency, I remember being considerably irritated by a long list of his attitudes: from his threats to leave NATO and his constant mistreatment of allies to his inclination to meet and even laud authoritarian leaders like Putin or Kim to the detriment of the West's core values and interests, not to mention his demagogical style. However, the decisions Trump took that shocked me the most were the withdrawals from the Iran deal (JCPOA) and from the Paris climate agreement. This is basically because, beyond any other consideration, his decisions simply did not make sense.

The JCPOA was the result of a unique joint diplomatic effort of the five permanent members of the Security Council, together with Germany and the EU, negotiating directly with Iran, the goal of which was to ensure that the country's nuclear programme would be exclusively peaceful. The EU High Representative – Catherine Ashton until almost the end, and briefly her successor, Federica Mogherini – was asked to co-ordinate and lead the talks. The American administration, needing to have intense bilateral discussions with Iran, held a series of meetings in Oman that developed the framework for an agreement. A painstaking effort over many months enabled the permanent five plus Germany (P5 + 1) to reach an interim deal and ultimately a final agreement. The secret American contacts were folded into the mainstream of the negotiations, thanks to the tireless work of John Kerry, Wendy Sherman, Bill Burns and others.

I had a first direct interaction with the Iran file while in Washington. Soon after my arrival, in 2010, I was confronted with a great deal of scepticism in Congress regarding the capacity of the EU to impose sanctions on Iran, a crucial element in the process of bringing Iranians to the table with a serious attitude. For the first time ever for an EU representative in DC, I was invited, together with the relevant EU member states' ambassadors, to a hearing of the Foreign Affairs Committee of the House of Representatives, chaired by a Democratic congressman from California, Howard Berman. I led the discussion on our side, which soon focused on the planned EU sanctions package against Iran.

Berman was so doubtful of the likelihood of the EU adopting sanctions, given the well-known divergence of views and interests of its member states – but also as a reflection of his own underestimation of the EU's role – that he was ready to bet against it. I was, of course, more than certain that the contrary would happen. I won the bet, which involved a bottle of good French Champagne or a dinner, I can no longer remember, partly because we never saw our bet through ... unlike the EU ministers who approved a series of tough sanctions against Iran.

A few years later, in the spring of 2014, another moment illustrated the very high stakes of the negotiation – and the critical importance that Barack Obama attached to it and to the EU's role in it. A few months before the end of her mandate as High Representative and co-ordinator of the Iran negotiations, Cathy Ashton was visiting Washington and had scheduled a meeting with the president's National Security Advisor, Susan Rice, at the White House.

We gathered in Rice's office, one of the largest in the otherwise very compact (and crowded) West Wing, together with her deputy, Antony Blinken, the Under-Secretary for Political Affairs and American negotiator, Wendy Sherman, and a few other American officials. Apart from me, Cathy was, as always, flanked by her loyal Chief of Staff, James Morrison. Strangely enough, I noticed that there was an empty chair at the top of the table.

The High Representative, working with the P5 + 1, had successfully managed to produce an interim deal in 2013 and the negotiators were then working on the very final version of a permanent agreement. The meeting was important and timely as the negotiations were at a critical stage. Halfway through it, a surprise happened. Cathy Ashton has a clear memory of it:[9]

> We had talked for some time about Ukraine when the door opened. I had my back to the door and I looked round and immediately everybody stood up as it was POTUS [President Obama]. I then realised that at the head of this table was an armchair that fitted the table. I just thought it had been left empty. James said that earlier someone had mentioned that someone might join the meeting but I had missed this. POTUS gave me a big hug. He asked me about Ukraine, and he talked about talking to Merkel about it. We talked for about fifteen to twenty minutes about this and then he switched subjects to Iran.

In his distinctive relaxed style and articulate discourse, Obama told Cathy Ashton what high expectations he had of her personally and of the EU's role, asked for her assessment and encouraged her firmly to pursue a deal.

'He said he wanted to give me some messages for me to give to the Iranian team, and how confident he was in me,' Ashton recalls. 'That he would sell this deal but it had to be good enough and that they needed to understand this was a difficult environment to do it. But he would do it if he felt it was good enough.'

Obama was portraying a realistic concern: he wanted to make sure any agreement would be well received in the USA. He understood the strength of opinion within the P5 + 1 and feared that some might well settle for less, which could easily leave him isolated. He needed the most from any negotiation in order to feel confident enough to fight for a deal that achieved the goal of a peaceful Iranian nuclear programme.

Cathy Ashton made it clear that there was one negotiation and that, as far as Iran was concerned, the USA was the most important player in this. More importantly, the six countries understood that it was the sum total of their efforts that mattered, not the individual parts. The deal only worked if everyone agreed that it worked. And anyway, 'no matter what anyone else did, only the USA could lift its own sanctions – and that mattered most to the Iranians', Ashton clarifies. 'So, I told him, he didn't have to worry as for Iran it would not matter if everyone else agreed and not the USA as the USA is what they need.'

Before leaving, after more than half an hour in the room, the president told us that there was no other negotiation going on, wished Cathy Ashton good luck and told her next time they met they should have lunch.

Concluding the meeting after a detailed stocktaking on Iran, Susan Rice asked whether it would help Cathy Ashton if they put out the picture of Obama with us. The answer was obvious as Ashton's success would not have been possible without the confidence of all partners, Iran included, and particularly without the trust of the White House.

The JCPOA, finally signed on 14 July 2015, was a remarkable example of international co-operation and diplomatic ingenuity.

Unfortunately, the following tenant of the White House, Donald Trump, destroyed it without a shadow of regret, in the blink of an eye – in the view of many, simply because Obama had done it. Today, there are few doubts about Iran's capability now or very soon to weaponise its sophisticated nuclear assets. A terrible waste. That's on Trump.

The 2015 Paris agreement on the fight against climate change was another crucial diplomatic achievement, a promising outcome of decades of international discussions. And it was another one that Trump dismissed, sending the worst possible message to the international community on a topic of existential relevance.

I had engaged in climate negotiations since the first top-level international gatherings in the spring of 2009, in the run-up to the Copenhagen climate summit to be held in December. At the beginning of his mandate, President Obama was very hesitant and cautious on climate, not yet ready, in this domain, to distinguish himself too much from his predecessor. We were still very far from the full commitment he would reveal during his second term. In fact, when Commission President Barroso first met President Obama and Secretary of State Hillary Clinton in Prague, during Obama's first visit to Europe, the exchange of views on climate was very tense. The meeting started off well, but once we raised climate I realised the new president was uncomfortable with EU pressure on him to act. Obama claimed, in slightly agitated fashion, that we were asking for too much and were not aware of how difficult his domestic context was on climate.

His call for the Major Economies Forum on Energy and Climate (known as MEF) representatives to meet ahead of Copenhagen was part of his response to our request. It was a very timid move as seen from Europe, where we had already approved an ambitious energy and climate strategy back in 2007, but a necessary one for the USA: in Obama's view, industrialised countries alone should not pay the price of climate action and other major economies – the emerging ones, like China and other members of the G20 – would need to contribute as well. Copenhagen would be a lot about this debate.

Leaders' personal representatives ('sherpas') held the first pre-
paratory meeting in Washington. Seventeen major economies
were represented, including the EU. This was the beginning of
the road to Paris as far as the position of major economies was
concerned. What followed until Paris and beyond turned out,
in fact, to be better than we had expected when we gathered in
Washington, where our hope regarding the American position
was still limited. I had a brief and very pleasant bilateral exchange
with President Obama at a reception he hosted for delegates at the
White House. It was my very first direct contact with him, ahead
of other opportunities in the margins of G8 and G20 summits, and
a year before my formal presentation of credentials to him, in the
Oval Office, in August 2010.

President Obama told me that he counted a lot on the MEF as a
stepping stone to a wider global convergence on climate change. In
retrospect, he was right, particularly regarding China, as we could
witness in Copenhagen. We were then still a long way from Paris,
in 2015, where a global agreement would be reached. However,
what neither of us would have suspected is that a few years down
the road, because of Donald Trump, the USA would step out of an
agreement that had taken such a lot of investment to accomplish.

Trump's behaviour on the Iran and climate change files are tell-
ing illustrations of his peculiar approach to international relations
and his interpretation of the core interests of his country. It represented an enormous waste – hazardous waste – of intelligence,
energy, inventiveness and international co-operation.

However, in his own unsophisticated way, Trump was not too
far from reflecting a deeper undercurrent in American public opinion, not far from what had made Obama ignore his red lines on
Syria's chemical weapons.

AMERICANS, THE EXCEPTIONAL ISOLATIONISTS

In post in New York during the first three years of Trump's term
in office, I had to make an effort not to be too overwhelmed,

distracted and misled by the president's histrionics. The risk was to ignore a deeper, more relevant reality. What we were witnessing then was more than a display of a salesman's showbusiness abilities. If there is one thing Trump is good at, it is 'reading the market'. And what he read was that the USA wishes to retreat from the interventionist global leadership role it has regularly played in recent decades, under different presidents, and is resistant to seeing its sovereign room for manoeuvre constrained by multilateral institutions or commitments.

I had had the chance to observe deep America. As ambassador in Washington between 2010 and 2014, I made a point of visiting all fifty American states, as well as Puerto Rico. I met state governors and local mayors, elected senators and members of Congress, discussed with business people and exchanged views at think tanks and universities. And I talked to 'normal' people. In the subsequent four years as Ambassador to the United Nations, in New York, I closely followed the unexpected Obama/Trump transition and the intense debate it triggered, and watched the unfolding of a unique, previously unthinkable way of governing the USA.

I empirically confirmed that the USA is not two sophisticated and globally minded coasts separated by big parochial plains, as some in Europe tend to believe. The USA is a complex sociological and cultural reality, in constant evolution, full of energy and creativity, very rich and very poor, uniquely cultivated and astonishingly underdeveloped, capable of consecutively electing such antipodal personalities as Barack Obama and Donald Trump (and again put Trump ahead in election polls in the middle of several court trials and with convictions against him).

World-renowned scholars, scientists, artists and tech developers coexist with many middle- and working-class Americans who hold no passport and have never even travelled throughout their own country. In most parts of the USA, even Washington DC is seen as a foreign land, so common is the suspicion regarding coastal elites and the federal government, and so real is people's attachment to their local community and their own state. The general knowledge of global geography in the USA is the source of many unsympathetic jokes, which are not that far from the truth.

Beyond anecdotes and prejudice, the fact is that for most Americans, the world is the USA, and the USA is the world. The majority of them simply do not feel the urge to worry about 'the rest', let alone take care of it or be contained by it. Aware of the risk of generalising, I would dare to admit that deep America is as parochial as coastal America is global, but at the end of the day, all America is ... American (in all honesty, can all Europeans claim to be that different?).

The USA is a country immensely proud of its achievements that considers itself to be exceptional under God – but which is today tired of its global responsibilities.

Mind you, American isolationism is not new. It has in fact been a major feature of the country's political culture and mindset, which has often surfaced in its foreign policy pronouncements. It is founded on collective pride and self-esteem and on a sense of uniqueness and virtual invincibility. Protected by a buffer of two large oceans to the east and to the west, comforted by friendly or harmless neighbours to the north and to the south, aware of their country's unique and formidable military might – not to mention its economic, technological and soft-power clout – Americans can afford to focus inwards and that comes naturally as their default attitude. Unless it is attacked – as at Pearl Harbor or downtown Manhattan – or led to believe that its fundamental strategic interests are at stake beyond its territory, the USA would for most of the time rather stay put.

Occasionally, though, isolationism is trumped by the other side of the coin: 'exceptionalism'. Occasionally, the USA decides to toss the coin and chooses to venture abroad, in pursuit of noble – and sometimes less noble – goals. To end suffering, to save lives, to prevent genocide or at the request of allies that safeguard American interests, strategic or economic. With or without international legal cover. Alone or in good company.

The driver of interventionism is always the sense that the USA is an exceptional country, called upon to use its might to do right, to do what others are not capable or not willing to do, and to protect and exercise its national sovereignty even beyond its borders. A sense of mission or a selfish survival impulse, or both at the same time: interventionism is to a large extent an expression of exceptionalism.

I was often asked how I felt about the USA's role in the world, about the country's 'exceptionalism'. My favourite reply in private exchanges was as contradictory as the American positioning. It would go like this: 'I think we would like and need you to remain an exceptional country but would prefer that you don't overdo it – and don't brag too much about it either.'

At the dawn of the century, deeply touched by the Twin Towers attack, the USA chose the other side of the coin and reacted with wounded animal instincts: when your honour as 'top dog' is at stake, attack is the best defence and taking action is inevitable, even when it is not necessarily the most rational option. Invading Iraq and Afghanistan made sense for the American leadership on those grounds and on the basis of contemporarily available evidence (or what was presented as such). One can claim that there were maybe better and less harmful alternatives for expressing revenge and that, in any case, the 'day after' those military operations should have been considered in all its complexity. However, it is difficult to deny that something had to happen at that point in time. We should also remember that the White House was not alone in its judgement and decisions, far from it, even if some try to forget that today.

The impact of the American reaction to 9/11 would, however, turn out to be significantly detrimental, if not disastrous, for the perception of the USA and its allies in large parts of the world. After initial wide support from American public opinion and political forces, George W. Bush faced increasing criticism and scepticism at home. When subsequent Republican and Democratic presidents prepared and eventually concluded the withdrawal from Iraq and Afghanistan, even if in a less than optimal and even clumsy way, this reversal of previous decisions was widely supported by a tired public opinion. In the process, damage had been done to the USA's external reputation and fuel had been poured onto the fire of isolationism at home and anti-Western feelings abroad, while the announced and expected positive effects on the target countries had not materialised.

Invading Iraq the way the USA did had another important effect: to divide Europeans among themselves and create gaps between some European leaders and Washington. It was not a happy moment either for the EU or for transatlantic relations. Fortunately, we were all able to overcome those divisions even if some degree of mutual reserve still exists.

It is against the background of the USA's historic tension between isolationism and interventionism that we need to consider President Biden's reaction to the Russian war on Ukraine in 2022. The fact that this time the US president did not blink or react impulsively, that he thoughtfully chose to act on behalf of a noble cause, not simply out of narrow self-interest, is to be commended. The fact that he opted to support Ukraine, albeit with great caution, can be explained by the sheer magnitude of Putin's provocation, the relevance of Russia for American strategic interests and the clear and sincere commitment of Joseph Robinette Biden Jr to European security (Biden is by far the American politician who best knows and 'feels' Europe).

American public opinion reacted positively in the early days of American support to Ukraine. However, the prolongation of the conflict and the huge cost of supporting Kyiv, combined with the alarming situation in the Middle East since 7 October 2023, as well as the Trump-driven evolution of Republican positions, have eroded the initial consensus. This has enhanced the underlying unwillingness to intervene, particularly in theatres, like the European one, where Americans believe others should assume greater responsibility. The case of unconditional support to Israel is, of course, a different and unique one, respecting its own distinct rationality – but even that had trouble resisting the Israeli government's hardline behaviour in Gaza.

On balance, and beyond the differences in semantics and ideology of Bush, Obama, Trump and Biden's White Houses, regardless of the distinct contexts in which they operated, what is likely to remain from the first quarter of the twenty-first century is the confirmation of an overall trend towards the USA's unwillingness to act on the international scene, unless action corresponds to a direct national interest and is pursued autonomously from multilateral constraints.

Today, as we start a new quarter of the century and new political cycles begin in the USA and Europe, within a highly volatile international context, serious questions haunt Europeans: what will the USA ultimately do and how much should Europeans count on them? How is American exceptionalism reflected in the country's international posture? As interventionist or isolationist, or something in between? Or would it act out of simple self-interest? We could be witnessing the dawn of the 'age of American unilateralism'. And this is a major factor, in times of divorce, in assessing the likelihood of more serious deterioration.

This should be seen as a serious wake-up call for the USA's allies. 'We are going to see an America which continues to be reluctant to intervene overseas where this involves boots on the ground', says Kim Darroch, now a member of the House of Lords and former British Ambassador to the United States and the EU and National Security Adviser.[10] 'The US in turn will simultaneously demand complete loyalty and support from Europe in its confrontation with China.'

My expectation is that the USA, regardless of who occupies the White House, will gradually impose a race to the bottom on foreign conflicts – less American interventionism and more pressure on allies to step in – and a race to the top on China – tougher measures to contain and counter Chinese power, be it economic or military, and more pressure on allies to support the American drive, by raising barriers and constraints on Beijing. For Europe, particularly if one considers Ukraine as part of the 'race to the bottom' and one bears in mind how dependent the EU is on trade with Beijing, this is not a promising scenario. Joe Biden could well go down in history as the last 'transatlanticist' American president.

One caveat though: American exceptionalism will always shadow American isolationism and ultimately mitigate it. As much as American public opinion is reluctant to take care of other countries' problems and leaders tend to follow this inward-looking instinct, the fact remains that there is hardly any major crisis in the world that can be overcome without an active American role and there is hardly any major crisis in the world that does not affect, sooner or later, the USA's vital interests. And when that happens, the cavalry is never too far away ... There is a price to pay for being exceptional – as much as there is always a risk that a great power succumbs to imperial temptations. Will the former benign hegemon wish to become an imperial superpower?

HU OUT, XI IN, HU OUT (FOR GOOD)

Hu Jintao always impressed me by his composure, his professionalism and his total lack of charisma. In several bilateral and multilateral summits where he represented China, rarely did I see an expression of feeling on his face. His handshakes were brief and flabby and exhausted the extent of his physical contact with his interlocutors. He never spoke off-script or in English, there was no small talk beyond the weather and there were no personal remarks of any kind. But he smiled, he was reassuring, he made Europeans feel confident about China's intentions.

As Secretary-General of the Chinese Communist Party and President of the People's Republic of China for ten years, between 2003 and 2013, Hu embodied the Chinese Communist Party's meritocracy and projected a relative predictability about his country's future and international behaviour, throughout the first half of the first quarter of the century. We had our issues and our differences, obviously, but there was a general impression of normality as we got accustomed to, and also benefited from, the rapid opening of the Chinese market and observed the country's increasing protagonism in the global scene. We were beginning to feel the impact of the competitiveness of its economy, but alarm bells were not ringing yet. We heard clear messages about Taiwan, but we expected these to be more rhetoric than a real threat. When Hu's time came to an end, respecting a regular and well-choreographed Chinese change of guard, the best expectations in the West were that his successor would ideally represent a copy and paste version of him.

Eleven years after his retirement from the top position, in October

2022, in the Great Hall of the People where the Communist Party was holding its twentieth congress, Hu Jintao was seated to the left of Xi Jinping when he suffered an ultimate humiliation that fully revealed the true nature of his successor. For reasons never officially explained but that were obviously contentious, Hu was prevented from opening a file placed on the table in front of him and was physically removed from the room by a couple of handlers, visibly against his will and without any sign of explanation or solidarity from any of the top brass of the party, let alone from Xi Jinping himself.

This display of infighting at the highest level of the party and state hierarchy took place in front of thousands of delegates and eventually made its way to the internet. It was the symbolic end of the road for Hu and for the cycle in Chinese history that he had embodied, but also the visible demonstration of the consolidation of power of the new leader. And Xi Jinping wanted it to be known and taken good note of.

The first quarter of the twenty-first century witnessed a qualitative change in China's position on the world scene that will have an impact for decades to come. President Hu was the last rotating leader, the last representative of the Deng years. Xi is the foreseeably long-lasting face of a more assertive, more confident, more powerful China.

President Xi has recently started his third term in office. More will be added, probably until the end of his life, or close to that, who knows? The possibility of extending his mandate was confirmed in 2017. Xi approaches his role at the head of party and country with a double 'conservative' mindset. Conservative in line with his upbringing in brutal family and social conditions, suspicious of private wealth and capitalism in general, not keen on social innovation. Equally conservative in the sense of preserving, above all, the power of the party and its leadership elite.

His agenda 'is driven by 'ultra-realist' interests and an explicit rejection of 'universal' values, which China calls a Western, quasi-colonial imposition. 'Xi's China tolerates those international principles that assure the survival of the system he has been charged with managing,' says David Rennie, a senior journalist/

columnist at *The Economist*, who headed its offices in Brussels, Washington and until recently Beijing.[11]

Most importantly, President Xi believes time is on China's side. After all, China waited for so long to return to the top of the world, to overcome what it considers humiliation and marginalisation by the West, that it can wait a little longer for a full vindication. Not too long, though.

A higher level of self-confidence than his predecessors was perceivable by Xi's interlocutors. When José Manuel Barroso, the President of the European Commission, met him for the first time at a bilateral EU–China summit, he recalls[12] having been impressed by the fact that President Xi made his initial remarks without reading notes, something his predecessors, and Hu in particular, would not have done. Later, the new Chinese leader would also become the first to pay an official visit to the European Commission in Brussels. Signs of individual control and statesmanship. And power.

Today, the stage is thus set for what could be an amazing 'poker game between China and the West', as David Rennie puts it.[13] Within the battle of de-risking and potential de-coupling, against the background of an ever more likely confrontation in the South China Sea, at the height of technological rivalry and open competition between systems and models, resilience will be the name of the game. Chinese leaders expect Western countries to accommodate the rise and new role of their country because they need its market too much to risk destroying it. Western leaders expect China to control its rise because it needs Western markets too much to risk destroying its access to them. Who will blink first? Will it happen soon or will we be watching a long-lasting gamble?

PANDEMIC SCARS

The Covid pandemic of 2020–22 will feature in historical records as a major event in the first quarter of the twenty-first century, with domestic and global consequences – and lessons to be learned. We had a vague awareness of the health risks of the galloping interconnectivity of the globalised world. Images of medieval plagues or of the more recent Spanish Flu pandemic had crossed our minds when warned by Bill Gates, among others, about the likelihood of a swift spreading of viruses on a global scale. And yet, Covid-19, or Corona as it was known in its early days, triggered the pandemic of our lives to our collective surprise.

The pandemic irrupted in the first quarter of 2020 and coincided with Brexit – and with the start of my tenure in London as EU Ambassador to the United Kingdom. The first lockdown was announced six weeks after my taking office in London and forced me to return to Brussels, together with most of my colleagues, who subsequently scattered around Europe for a few weeks, working from their respective capitals in a first experience of remote diplomacy.

As much as the virus itself could not be contained within national borders, it would have been naive to expect that the political ramifications of the pandemic would not affect international relations (and, of course, also EU–UK relations). This was particularly so when a justifiably excited public opinion started focusing on vaccination.

It was all about the competition for supplies and protection of the needs of respective populations, within a very unbalanced and restricted market where only a few producers were able to conceive, produce and deliver the needed goods. No politician in any country could afford to be seen as less keen than others to ensure that their fellow citizens would have access to vaccines as soon as possible and in appropriate quantities, whenever they became available. Those countries that had better prospects for taking the lead had no alternative but to satisfy first the demands of their populations. However, in the process, many in the rich, industrialised North forgot how others would perceive our focus.

The management of the Covid pandemic is a good recent illustration of how domestic considerations impact upon foreign policy and external relations in general. The reverse is equally true – and more and more so, since we have witnessed how the Russian invasion of Ukraine and events in the Middle East have impacted the domestic political debates at national level. Blurred lines all over.

Covid vaccination was a particularly challenging issue within the EU. We basically had two options: allow for a first come, first served model and risk having our smaller member states ending up with no vaccines or getting them too late, for lack of adequate financial agility and bargaining power; or, as wisely decided, create a new mechanism of centralised procurement and equitable distribution, according to the needs and not the means of each country.

The model chosen implied a tough, complex negotiation with vaccine producers and a tight control of contractual arrangements, to prevent any diversion of trade before the delivery of contractually agreed quantities to EU countries, out of respect for legal obligations and the huge amounts of taxpayers' money involved. For all those reasons, a system of export surveillance and monitoring was necessary. This was not about export prohibition, as exports were never forbidden and only a very tiny amount, in one single instance, was blocked. At the end of the most critical phase, we were indeed proud to claim that the EU had catered for the needs of its population and at the same time had been the biggest exporter of vaccines.

It had not crossed my mind that the EU export surveillance technical tool designed to address an extremely sensitive health situation and guarantee good delivery for our citizens would be the source of one of the toughest moments in our relationship with the UK in the early post-Brexit era.

That afternoon and early evening of a Friday in late January 2021 is difficult to forget. It was my birthday, I had commuted from London for the occasion and as we were preparing for a relaxed dinner in Brussels, messages started appearing on my iPhone screen with alert signs. In the urge to implement the export monitoring and surveillance system, someone in Brussels realised that we had a long and open land border with a third country called the United Kingdom and thus there was a need to foresee the possible triggering of Article 16 of the protocol on Ireland and Northern Ireland, which allowed the suspension of the protocol to make sure that no vaccines would unduly cross the border between the south and the north of the island of Ireland. And this was included – without any prior consultation of our partners across the Channel or of the most directly interested member state, not to mention yours truly – in a first draft of the Commission document that would be circulated for internal decision. As often happens, it leaked.

Alarm was immediately raised concerning the sensitivity of using the 'nuclear weapon' of the protocol in such a situation. Admitting the possibility of the EU unilaterally using Article 16 to protect its trade interests, even if presented as health ones, would be perceived in London and particularly in the Northern Ireland unionist camp as a confirmation that the EU would use that provision of the protocol for its own internal purposes regardless of local interests and without prior consultation and agreement. Our credibility and goodwill were in question.

After a couple of hours of phone contacts and with the help of many in Brussels and Dublin, the reference was extracted from the draft and explanations were provided. The accidental mistake lasted overall less than four hours. I soon realised it had been four hours too long. The damage had been done.

Over the weekend, we had some indication that London would not exploit the incident beyond its factual dimension. However, on Monday things changed for the worse and the Article 16 incident haunted the relationship between the UK and the EU for months and years to come. It would be used by the UK to denounce – unfairly – our alleged bad faith and diminish our arguments against the use of Article 16 or any other unilateral measures. This was undoubtedly a Brussels own goal that I could have happily lived without. But it was also an example of the weaponisation of a very delicate and sensitive issue – Covid-19 – for the purpose of scoring short-term political goals.

Vaccines were at the heart of another difficult moment that involved one of my presidents, Charles Michel, from the European Council, and almost provided me with a first opportunity in my career as ambassador to be summoned by the hosting government.

On 9 March 2021, late in the afternoon, I was told that London was 'furious' with a statement by President Charles Michel. The issue was serious enough to justify the message that came in some minutes later: 'FCDO [Foreign, Commonwealth and Development Office] called. Raab wants to call you in over Michel's remarks on British vaccine exports.' Dominic Raab, the foreign secretary, wanted to summon me to ask for an explanation of Michel's comments and, more importantly, to tell me what the British government thought about it.

In his weekly newsletter, Charles Michel had refuted attacks on the EU that had surfaced in the UK. 'I am shocked when I hear accusations of "vaccine nationalism" against the EU ... The UK and the US have imposed an outright ban on the export of vaccines or vaccine components produced in their territory ... The EU has never stopped exporting.' His remark was accurately based on the contractual arrangements between the British government and the vaccine producers, which prevented them from exporting outside the UK.

I took due note of Dominic Raab's request and relayed informally elements of context to help de-escalate the incident. But I also took note of the fact that the foreign secretary was about to summon an ambassador whom he had not yet fully recognised as such (for more details, see Chapter 4).

The awkwardness of Dominic Raab's summons did not escape the attention of a former British Conservative Member of the European Parliament, Charles Tannock, who tweeted: 'Not sure whether to laugh or cry over this tragicomical situation. @ValedeAlmeidaEU must be having a laugh at this one.' He was half right. It was just a smile.

To confirm that chance plays a role in history, I was away from London that week and it fell on my deputy to meet not the foreign secretary but the permanent under-secretary, Philip Barton. As always, Nicole Mannion did it very professionally the following morning and was met by Barton at 8.30 a.m. in his office, with no water or coffee. The only thing on offer was a one-page aide-mémoire repeating the arguments contained in a letter sent in parallel to Charles Michel.

This was how a foreign minister escaped the embarrassment of inconsistency and I missed the last opportunity in my career to add 'summoned by' to my ambassadorial bio. This incident had at least one advantage: it brought to the surface of the political debate the issue of transparency in the Covid-19 vaccines market. And in this area, we had a relevant story to tell – which we did.

The revelation of the magnitude of EU vaccine exports laid bare an asymmetrical reality: up to then the UK had exported zero vaccines. I had to be very clear in my communication, which I was on ITV among other outlets: the EU does not practise vaccine nationalism and would expect other countries to behave likewise; we need more transparency in vaccines exports and we must make vaccine producers more accountable for the sake of the safety of our citizens and the protection of taxpayers' money. Keen to avoid escalation, I chose not to highlight another fact: during the month of February, the UK had partly relied on EU-produced vaccines to inoculate its own citizens.

These two 'vaccine war' episodes illustrate the extreme sensitivity of sanitary and health issues and the overlapping of domestic and foreign agendas in today's world. Domestic policy choices, be it in the health, taxation, environment, climate, energy or regulatory domains, to cite only a few, now directly impact external relations as never before.

Covid-related disputes, the ones I have briefly described and others related to North–South imbalances (to which I will refer later), created wounds and left scars. They were warning signs of things to come, now that trade and economic relations had left the cosy, technocratic offices of experts and sectoral ministers, and had become part of the list of key issues brought to the attention of leaders.

FOREIGN IS THE NEW DOMESTIC

As exemplified above, and as I witnessed in dozens of summit meetings at European and global level in the last twenty years, the international agenda increasingly reflects the blurring of lines between domestic and foreign policies. No responsible president or prime minister, from big or small countries, can afford to neglect such cross-interaction: in assessing measures to take on the domestic front, they need to calculate their foreign impact, and vice versa, upfront and not as a side issue.

This is inevitable in today's interconnected and interdependent world and in the context of a globalised economy. In recent times, the financial crisis, Brexit, the pandemic, climate change, energy, migration, supply chain disruptions, the inflation surge, the increased assertiveness of China, the Russian war on Ukraine and the violence in the Middle East have, in different ways, exemplified this blurring and illustrated how complex and difficult it is to manage. If not well thought through, however, the cross-pollination between the domestic and foreign risks jeopardising rational and effective policy making and could ultimately weaken both tracks of political action.

An example of this is today's temptation to approach external economic relations purely from the angle of 'strategic sovereignty' or 'strategic autonomy'. The debate is now taking place in Europe, even if it had already started in Japan some years ago, and these expressions have now infiltrated national discourses around the world, with different colorations and connotations, and are actively exploited by populists, feeding their obsessive 'national' versus 'global' narrative.

In the EU, the general public's awareness of the autonomy/security relationship dramatically increased in the early days of the pandemic when we realised how dependent we were upon medicines entirely produced in the South and particularly in China and India. When the pandemic wreaked havoc among a panicked public opinion, Europe was not able to produce a single tablet of paracetamol, the drug used to alleviate the symptoms of Covid – it all came from abroad. It was highly symbolic.

Obviously the concern had already surfaced in political and economic circles well before the pandemic and was not exclusive to the pharmaceutical industry. Our industrial capacity had been delocalised for the sake of supply chain efficiency and overall competitiveness. This was a main feature of globalisation, which created millions of jobs in emerging economies and enhanced business competitiveness and benefited consumers in developed countries. However, its downsides were real. The double shock of the financial crisis and the pandemic made these disadvantages more clearly visible to a larger number of people and confirmed a new reality: the political and social cost of global supply chain efficiency became difficult to sustain, particularly in the light of the increasing assertiveness of China, the major beneficiary of the transfer of production capability. Economic dependence became an inevitable source of insecurity, or at least of the perception of it. And this is fertile ground for populists.

The pandemic opened the Pandora's box and offered protectionism a real opportunity. The Russian invasion of Ukraine, which followed immediately, and particularly the economic and inflationary consequences of the war, added to the problem. The competition from China, previously seen as a benign new trading partner but now increasingly perceived as a threatening, non-like-minded systemic rival, completed the picture: there was and still is considerable pressure on governments to be 'protective' of their respective economies.

Having worked for the EU long enough to remember the mantra of free trade, open borders and fair competition as a foundation of our economic and political model, it is not without some concern that I now witness a drive towards selective closure of markets and targeted export and import restrictions on the borderline of the rules-based global trade apparatus that we helped put together. In parallel, the debate about industrial policy and European or national 'champions' involves the risk of market 'dirigisme' and distorted competition, potentially leading to unsustainable and non-competitive choices and precipitating the fragmentation of the EU's single market.

Particularly in the US, but not only there, tariffs are increasingly seen as the 'panacea'. This can be a dangerous *fausse bonne idée* (in French for not innocent reasons ...). Tariffs on imports can potentially do more harm to domestic consumers and to the competitiveness of one's own producers and exporters than to the initial intended targets. In the US alone, 41 million jobs depend on trade. Over 10 per cent of American jobs have been created by foreign investment, a lot of it coming from EU countries.

A thin line separates fully legitimate trade defence, anti-dumping tools and export controls from protectionism, and de-risking from de-coupling. We need to remain attentive to avoid undermining the interests of export-dependent economies like the European ones, most of them small or medium sized and unable to operate expensive and potentially distorting state aid mechanisms. We need the right balance.

• • •

On the political and institutional front, there have been, inside the EU, some ramifications of this new mindset that bundles domestic and foreign agendas.

Since José Manuel Barroso's first mandate, Commission presidents have been seeking to reposition the Commission more as a 'political' actor, which is understandable and even obvious, given that the College of Commissioners is made of politicians from several party-political families and the College is confirmed by elected bodies. They have had to keep in mind, at the same time, the need to avoid an excessive 'party-politicisation' of the Commission that would jeopardise the careful balance sought by the founders of the European Community when they created the supranational Commission as a *sui generis* entity. The Commission is in fact asked to act simultaneously not only as the sole initiator of legislation and policies, but also as the legal guardian of the treaties, as an independent administration and as a regulator of the single market – all critical functions requiring a certain degree of objective and even technocratic impartiality (as well as a clear perception of it by public opinion).

The need for the right balance is particularly true of the international dimension of the Commission's activities, where the consideration of the external and strategic ramifications of its actions goes in parallel with the respect for the prerogatives of other EU actors – first and foremost the President of the European Council and the High Representative – and the sovereign rights of EU member states in the foreign policy and defence domains.

The right balance between 'domestic' and 'foreign' dimensions and among the different institutional actors is not always easy to strike and the external perception of those difficulties can even become problematic for the image of the Union, as we have witnessed in the last few years. President von der Leyen was able to use the large array of capabilities and resources available to the Commission – not existent in any other Brussels-based institution – as well as her personal abilities, in support of the EU's external profile. This was done not without some internal resistance but somehow reflected a need for the concentration of roles, for critical mass in critical times. Seen from outside, and certainly from Joe Biden's White House, it was a rather welcome clarification of interlocutors. However, it should not distract EU institutions and respective leaders, as their new mandates start, from seeking an even better co-ordinated and more results-oriented division of labour among them and avoiding self-inflicted wounds to their international credibility.

Overall, the EU can definitely do better in projecting its influence and capacity to act externally. Inserting a political and geopolitical dimension into internal policies and economic agendas, and vice versa, is the way forward and both European and American governments, and political leaders have been aiming at that recently. As has been said, however, there are some risks involved, as the inbuilt logic of this process has been inherently 'protective' and could trigger protectionist temptations that might backfire and negatively impact not only relations with third parties but also relations between them (as seen in some recent sensitive EU–US trade disputes).

Moreover, the current defensive and protective trend may also be detrimental to and contradictory with some other central objectives. Take the valid goal of 'de-risking' trade and investments with China for the sake of economic security and sovereignty. The only way for the EU to reduce the negative impact of such a strategy is to increase diversification of its trade and investment patterns, away from China and towards other markets, other suppliers of raw materials and other enablers of supply chain efficiency. Well, paradoxically, the same overarching concern about protecting some of the EU's economic sectors prevented, for decades, the conclusion of a trade deal with the Latin American, South Atlantic countries of the Mercosur/Mercosul group,[14] whose potential as alternative partners to replace or at least compensate for China is second to none.

Further north in the Atlantic, Biden reacted to the inflationary effects of the war in Ukraine and competition from China – as well as populist discourses from right and left – with a more intelligent package than his predecessor's but with equally detrimental impact on European countries. Cleverly wrapping its policy in an anti-inflationary and climate-friendly guise, the Biden administration acted fundamentally, as it confessed, in the service of American companies and jobs, combining the impact of internal and external policy initiatives.

Jake Sullivan, the brain behind Biden's foreign policy writ large, put it very explicitly in a now famous speech where he advocated a 'foreign policy for the middle class'. Speaking at the Brookings Institution, Democrats' favourite think tank in Washington DC, in April 2023, Sullivan started by realising how odd his position was:[15] 'I want to start by thanking you all for indulging a National Security Advisor to discuss economics.' He then went on to talk extensively about economic policies from a foreign relations angle (and actually quoted Ursula von der Leyen several times, as if to confirm that the same reasoning was being pursued in parallel on both sides of the Atlantic).

Sullivan acknowledged that an international environment defined by 'geopolitical and security competition' had 'important economic impacts' and admitted that 'economic integration' of the first decades of globalisation had not stopped 'China from expanding its military ambitions' or 'Russia from invading its democratic neighbours'. 'Neither country had become more responsible or co-operative,' he added.

His underlying focus was, however, on the impact in deep America, and specifically on its manufacturing capacity, which had been 'hollowed out', and on inequality. 'The American middle class lost ground while the wealthy did better than ever,' he said. Hence the need for an industrial strategy, for 'resilience and security' in supply chains and for common action with American partners to achieve the same goals.

This was not new, though. Seven years earlier, I had detected this trend among Democrats, just days before the presidential election of 2016. In a private small-group conversation at Columbia University, in New York, Sullivan, then Hillary Clinton's most senior policy adviser and her putative National Security Advisor, was already very clear: 'the first foreign policy priority that emerged in discussions with American citizens during the campaign was geared toward trade policy. Second to that was the fear of another war entanglement, in conjunction with some acute perception of the dismal realities of the world.'

Jobs and no boots on the ground: that is how Democrats perceived their voters' priorities as regards foreign policy before they lost the vote to Trump – and Trump carried out that exact agenda.

More globally, the blurring of lines between domestic and foreign policies affects the West's relationship with developing countries. A recent example of that is the Covid pandemic. Regrettably, it added another layer of suspicion and mistrust to the way the South perceives the northern hemisphere.

As illustrated above, when I referred to the difficulties involved in vaccine policies, the priority for our leaders had to be to provide vaccines to their citizens. There was no way around that. That said, in order to achieve this goal the EU did not impose any restrictions on exports to third countries, once contracts with the EU had been respected. We actually became, through companies established and producing in our territory, the largest exporter of vaccines to the rest of the world.

Did people in the South realise that? I hope they did, but I am afraid that their focus was rather on the scarce quantities of vaccines that reached their countries, regardless of their origin, compared to their availability in the North. The need to ensure that domestic concerns do not unduly prevent fairer access to vaccines around the world – for instance, by supporting and pro-longing the efforts of valuable organisations like GAVI[16] – is indeed an important lesson to learn for the global management of the next pandemic.

Health is rising to the top of the list of domestically sensitive and foreign policy-relevant domains, joining trade, energy, technology, climate, transport, migration, regulation, finance and development aid and many other sectors. The world is definitely increasingly complex to govern and the stakes are becoming higher for political leaders. And so is the risk of divorce.

3

What's in a Quarter?

The episodes and issues described and commented on above, and what we can read into them, highlight relevant undercurrents of the first quarter of the new century. There is, however, more than that to a period of time as eventful as this one. There are critical stages and landmark events – and some very curious calendar coincidences – that complete the picture. It is worth recalling and contextualising some of them. I choose to do this around four key years: 2001, 2008, 2016 and 2022, as they encompassed a lot of what will remain as the legacy of the first decades of the century.

CALENDAR COINCIDENCES (OR NOT)

Calendars speak volumes. Like maps, they reveal hidden facts and connections, and open the door to further reflection. The calendar of the first quarter of the twenty-first century is no exception.

As has been said, Vladimir Putin's invasion of Ukraine in February 2022 concluded a dramatic sequence of increasingly serious challenges to the terms of coexistence among nations and within nations during this period.

Within this time span, four individual years – 2001, 2008, 2016 and 2022 – were particularly illustrative, partly because they contained curious, and revealing, calendar coincidences.

Only a few weeks separated, in 2001, the attack on the Twin Towers in downtown Manhattan from the accession of China to the World Trade Organization. The latter event marked the reawakening of the sleeping giant and its re-emergence as a great power as well as the unleashing of hyper-globalisation, lifting millions out of poverty in China and beyond, but also creating new pockets of poverty and inequality in the developed world. The events of 9/11 profoundly wounded the unipolar power, caused global shock waves, introduced new forms of non-state terrorism and eventually provoked a reaction whose effect still reverberates today. Interestingly, it was also in 2001 that Jim O'Neill coined the term BRICS to designate the leading emerging economies of Brazil, Russia, India and China, later expanded to include South Africa.

In 2008, there were again only a few weeks between the invasion of Georgia by Russia and the fall of the Lehman Brothers bank in the USA. The latter triggered the greatest financial and economic crisis of our generation and revealed the regulatory and accountability gaps between global, sophisticated markets, on one side, and inappropriately equipped national governments and fledgling instances of global governance, on the other. It also tarnished the reputation of banks and bankers, and enhanced the perception of inequality and injustice around the globe. The former represented the earliest violation of the post-Cold War territorial integrity dogma, a ground test for the ability of Russia to reverse its past alleged 'humiliation' that would culminate in a 'special military operation' of great proportions and meaning, fourteen years later. While Russia invaded Georgia, another calendar coincidence is worth noticing: in the same month of August, China hosted the Beijing Olympic Games – its coming of age, its initiation ritual as a member of the global league.[1]

In 2016, the British people followed the advice of those who maintained that leaving a huge market next door and separating from one's best friends and neighbours would solve deep-rooted identity problems and provide solace for an unfair domestic share-out of the benefits of globalisation. Five months later, across the Atlantic, and to the surprise and disbelief of many, Americans elected Donald Trump as the successor to Barack Obama. The two events meant the formal induction of populism into the political Hall of Fame and were a major contribution to the divorce among nations and within nations.

When Vladimir Putin gave the order to invade Ukraine, on 24 February 2022, the world was still painfully extracting itself from the worst pandemic of our lives, two years after the first lockdown, and our economies were still struggling to recover. While we were happily resurfacing out of confinement, Putin was keen to plunge us into the troubled waters of open confrontation. Putin's action was the last nail in the coffin of our illusions about his regime.

2001: AN EARTH ODYSSEY

For my generation, Stanley Kubrick's film *2001: A Space Odyssey*, co-written with Arthur C. Clarke, remains a revealing and pre-monitory moment. In the late 1960s and early '70s, many of us came out of cinema halls thinking: 'These guys are going too far. How can you believe that a computer will ever speak? And take decisions on its own, without human control, and against humans? In thirty years from now?!'

We had to wait a little longer than foreseen by Kubrick and Clarke for their premonition to materialise fully, but when we reached mythic 2001 another dimension of disruption that we did not think possible awaited us. Albeit in a different way, 2001 lived up to our expectations: we were embarking on a real odyssey, this time on Earth.

In Downtown Manhattan

Nothing could have been more terrifyingly symbolic. Nothing could have better demonstrated the fragility of our Western comfort, the relativity of our power and the vulnerability of our presumed security. Within a few minutes on a typically beautiful blue-skied morning in New York, a few Arab terrorist hijackers, licensed as pilots by flying schools in the USA, equipped with box cutters and orchestrated by Osama Bin Laden, threw American planes against the tallest buildings of the financial centre of the Western world, provoking massive clouds of dust and tons of rubble, killing thousands of innocent people, and leaving families destroyed all over the world. Just as simple and devastating as that.

I missed the first wave of the attack but caught the second one live on screen. My wife and my youngest son alerted me first. Then my father, who called me right after the news broke: 'Switch on the TV!' he shouted from Lisbon. 'You would not believe what is happening.'

'What is happening?' was the first question we all asked. 'Must be a massive publicity stint for a new Hollywood blockbuster', some of us thought, trying to be positive. Special effects, as we called them back then. It immediately became clear it was for real and the news kept pouring in, repeatedly, of other attacks elsewhere in the USA, revealing the tremendous impact of the events of that day.

'Who dared to do this?' became the next obsession, until a new, as yet obscure non-state enemy with a name that was difficult to spell revealed its identity.

Nothing could have been more traumatising for the USA and more worrying for the world. By mid-morning in the USA and mid-afternoon in Brussels, we had realised that things would never be the same again. What we could not yet assess was the magnitude of its significance. We could not have imagined then that 9/11, with drama and uproar, was the actual beginning of the new century. A delayed millennium bug of huge proportions.

The next question we started asking on that 11 September, once the paralysing shock had been replaced by an attempt to understand the consequences of what had happened, was 'What will Americans do now?' How would the USA react to the worst ever attack on its soil and on its pride? We would soon realise that the response to the attack, in Afghanistan and Iraq, regardless of its legitimacy and justification, would also seriously affect the course of events in the first quarter of the century.

David Rennie, from *The Economist*, puts 9/11 in historical context: 'Bin Laden, as terrorists do, managed to leverage astonishingly modest resources to provoke the American hyper-power to overreach. That ushered in an era of nation states defending what they see as vital interests while ignoring multilateral constraints.'[2]

The attacks in downtown Manhattan influenced the American and Western psyche to an extent only comparable to the damage done by the USA's reaction to it, in terms of our own global credibility as standard bearers of universal values. This is an assessment of the impact, not the value, of the decision to go into Afghanistan and to invade Iraq, or to support both moves. I know extremely well the context in which the decisions were taken in Washington and how much the imperative of solidarity with the USA motivated those who aligned with George W. Bush.

As I often tell my American friends who have some pleasure in teasing Europeans about their defence budgets or their commitment to the Atlantic alliance, 9/11 was also the first occasion ever that NATO's famous Article 5 was triggered. It was done by Europeans and Canadians in support of and solidarity with Americans. The allies that triggered Article 5 did not all agree with the later invasion of Iraq, but they shared the same spirit of solidarity with those who did.

The fact remains that the consequences of action taken then – and particularly the invasion of Iraq, the removal of Saddam Hussein and what was left behind – still reverberate in the image and reputation of the USA and in the collective memory of the non-Western world. Today, it continues to be used by the adversaries of the USA and its allies, and of the 'West' in general, to accuse us of incoherence and double standards, and it weakens our legitimate quest for the respect of international rules.

The combined effect of Al-Qaeda's attacks on American soil in 2001 and the USA's reaction left an indelible mark in the relationship between 'the West and the rest' and is central to understanding what has happened since.

In Downtown Beijing

September did not, however, exhaust 2001's capacity to shape the century. The odyssey continued in October. Exactly thirty-five days after the attacks against the Twin Towers, China formally became a member of the World Trade Organization (WTO). Separated from it by just a few weeks, what went relatively unnoticed at the time was destined to produce an impact on the beginning of this century that was as important as 9/11. China had already started its opening up a couple of decades before under the inspiration of Deng Xiao Ping, but the formal accession to the WTO was the confirmation and legitimation of China's entry into the global capitalist economy as a full member.

And what a resounding entry it was. From a relatively anonymous cast member, China moved to lead actor on the global stage in a matter of years. From a discreet, voluntarily shy second or third fiddle, it evolved into an assertive soloist, claiming its fair slice of glamour and applause. And power.

In Brussels and other Western capitals, there was a certain degree of naivety in our hope that China's entry into the global market as an equal player would determine its own internal evolution towards our patterns of democratic governance and open societies. President Bill Clinton famously stated in 2000, when advocating China's accession to the WTO, that it 'will move China faster and further in the right direction. It will advance the goals America has worked for in China for the past three decades. So, if you believe in a future of greater openness and freedom for the people of China, you ought to be for this agreement.'[3] We in Europe thought pretty much the same, with the additional authority of experience. For the EU, open borders, intensified trade and free circulation of factors of production had been a trigger and a guarantee of co-operation and peace among former foes. It should also work for China and its relationship with the West.

There was also a certain degree of greed, to be honest. China's joining the WTO was in the West's self-interest. A potentially huge market and a particularly useful, inexpensive assembly hub looked like a win-win operation for American, German or French investors, a growth factor for our economies and an advantage, price-wise, for our consumers.

The Chinese leadership's behaviour at the time of joining, and for some years beyond, reassured everyone, even those most pessimistic about China's resurgence. The underlying message: let us grow, it will be good for us and for you. And: if you do not bother us with our internal issues, we will not be a problem for you else-where. Hence, an overall Chinese abstention in international fora from taking sides or antagonising us. No diplomatic 'wolf warri-ors' in sight, then.

I began to see a change in diplomatic behaviour while in New York, between 2015 and 2019. During my four years there, as EU Ambassador to the United Nations, I had to deal with no fewer than three Permanent Representatives of China, a degree of rota-tion that was totally unusual for Chinese diplomatic practice. Ambassadors normally stay in their posts longer than those from Western countries. When I later arrived in London, the Chinese ambassador there had been in post for more than ten years. But he left soon after.

Even more relevant than the duration of their postings, what impressed me was the personality and the patterns of behav-iour of my Chinese colleagues. There was a clear evolution from discreet and smooth operators to much more assertive and out-spoken individuals – and better English speakers. The change was so pronounced that even some of the individual ambassadors felt slightly odd having to adapt to a new profile. Others exaggerated in their zeal and became known as 'wolf warriors' before a correc-tion in style was issued from Beijing. What remained, in any case, as the pattern of the new Chinese diplomacy was a higher degree of self-confidence and assertiveness.

Ashes and Foundations

It is pretentious to claim that we knew by then the true sig-nificance of these two events of 2001 for the shaping of the new century. Today, it is difficult to deny their combined impact. The year 2001 closed off a period of unipolar dominance and unchal-lenged predominance of the liberal order. Ten years after the end of the Soviet Union, the world would now enter not only a new century but also a new cycle.

The USA would never be the same after the attacks on the Twin Towers: that at least was clear at the time. Wounded, the USA would have to counterattack but would also care less for other countries' problems and focus more on safeguarding its internal security and prosperity. Wounded, the USA would be more vulnerable to extreme interpretations of its national interest and the fluctuation of different approaches to foreign and security policies.

Within the coming twenty-something years, the USA would move the pendulum of its foreign policy back and forth. First came emotional activism, during the 'neo-con' Bush years, then rational retraction with Obama and erratic gesticulation with Trump, and finally a more traditional 'foreign policy establishment' attitude with Biden. All colours of the spectrum were covered as the nation sought to find a new balance, but one common trait emerged: protect the USA from any threats, wherever they came from – even if they resulted from the country's own impulse to act. What will come next?

Smoothly and discreetly entering the WTO gave China the credentials and tools it needed as a 'new kid in town' to enable it to start preparing its coming of age as a main player in the geo-economic and soon geopolitical scene, while avoiding any backlash or opposition. As Deng Xiao Ping would put it, 'Keep a cool head and maintain a low profile. Never take the lead – but aim to do something big.' What China did following its formal leader's guidance was to become a central feature of the first quarter of the new century.

As downtown Manhattan was painfully rebuilding from the ashes, downtown Beijing was hastily and methodically setting the foundations of an economic powerhouse that would soon reclaim what it believed to be a legitimate global centrality.

The year 2001 was also about a meaningful new acronym. A few weeks after China joined the WTO, Jim O'Neill, then a top manager at Goldman Sachs and a future minister in David Cameron's Conservative government, seized the moment and was the first to coin a new acronym that would symbolise the nascent change of paradigm. He invented the BRICS, the shorthand for a new group of countries bound to challenge the old masters of the international community. The formal group was created in a summit in Russia in 2009 and initially included the host country and Brazil, India and China. South Africa would be added a year later and the S for plural would also stand for the only country representing Africa there. Significantly, South Africa was invited in by China without it having consulted another member with particular relations with the African continent, Brazil. Since then, and recently, other countries have joined: Egypt, Ethiopia, Iran and the United Arab Emirates, and more are to follow. After a period of relative obscurity, reflecting their own internal contradictions – which still remain – the BRICS have recently gained new clout, in the wake of Russia's war on Ukraine and the deterioration of the international climate that followed, and as a result of renewed Chinese–US rivalry.

Thus, 2001 closed a chapter we knew well and opened a new one we would soon discover in all its challenging complexity.

2008: THE FALL OF LEHMAN AND THE RISE OF PUTIN

Another curious (or dramatic) calendar coincidence revealed a major trend: nothing should be taken for granted in this passage of centuries.

Between August and September 2008, just a few weeks separated Russia's invasion of Georgia, marking the beginning of Putin's openly belligerent attitude, and the fall of the Lehman Brothers bank, triggering the worst financial crisis since the Great Depression.

When Lehman Brothers was dropped with a bang by Hank Paulson, the US Treasury Secretary, on 15 September 2008, I spent a weekend on the phone at our family home in a quiet Brussels neighbourhood, helping to connect the EU dots in the first hours of the crash. The nervousness in the political and financial circles I was in touch with, as we tried to assess the magnitude of the event, contrasted with the placidity and mild temperatures of late summer in Brussels. I must have walked for miles around my garden with my Nokia phone glued to my ear. I'm sure my neighbours (not to mention my dog, who quickly decided it wasn't worth following me in circles) were completely unaware of the anxiety that had gripped European capitals, Washington and New York.

A week before, I had travelled to Moscow and Tbilisi with similar anxiety, but for different reasons. The President of the European Commission, José Manuel Barroso, was joining Nicolas Sarkozy – who was occupying the then rotating presidency of the European Council of EU Heads of State and Government – on a hastily organised trip to the capitals of Russia and Georgia in the wake of the Russian invasion of the latter's territory, which had happened a few weeks earlier, allegedly in support of a Russian minority.

It was a remarkable 2008 *rentrée*. Two major global crises were unfolding as summer was coming to an end. Two official trips were lined up to try to understand better and influence the future course of events (see in Chapter 2 the visit to Camp David to discuss with George W. Bush the response to the financial crisis).

The trip to Moscow and Tbilisi turned out to be a fascinating immersion into the new reality of post-Cold War conflict resolution and a colourful illustration of the role of personality profiles in power relationships.

Dimitri Medvedev had recently started his five-year stint as President of the Russian Federation. His elevation from prime minister to president and the accompanying demotion of Vladimir Putin to prime minister was orchestrated by the latter to accommodate the provisions of the Russian Constitution, while preserving his control of the levers of power. He had hinted at that over dinner at the St Petersburg G8 summit, two years earlier.

Out of respect for the newly established hierarchy, the EU leaders had no alternative but to talk to Medvedev even though they knew full well that Putin was making the ultimate decisions – and that was certainly the case concerning the invasion of Georgia. After a first meeting with Medvedev at the Meiendorf Castle, outside Moscow, lunch also included the Foreign Minister, Sergey Lavrov, a close ally of Putin. It was a long Russian lunch, lasting for almost four hours, and was full of drama (and caviar and vodka, of course). It was followed by another flight to the capital of Georgia and a late and long dinner with the then leader Mikhail Saakashvili (with no caviar or vodka but mountains of nuts, eagerly swallowed by the handful by equally agitated Sarkozy and Saakashvili). Drama was in the air as we drove our cars along the George W. Bush avenue in the capital's downtown and was on full display during the meal. The return to Brussels happened in the very early hours of the following day. Arriving home, I felt I had returned from another world and enjoyed the Belgian capital's peaceful dullness.

This visit highlighted the inbuilt instability and volatility in Europe's borders, be it in the south or the east. It also served as an illustration of the diplomatic potential of the EU and its political actors: following the visit, a ceasefire was obtained, as well as a withdrawal of Russian troops from Georgian territory beyond the disputed areas, and a process of dialogue started in Geneva. Unfortunately, the 'Geneva International Discussions on the conflict in Georgia' are still ongoing more than sixty rounds later.

Thousands of miles away, another meaningful event would also mark 2008: the Beijing Olympic Games, the first ever to be held in the country. China was at the top of the world. And intended to stay there.

2016: THE POPULIST TAKEOVER

If it had to be given a title by those who decide what a particular year should be known for, 2016 would be the International Year of Populism. It was the year during which populism gained its credentials as an impactful political phenomenon, via two significant events happening on each side of the Atlantic, separated by only five months. As the future would confirm, it was to be a long-lasting reality.

The Mother of All Divorces

Like many, I went to bed on 23 June 2016 believing the UK would decide to remain in the EU but woke up a few hours later to the shocking news of its withdrawal. I was in New York and my 'morning after' was painful. 'Do you still have a job, João?' and 'What is the next country to leave the EU?' were two of the ironic, cynical questions thrown at me by fellow ambassadors from less EU-friendly countries as I walked through UN corridors later that morning. Those closest to us expressed sadness and solidarity. All were in shock.

I had no alternative but to react with panache and serenity, even if my real feelings were disappointment and unhappiness with the Brexit operation. Matthew Rycroft, my British colleague at the time, was in an even worse position than me. I felt that he had received no particularly convincing instructions from London other than to say it was the will of the British people to leave the EU and that the UK would remain a committed member of the UN regardless of Brexit. We both faced the arduous task of managing a few years of transition as our shared goal was to limit the damage done to our common interests and values at the heart of the multilateral system, in which we did not only have good friends.

A few days later, chairing our weekly EU ambassadors' meeting, as I did for four years every Tuesday at 9 a.m. on 666, 3rd Street, I made Brexit the first item on the agenda. I had by then, over the weekend, experienced all the post-traumatic stages in reaction to the outcome of the British referendum. By the time of the meeting, determination was the dominant driving force. And it was totally shared by my colleagues. No complacency about a dramatic situation and the magnitude of the challenge, but no depression or panic either. Respect for democratic choices, solidarity with highly competent and European-minded British colleagues and focus on effective EU co-ordination inside the UN.

I summarised my state of mind in my remarks: surprised, sad, but determined. 'These are extraordinary times, even dramatic, for the UK and the EU. We should not minimise the significance of Brexit nor the magnitude of the challenges. This being said, we need to stay serene and determined and not provide further ammunition to our critics who are already trying to exploit the situation.'

'Let's not provide our detractors with the additional pleasure of our division', I added. 'Let's stick together.'

I recalled the detailed procedures to be followed in case of withdrawal, including the need for the departing country to introduce a formal demand and the strict timings associated with it. These provisions had, ironically, been drafted by none other than the former

UK Permanent Representative to the EU, Ambassador John Kerr, in his capacity as Secretary-General of the European Convention, which drafted the Constitutional Treaty for the European Union. The Constitution was eventually discarded after two negative referenda in 2005, but some of its provisions found refuge in the Treaty of Lisbon, signed two years later. The ones relating to the possible withdrawal of a member state, which were not part of any previous EU treaty, became the now famous Article 50.

Visiting Dutch foreign minister Bert Koenders, whom I had invited to the EU Heads of Mission meeting as a guest speaker, gave us an insight into what was happening back home and insisted on a message of unity. Later in the day, together with his Italian counterpart Paolo Gentiloni, he would deliver an appropriate illustration: the Netherlands and Italy, instead of prolonging a senseless fight for a place in the Security Council, decided to split the two-year mandate (for more details, see Chapter 6). Everyone in the UN got the point: the EU was still in business!

My colleagues reacted unanimously in supporting the line I had proposed and we all left the meeting aware that we would be navigating in uncharted and challenging waters from now on.

I could not, however, totally push aside my deep personal feelings. For someone who believes in the European project and has dedicated most of his professional life to it, the departure of the UK was and still is a big blow, a major source of frustration. I understand, as this book tries to explain, the reasons why it happened. However, I can't help thinking that it is a lose-lose operation that will be detrimental to the common interests of the UK and the EU.

Brexit is key in understanding the epoch-making trends of the first decades of the new century. It encapsulates the interaction between external and domestic factors, the prevalence of simplistic and seductive slogans above elaborate rational arguments and the accumulated frustration and sense of exclusion in working and middle classes outside global cities, in the face of rapid cultural and moral shifts and economic disruption. It demonstrates how populist politicians can unashamedly explore a favourable context, while more moderate ones are incapable of adapting to the new realities of political communication and of abandoning politically correct dogmas. But it also highlights how much traditional political actors and institutions have distanced themselves from the grassroots, to the point of either not detecting or misreading the signals coming up from lower decks.

That is why the first three years after Brexit deserve particular attention. My 1,000 days in London as the first EU ambassador – from Brexit's day one to Rishi Sunak's week one – turned out to be fascinating, educational and revealing. I watched the UK from Margaret Thatcher's window in Smith Square, Westminster, travelled around the country as much as Covid allowed and interacted with three prime ministers and several foreign secretaries. Those were challenging years. Relations with the EU went through their lowest levels of mutual trust. As I will detail in Chapter 4, my job was to help keep them afloat until common sense replaced histrionics. When I left London at the end of 2022, I wished my successor less excitement and more boring times ...

Meteorite Trump and Comet Haley

Five months after the Brexit referendum, on 6 November, another momentous event marked 2016 as a historic year. This time I did not need to wait for the morning to be shocked by the news. It gradually became clear, as I watched television in the late evening at my 50 UN Plaza apartment that, contrary to expectations, Hillary Clinton would not return to the White House, sixteen years after she had left it with husband Bill. Its new tenant would be Donald Trump. Shock and awe followed, in the USA and beyond.

Things started to change around 9.30 p.m., the trend looked irreversible two hours later and the outcome became official by 2.30 in the morning. The surprise of the outcome and the extent of its impact were confirmed by Hillary's decision to depart from tradition and not appear in public that night to concede defeat. It was too much for her to swallow. She had to sleep on it.

Trump's win resonated loudly inside the UN for the remainder of that week, and doubts and concerns accumulated concerning how he would deal with multilateralism. It is fair to say that most ambassadors had not wished for a Trump victory, not least for fear of American disinvestment in the UN.

These concerns were fully vindicated a few months later, in September 2017, at the UN's General Assembly, known as UNGA, the annual jamboree of world leaders. I recall that it looked to me like the first week of the rest of the 'post-post-Cold War era', or the beginning of the end of the international liberal order as we knew it.

It was in any case the first appearance of both António Guterres, the Portuguese and EU citizen recently elected United Nations secretary-general, and Donald Trump, at the high-level opening of UN's General Assembly. Their speeches, within an hour's interval, as well as their underlying visions of global order, could hardly have been more distinct. It was also the first time I remember (and most likely the first time ever) that the EU delegates, me included, did not applaud, not even once, the leader of the host country. And we were far from being alone in our discretion.

It is thus very tempting to describe that week of September 2017 as symbolically signalling a major shift in anticipation of very different times ahead. National sovereignty as *the* guiding principle of external relations versus co-operation in search of common solutions to shared problems, the pursuit of national interest defined on a case-by-case assessment versus the staunch defence of internationally agreed rules and norms underpinned by universal values: *voilà*, the new fault lines of the twenty-first century.

The contrast between Trump and his predecessor added to the perception of qualitative change. The Obama administration's commitment to multilateralism had been second to none, even if not perfect. People admitted that Hillary Clinton would have been more 'realistic' and less 'idealistic' than Obama, but still a totally committed partner. Trump was a big question mark, a scenario that anyway people wanted to avoid. If some campaign statements ever became policy, the prospects would be gloomy. We had hoped, like many American voters, that governing would prove different from campaigning, and we were ready to give Trump a chance. Whatever happened, one point was consensual among my colleagues: we would miss Samantha Power.

Samantha, Obama's envoy to the UN, with whom we constantly shared positions and often aligned and whom I knew as White House adviser from my times in Washington, was replaced by Nimarata ('Nikki') Randhawa Haley. I had come across Nikki Haley during my previous posting in DC on the occasion of a visit to her office in South Carolina, where she was governor for six years. I had been impressed by her professionalism, charisma, self-control and ability to socialise easily without ever risking potentially contentious topics of conversation (not to mention her power dressing). These were very much the traditional qualities of an ambitious American politician.

When Haley moved to the same building in which I had recently occupied my official residence, contact became easier. She was living a few floors above in a larger apartment than mine (even buildings respect hierarchies), with her son, her dog and her husband Mike, whenever his military professional duties allowed. Nikki's appointment was received with some relief in the UN by those who feared the return of John Bolton, who had left sour memories from when he was there representing 'W' in 2005–06. And yet, although charming and likeable, Ambassador Haley was not able to compensate for her boss's attitude towards multilateral institutions even if she tried hard.

Inviting the members of the Security Council to the White House and having President Trump attend and chair the Council meeting in New York when the USA held its presidency were among the laudable initiatives she took. However, Trump's degree of antagonism towards any multilateral institution from NATO to the UN, plus the withdrawal from JCPOA (the Iran deal) and the Paris climate agreement, set the bar too high for Haley to be able to salvage Trump's reputation (if he was ever concerned by that, which I doubt). After two years in the job, she felt that it had been long enough to polish her curriculum and to give herself an international and foreign policy credibility. A longer stay would have tarnished her image and identified her excessively with Trump's disruptive international mindset. Already then, her mind was set on the White House.

When Nikki Haley arrived in New York, I said to many colleagues who had never met her that I thought she had presidential DNA. The daughter of immigrants from India, the first ever Indian American to serve in a presidential cabinet, an accomplished professional and politician, in possession of all the tools of the trade, she embodied the American Dream. She just needed to go deeper into files and acquire on-the-job diplomatic and international experience.

I once came across her parents, a middle-aged, discreet, 'normal' couple. In the very first days of Nikki's stay in New York, they came to visit her for the first time at our building, a Foster & Partners-designed, modern forty-five-storey tower just across the street from the UN headquarters, with stunning views over the East River and Long Island, as well as lower Manhattan. I was coming out of the building to take a seat in my car as they arrived. They stepped out of their chauffeured car, wearing distinctively traditional Indian clothes, looked up and, with a proud smile on their faces, took a selfie, with the building as background. Their daughter Nikki was not there physically but she was very much in their minds. Her appointment to the UN made sense of their hard work, building up their American Dream.

I said hello: 'You must be very proud.'

'We are', they replied, visibly happy but shy and modest. I understood better what my new American colleague represented.

Nikki Haley was eventually replaced by the wife of a major donor to Trump's campaign. I am not sure anyone still remembers Kelly Craft in the UN corridors, but everybody remembers Nikki. Like the comet that goes by the same name, Mrs Haley is bound to appear again ...

John Bolton, whom we feared could be appointed for the New York job, eventually reappeared in an even more influential position at the White House as National Security Advisor, but it soon became obvious that no one other than Trump was really in charge of foreign policy – well, in fact, maybe not even he was in charge. Bolton lasted a year next to Trump and is today a vocal critic of his former boss.

His policy inconsistency and doubtful attraction to traditional adversaries of the USA, combined with his contempt for traditional allies and friends, made Trump's four years a negative period of

American foreign policy history. Hence the anxiety prevailing in chancelleries in the Western world regarding the potential for a Trump return in the run-up to the presidential election of November 2024. A populist American foreign policy, potentially 'on steroids' compared to Trump's first term, would be equivalent to a new meteorite whose vertiginous fall onto the planet's surface would be capable of causing, once again, considerable disruption.

The Populist Poison

The year 2016 did not mark the beginning of the populist wave. But it made clear, for the first time at a global level, that the divorce of nations was being complemented and influenced by another layer of division and fragmentation, this time not at the international level but rather at the intra-national level: a divorce within nations.

Its roots are multiple and complex; its nature is political and social as much as cultural. Our societies became more diverse and more divided, sometimes even almost tribal, as people sought their true identity not on the basis of what they had in common as part of traditional larger communities, such as a nation or a 'people'; not solely on the basis of their economic status, such as a social class; but rather on what differentiated them on a much smaller scale, such as ethnicity, sexual orientation or views on concrete political topics. But even when they did find a large degree of common ground – again, on topics like nationhood – that often led to a radical vision of it and the rejection of its opposite: in this case, nationalism versus international co-operation or integration. The process of deconstructing traditional identities – or exacerbating them to the extreme – happened in parallel with the erosion of the credibility and weight of intermediary bodies and reference entities – political parties and trade unions lost support and representativity, and media, experts, regulators and supervising authorities lost trust.

Obviously, governments did not escape. They were particularly damaged by their perceived incompetence in the management of events and phenomena outside of their governance remit – the financial crisis of 2008–09 and to some extent the pandemic

– and by their lack of reaction to the negative effects of hyper-globalisation in the rust belts and farmlands of our countries and among parts of our working and middle classes. The political sphere underestimated the downsides of globalisation and failed to address its domestic consequences; in turn, the public discounted its upsides and did not associate the benefits they felt as citizens and consumers with the advantages of free trade and open economies. Overall, increased openness, diversity and inequality in our societies required a degree of adaptability to new realities that was scarcely available.

As a result, public opinion and media gradually became vulnerable to the populist discourse coming from the far right and the far left: simple solutions to complex problems, aversion to facts and reason, blaming of elites, bankers, free trade, greed, globalism and migrants, not to mention politicians in general, for all of society's evils. Social media induced and exacerbated culture wars did the rest. All this came together to present an extremely complex and entangled puzzle at the national level.

Mainstream political leaders were not – and still are not – immune to this evolution in domestic public opinions. The political agenda gradually reflected this bottom-up pressure, which did not spare foreign, security, defence and trade policies, among others, creating a total blurring of lines between 'domestic' and 'foreign' realms of policy making (and huge challenges for diplomacy, if I may add in defence of my embattled corporation). If this wave of populism, nationalism and protectionism is confirmed, we could be bound for a vicious circle from which it will be increasingly difficult to extract our countries.

Dealing with populism presents a huge dilemma for mainstream politicians: you either challenge it up front and rule out any co-operation or association between those forces and the sphere of power (what is called in French a *cordon sanitaire*) or you try to accommodate its discourse and ultimately involve populists in the exercise of power to take the steam out of their opposition (but at the risk of being polluted by them). The middle ground is difficult to find.

My experience in dealing with similar forces in the UK and what I observed in the USA, first with the Tea Party movement and later with Trump, taught me a few lessons: never give up on your principles and positions; never respond to provocations with counter-provocations and always try to stay cool, explain and contextualise; trust the intelligence of public opinion even if you often doubt it; combat populist solutions but never underestimate the problems that motivate people who vote for populists; and last but not least, learn from populists the best ways to talk and listen to citizens in this age of narrow attention span and fragmented, instantaneous means of communication.

We urgently require an antidote to the populist poison if we want to avoid further divorce within our nations.

2022: THE BURIAL OF AN ILLUSION

At a room adjacent to the one where the foreign ministers of the G7 were meeting in Liverpool, in December 2021, under the chairmanship of Liz Truss, I sat among the political directors to draft the ministers' final statement. We were all wearing masks (those days seem so far away now) as the pandemic was still stubbornly resisting mass vaccination, secretly hoping that another even more consequential crisis would not soon replace Covid on the front pages.

I was acting on behalf of the EU's High Representative, Josep Borrell, who had asked me to replace his political director, retained in Iran talks. We were two months away from Putin's invasion of Ukraine and the main point of discussion was what to say to dissuade the Russian president from taking that step. From the start it became obvious that there was no consensus in the room on how to do it.

Together with my colleagues from the EU members of the G7 (Germany, France and Italy) we wanted to be tough but not unnecessarily rough. Americans and British had a more radical approach. But we all knew that our job was to find consensual language. After all, having a common G7 position was even more important than the detailed words chosen to send a unified, strong message to Vladimir Putin.

As I stated at one point, reacting to a very assertive American colleague, Victoria Nuland – with whom I had sparred while in Washington a couple of years back, even if we stayed on good terms – our purpose was to send a clear message to Moscow but also to preserve an essential asset: the EU's unity of action. On our side, that meant not prejudging the sanctions decision, which we could only take after the invasion and bearing in mind the different positions inside our camp. 'As you well know, sanctions against Russia are only meaningful if they are European and to be European they need to be adopted unanimously by the twenty-seven,' I noted. Hence the caution and the need for balance at that stage. Nuland was not convinced, repeating that Washington was adamant that the risk was imminent and the language should be absolutely blunt about what Putin should expect if he invaded Ukraine.

We ended up with a quite strong consensual formula: 'Any use of force to change borders is strictly prohibited under international law. Russia should be in no doubt that further military aggression against Ukraine would have massive consequences and severe cost in response.'

The content of the meeting reflected a deeper reality, even more important than the conclusions: there were diverse degrees of appreciation of the likelihood of Putin's invasion and distinct sensitivities back home. The Americans and British were more convinced of the inevitability of the invasion than us. The EU camp was mindful of the self-fulfilling dimension of the insistence on referring to invasion and war, and the need to avoid prejudging Moscow's moves.

With hindsight I explain the gap in perception mainly by a different level of intelligence evidence – it is now known that the USA had received secret intelligence reports a few weeks before the Liverpool meeting that pointed to advanced preparations in Russia. In addition to our focus on preserving unity of the twenty-seven, the gap can also be explained by the psychological reluctance and resistance on the EU side to openly consider an invasion scenario, knowing all too well that its impact would be mainly felt in our member states and would have severe consequences for the security context in Europe.

This being said, in all honesty, the EU was not alone in its judgement of the unlikelihood of an invasion. Ten days before the beginning of the war, on Valentine's Day, I had invited a cross-section of London's political, think tank and media establishment for an informal dinner with Stefano Sannino, in his first visit to the capital since taking office, a year earlier, as Secretary-General of the European External Action Service (EEAS), the foreign service of the EU. I had opted for my preferred formula: a single conversation focused on precise topics to stimulate each guest's individual views. I suggested the state of the Union (not ours, theirs) and prospects for Global Britain, against the backdrop of the Russian/Ukrainian crisis.

This allowed for a very lively discussion, which started off with spirited remarks by George Robertson, former NATO secretary-general and now a member of the House of Lords, sharing memories of his dealings with Moscow, and went on with David Liddington and Gavin Barwell, respectively deputy prime minister and chief of staff to Theresa May, being very vocal about what they thought of the man who had succeeded their boss. Jonathan Hill, the last but one UK Commissioner and now active in high-level business and thinktank circles, Robin Niblett (Chatham House), Charles Grant (Centre for European Reform, CER) and Sarah Sands (Bright Blue, a liberal-conservative think tank) brought in other perspectives. The diversity of inputs was completed by the expertise of leading foreign affairs journalists, Gideon Rachman (*Financial Times*) and James Landale (BBC).

I closed the dinner with two focus group-type questions: Will the UK have a NATO secretary-general? Will Putin invade Ukraine? With different justifications, the majority of my guests thought there was no real chance of a British NATO secretary-general. Equally, the majority felt that Putin would not dare going into a full war against Ukraine.

Back to Liverpool: in spite of the difference in assessment, the main message coming out of the G7 foreign ministers' gathering was however, undoubtedly, one of unity of purpose and action. Events in the following months and years would confirm the solidity of the anti-Putin coalition. The good mood and the quality of friendship among the group, in spite of natural differences in 'nuance', was confirmed during the evening.

After their meeting ended, the foreign ministers moved to downtown Liverpool and to the Beatles museum. They toured it, had dinner in the club cellar and, most importantly, danced (and sang) to the tune of a Beatles tribute band. I discovered the hidden dancing talents of many of them as they, and I, enjoyed listening to many songs from our youth. Some might have been written for the event: 'With a Little Help from My Friends', 'Back in the USSR' and 'Come Together' echoed the G7 agenda.

Over dinner, at the political directors table, the discussion was about Putin, obviously. His motivation, his strategy and our assessment of his final intentions. I recalled my own experience of meetings with Putin, which always reflected his feelings of humiliation, non-recognition and mistrust.

Watching Putin acting and speaking nowadays, I realise that the leader who decided to invade Ukraine in 2022 has radicalised and strengthened the worst personality traits of the person I got to know between 2005 and 2010. The leader who invaded Ukraine in 2022 has taken the grievances and obsessions he had outlined before to a level that was unimaginable then, to a point of possible no return.

Twenty-two years after his ascent to power, Putin hit the summit of his trajectory of vindication and the zenith of his narrative of restoration. But he also put an end to all the illusions we might have had about the likelihood of Russia, under the present leader, becoming a closer partner to the EU or to the West in general, a country willing to deepen the democratic nature of its political system and to raise the levels of prosperity of its citizens, via the modernisation of its economy, the opening of its market and the investment and technology of industrialised countries.

At one point in the first decade of the century, I felt there was a chance that we could embark on a more co-operative path with Russia, even under Putin. We had established the unique principle of two EU–Russia summits per year, alternately in each other's territory, in order to pursue avenues of dialogue and co-operation. We had even launched an agenda of talks aimed at upgrading our existing Partnership and Co-operation Agreement in order to focus on modernising the Russian economy and strengthening the links with the EU (for which I was, for a period, the EU's chief negotiator). Younger advisers to then President Medvedev wanted to create a Russian Silicon Valley, attract Western tech innovators and venture capital, and through that stimulate what they thought was an urgent need of *aggiornamento* (updating, modernisation) of archaic structures and mentality. Putin's evolution towards further rigidity, centralisation and inaccessibility of the regime, together with his military interventions abroad, destroyed any hope of the modernisers and gradually eroded our trust in his willingness to co-operate with the EU for the sake of common interests.

The year 2022 marked the end of an illusion about the future of a post-Soviet Russia, at least for the foreseeable future. Combined with the still remaining economic, psychological and ultimately political effects of the Covid pandemic, the 2022 Russian war in Ukraine enhanced geopolitical and geo-economic tensions and laid another brick in the wall of international separation and fragmentation. Of divorce.

Margaret Thatcher saluting her supporters at Smith Square after her general election victory, London, 1987. (PA Images/Alamy Stock Photo)

By the window at Smith Square, a few days before my departure from London, autumn 2022. (Courtesy of Bart Vodderie)

At the EU–Russia summit at Sochi, Russian Federation, 2006 (with José Manuel Barroso, Vladimir Putin, Javier Solana, Wolfgang Schüssel and Konni). (Courtesy of www.kremlin.ru)

Exchanging views with President Barack Obama in the margins of a meeting of Major Economies Forum, White House, Washington DC, April 2009. (Author's collection)

With José Manuel Barroso and Catherine Day, then President and Secretary-General of the European Commission respectively, outside the European Council meeting room, in Brussels. (Author's collection)

Often a challenge but always a pleasure to engage with top-quality British journalists. Here in a relaxed atmosphere on the margin of the Conservative Party annual conference in Birmingham, 2022. (Author's collection)

With leaders, between working sessions at a G8 Summit. (Author's collection)

With President George W. Bush. (Author's collection)

Meeting of EU High Representative Cathy Ashton with President Obama and his National Security Advisor, Susan Rice, and colleagues, White House West Wing, Washington DC, June 2014. (Courtesy of The White House)

Sharing a relaxing moment with António Guterres, Secretary-General of the United Nations, commenting on the football skills of UN ambassadors, pictured in the EU Delegation yearbook, New York. (Author's collection)

Ambassadors' life is about multitasking, including on the football pitch. Here with colleagues from Germany, Sweden, Portugal, Czech Republic, Finland and Austria. The captain of our team for the occasion was none other than World Champion German player Lothar Matthäus. (Author's collection)

With Donald Tusk, then President of the European Council, at the EU ambassador's residence in New York. (Author's collection)

Family photo after a G8 'Sherpas' meeting at Chevening, ahead of the 2005 G8 Gleneagles Summit, hosted by Michael Jay (first row, centre). (Author's collection)

'In the room' at the G8 summit chaired by Italy, L'Aquila, June 2009. (Author's collection)

Speaking on behalf of the EU at the UN General Assembly hall, New York. (Author's collection)

With Boris Johnson at Carbis Bay, Cornwall, a few hours before the start of the G7 summit under his chairmanship, June 2021. (Author's collection)

EU leaders having a relaxed moment at Carbis Bay, Cornwall, between working sessions of the G7 summit, June 2021. (Author's collection)

Negotiating with David Frost. EU delegation led by Maroš Šefčovič, Vice-President of the European Commission, Lancaster House, London, 2021. (Author's collection)

Team photo at COP26 in Glasgow, celebrating good EU work at the climate conference, with Ursula von der Leyen, President of the European Commission, 2021. (Author's collection)

Meeting Keir Starmer, then leader of the opposition, London, spring 2021. (Author's collection)

Covid-times salute at a meeting with the Mayor of London, Sadiq Khan. It was a great pleasure to live in such a great city for almost three years. (Author's collection)

Exchanging a few words with then Prince Charles, visiting the Joint European Torus nuclear fusion research centre in Culham, Oxfordshire. (Author's collection)

With my wife Maria Ana, on our way to the presentation of credentials to Her Majesty, at Buckingham Palace, October 2021. (Courtesy of Bart Vodderie)

Breakfast at *BBC Breakfast*.
(Author's collection)

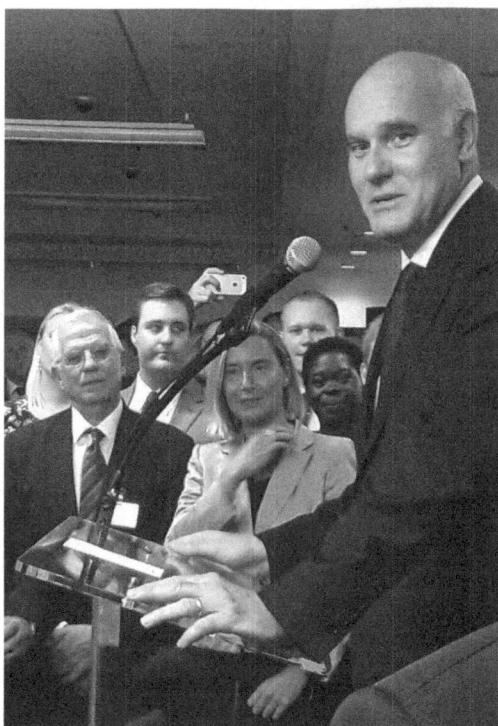

Welcoming guests to the EU
reception at the UN General
Assembly annual gathering
in the presence of the then EU
High Representative, Federica
Mogherini, and her successor,
Josep Borrell, then Spanish
foreign minister, New York.
(Author's collection)

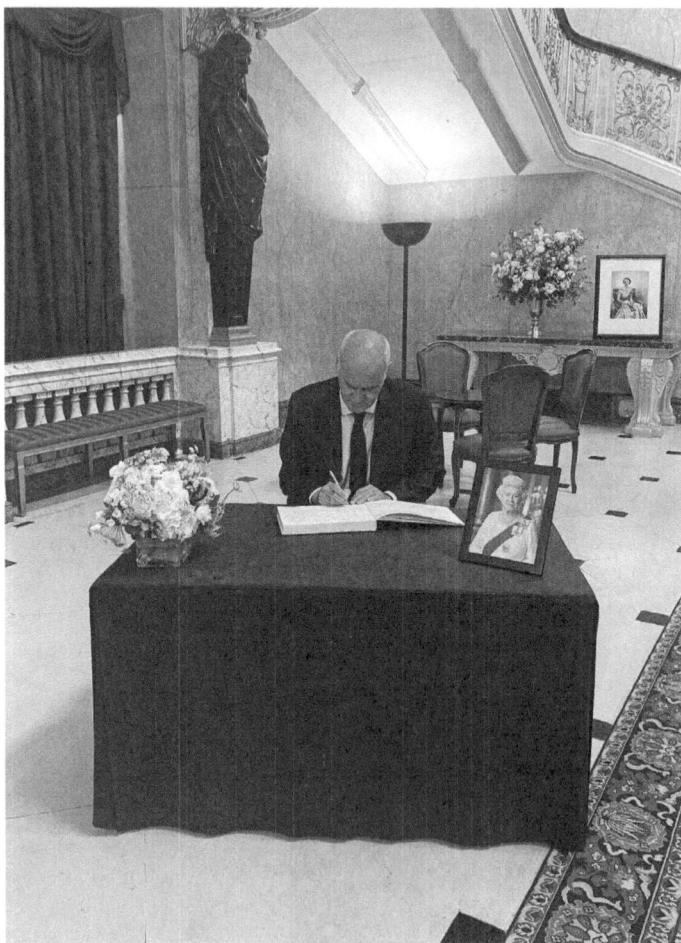

A sad day: signing the book of condolences on the death of
HM Queen Elizabeth II, at Lancaster House, London, 2022.
(Author's collection)

4

A Cautionary Tale: The First 1,000 Days of Brexit Seen from Thatcher's Window

Talking of divorce of nations, no other separation is more illustrative than the one taking place in recent years between the UK and the twenty-seven members of the EU. It was dramatic and traumatic, and convoluted. It deserves an inside look. What follows is my personal recollection of the first 1,000 days of Brexit Britain. Hold on for a bumpy ride.

St Pancras quickly became familiar. And its gigantic clock even more so. Loyal to the tradition of Victorian railway stations, St Pancras is spacious and luminous, and its gothic revival features have been made functional for cross-Channel commuting. It is London's home of Eurostar, and it was my transit hub between London and the European continent for almost three years. Every time I stepped off the train, I would raise my head and check the clock on the wall opposite. With one single exception, the clock showed the right time. Its precise timekeeping became a rare source of certainty in my otherwise unpredictable diplomatic life in London.

I arrived at St Pancras on Eurostar 9133, on the afternoon of 30 January 2020. Two days ahead of Brexit, 'to be sure you would still let me in', I joked with a British friend. I boarded 9132 back to Brussels, mid-November 2022, for the last time as the first EU Ambassador to the Court of St James's, 1,000 days later.[1]

There was a lot in my return luggage: I had survived one pandemic and outlasted two prime ministers; I had met the queen in private, celebrated her platinum jubilee and paid my respects on the day of her funeral, all within eleven months. Altogether, in less than three years, I had engaged with five chancellors, three foreign secretaries and six Europe ministers under the authority of three prime ministers and two sovereigns. In my last year in London, I had seen war returning to the European continent and inflation and national strikes returning to the UK.

As a diplomat, my 'never a dull moment' experience was packed with tough negotiations, unilateral moves and inflammatory rhetoric on the part of the UK, low trust and delayed ambassadorial recognition, and all part of a post-divorce drama played out across the Channel.

As a Westminster-based observer, I witnessed a vibrant parliamentary democracy producing its worst and its best. I observed a number of 'gates', 'red meat', 'dead cats', sleaze and sexual misbehaviour scandals, but also enjoyed substantial political debates at colourful annual party conferences, lively weekly sessions of Prime Minister's Questions in the House of Commons and top-quality reports by the House of Lords. More importantly, I saw the British people putting aside their differences and reuniting as one to pay tribute to their departing monarch, the only one most of them had known in their lifetime. I was impressed by 'the queue for the queen', an unforgettable display of resilience and national pride.

As a temporary resident in the country, I had a chance to know the UK better through travels and personal encounters in the four nations of the kingdom, stimulating exchanges in Whitehall corridors, in both Houses of Parliament and in business boardrooms, challenging debates in university halls and razor-edge interviews in television and radio studios. I discovered a dynamic community of resident EU citizens whose numbers, resilience and contribution to the British economy and society kept surprising me. I reconnected with old British friends, made many new ones, and experienced the joys of the Premier League and the pleasure of good hot tea, great theatre and long walks in London parks.

Mine was on all counts a fascinating 1,000-day journey in Brexit Britain. A journey into the drama and the trauma of divorce between nations, neighbours and allies in times of pandemic and war and of a change of paradigm in the global order. A journey into a multinational country proud of its history and its ingenuity, searching for a new beginning in the aftermath of a long relationship that did not end well. A journey into a cautionary tale about divorce.

Curiously enough, my viewing point was the same building at number 32, Smith Square, in Westminster, a couple of blocks away from the Houses of Parliament, that once had been the headquarters of the Conservative Party. It was from one of its windows that Margaret Thatcher used to wave to supporters to celebrate her electoral victories. Who would imagine that the first EU Ambassador to the post-Brexit UK would observe the country from Thatcher's window?

The building has in the meantime appropriately been renamed Europe House, which did not prevent me from saying, every time I hosted a Conservative minister: 'Welcome home!'

No intended provocation, of course. Just a diplomatic wink of the eye. Or more ...?

BETWEEN THE PALACE AND NUMBER 10

Boris Churchill, Liz Thatcher, Rishi Draghi?

My assignment began with a prime minister whom I had known well in Brussels as a talented and controversial journalist who had not contributed to the EU's reputation in the UK.

It continued with a prime minister whom I had known well as a bold and ambitious foreign secretary who had not contributed to the EU's trust in the British government.

It ended with a prime minister whom I had not known well, but who had been considered a reasonable and competent chancellor, who I expected could contribute to redressing the UK's relationship with the EU.

Boris Johnson had hoped to be remembered as an heir to Churchill, and Liz Truss did her utmost to be compared with Thatcher. Historians will tell us which one succeeded – if either. But one fact can already be established: neither of them matched the personal contribution to Europe of their model prime ministers.

Churchill and Thatcher were in diverse ways and in different contexts unquestionable key actors on the path towards European integration. Churchill inspired the ideal and encouraged others to pursue it, even if he chose to stay out of the process to deliver it. Thatcher, while opposed to superior levels of European integration, left her mark by providing a crucial impulse to the creation of a world-leading single market and to the consolidation of ambitious trade and competition policies.

Johnson and Truss, in contrast, took central stage during the least glorious act of the modern history of Anglo-European relations, presiding over the detachment of their country from its continental partners and doing little to build a workable alternative to membership. I am not sure their role models would recognise themselves in these aspiring heirs.

Rishi Sunak had always been a committed Brexiteer, but the fact that he replaced a prime minister who probably buried the hardest Brexit model allowed him to be initially compared with a reliable, orthodox and 'saviour' profile like Mario Draghi, former European Central Bank president (and euro rescuer) and Italian prime minister. After experiencing Boris and Liz, markets and public opinion welcomed Rishi and his 'dullness dividend'.

I did not stay long enough in London to form an on-the-ground objective and sufficiently close impression of my third prime minister. Would he refreshingly surprise or rather regretfully disappoint? Would Draghi recognise himself in Sunak? With hindsight, now that he has left Number 10, I don't think Sunak did better than either Johnson or Truss in living up to the reputation of the politician with whom people had compared him.

On bilateral relations, by the time I left I was happy enough to acknowledge that we had avoided a total post-divorce break-up and rebranded our presence in London, while at the same time creating the basis of a long-awaited improvement in the cross-Channel climate. However, it remained to be seen whether this new cycle in the long Conservative hold on power in British politics would simply prolong Brexit's 'basic instincts' politics or otherwise be a real break with the recent past and provide conditions for a better relationship with the EU and its member states, in full respect of Brexit.

I had worked to keep bridges open. I left London in November 2022, hopeful that it would soon be possible to see intense traffic on them again.

No IKEA Instructions

At the dawn of 2020, as I took my new position in Westminster's Smith Square, a few blocks away Boris Johnson was comfortably installed in Number 10, having just won an election by a landslide with a mandate to 'get Brexit done'.

He was expected by the British people to deliver on the Brexit-related promises he had made before and after the 2016 referendum. He was also expected, at least by us in the EU, to implement the treaty he had negotiated and submitted to parliamentary ratification and to the vote of his compatriots – and to be coherent with the associated political declaration he had signed.

In Brussels and in other EU capitals, the EU had done its homework, and we were ready for this new cycle. That meant, for a rules-and-law-based system like ours, respecting the commitments we had signed up to and engaging with the UK as a new outside partner. For us, decisions have consequences. For us, Brexit meant Brexit. We were ready for business.

I had come to London to be the face and the voice of the EU in the UK and to open, install and lead our new diplomatic mission during the first couple of years after Brexit. As an integral part of our preparation for a substantial change in our relationship, the presidents of the European Council and of the European Commission, under a proposal from the High Representative, had entrusted me with a great honour and a complex assignment: to be the EU's first Ambassador to the post-Brexit United Kingdom. The UK had become a 'third country' and, as happens with more than other 140 partner countries around the world, normal diplomatic relations were to be established, and an ambassador appointed.

Mine was, however, quite a unique assignment. One that came without a manual, as I commented once to Emily Maitlis in her excellent podcast *The News Agents*. No user's guide was available for the simple (and sad and regretful) reason that this was the first time in the history of the EU that a country had left it. Overnight, our relationship had changed dramatically and, as we would confirm, traumatically. Nothing would be the same as before in cross-Channel relations. Little in my job would be the same as in other diplomatic posts.

I came to London in the aftermath of a uniquely traumatic period. It was clear to me from the start that I had to shape and frame the EU envoy's job profile with full acknowledgement of the delicacy of the context, without undue interference in the domestic debate about Europe, still an extremely sensitive issue, while at the same time making sure our side of the story was heard. I should remain available to engage with both supporters and opponents of Brexit and those who were simply wondering whether it had really been the right choice. I was keen to avoid any 'provocation trap' and gradually and calmly to build our credibility and our usefulness as a diplomatic mission vis-à-vis the government, other political actors and the public.

This would be the best way, in my view, to project the image of the EU as a partner for new beginnings. A reliable partner, respectful of the democratic decision to withdraw from its realm and committed to the implementation of what had been agreed, while doing its utmost to strengthen our relationship within the new paradigm. Provided we could find a willing partner.

London would obviously be my base, but I had a firm intention of reaching out beyond the capital and Westminster, and visits to Northern Ireland (the destination of my very first trip outside England, as soon as Covid allowed), Wales and Scotland were a priority.

Another way to be helpful and useful was not to get directly involved in the actual negotiations of the Trade and Co-operation Agreement in 2020 (see Chapter 5).[2] In my first year in the job, the purpose was to keep enough distance to provide added value for my British interlocutors (and consequently also to my authorities and peers) but at the same time stay close enough to be well informed and able to influence. This was also the preferred approach of the then EU chief negotiator, who was concluding his term in office and was not too eager to change his habits and the role he had acquired in the first phase of the 'divorce deal'.

I chose – and it made a lot of sense – to be much more involved as we moved into the politically complex day-to-day handling of the Northern Ireland Protocol and its ramifications, from early 2021, in good complicity and personal chemistry with the newly appointed top EU representative, the Slovak Vice-President of the European Commission, Maroš Šefčovič (an excellent choice by President von der Leyen). Efficient interaction between the two of us (we had known each other for a long time) and our teams in London and Brussels allowed us to navigate, in full sync, the stormy waters of British politics and EU–UK relations during two very intense years.

Throughout my stay in London, I was, however, keen to preserve the individual – even pioneer – nature of my function and its risk-taking dimension, and was happy to benefit from the great autonomy and trust provided by my authorities. As someone who never liked following manuals or instructions (too many IKEA assembly traumas, I guess, and more importantly a vivid memory of restraints on freedom in my youth under a dictatorship), this clean-sheet job description was a tempting proposal I never regretted accepting.

In the Slow Lane to Buckingham Palace

I moved to London after more than eight years representing the EU on American soil, first to the United States, in Washington DC, and then to the United Nations, in New York. Before that I had spent almost thirty years at the European Commission, in Lisbon and Brussels, including as the president's chief of staff and Director-General for External Relations. As I took my new job, I felt humbled, privileged and happy, even if for the wrong reasons, to be the EU's man in London at such a critical moment. A historically first posting that was also a career's last.

Her Majesty the Queen summarised it perfectly when she welcomed my wife and me to the credential's audience at Buckingham

Palace: 'Well, this is quite new, Ambassador. You really are the first, aren't you?' (This friendly remark was the introduction to a very interesting conversation that will obviously remain confidential.)

My appointment was indeed a first and as such it carried a lot of – to put it mildly – stimulating unknowns. There was only one thing I knew for sure: my job would be at least as lively and demanding as it had been across the Atlantic – but possibly bumpier ...

The first bump would unexpectedly concern my own diplomatic status. It took me eighteen months to have the honour of presenting my credentials to the queen because the government – or at least someone on its behalf – was tempted by the idea of diminishing the EU's standing within London's diplomatic community, from the very start. The issue became public knowledge in late 2020 via James Landale, the BBC's diplomatic correspondent, who was very well connected in Whitehall. We had kept absolute discretion on our side about the matter and did not change our attitude after the leak. When asked in public, I would just say that I was sure an appropriate solution would be found.

The government argued that because the EU is not a country, its ambassador and respective mission should not be entitled to the status and privileges given to all national representations under the Vienna Convention. Those who advocated this in Whitehall forgot to acknowledge that their position was in direct contradiction of the previous official British stance as a member state regarding the status of EU ambassadors around the world, in full accordance with the Treaty of Lisbon's letter and spirit, and would thus be perceived by the EU as an hostile act liable for reciprocation back in Brussels (which temporarily did happen and seriously handicapped my counterpart, Lindsay Appleby, the head of the UK mission to the EU).

The EU is obviously not a country and can technically be considered an international organisation, but it is different from any other. It is indeed a unique, *sui generis* entity, holding elements of sovereignty delegated by its member states in many areas relevant to external relations.

To be fair, I should add that the government's initial official stance did not prevent me from exercising my normal duties before I was fully accredited as an ambassador. On some occasions, officials and ministers made an extra effort to signal that there was nothing personal in an attitude that some (if not most) of them disapproved of or at least had difficulties understanding. However, the political and institutional signal it sent was a negative one and we could not accept it.

Common sense and sound political judgment eventually prevailed. Our calm and discreet – but firm – rejection of the government's initial position and our openness to some compromise technical arrangements in the setting up of our mission contributed to a balanced deal. The issue was satisfactorily settled between the FCDO and our EEAS. Ironically, the prolongation of the stalemate made my position much more noticeable than it would have been, had the government abstained from challenging my status.

At the end of the day, I became not only a full ambassador but also a very visible one with regular media exposure and recognition. I was honoured to be voted by peers the 'Diplomat of the Year/Europe' in 2022 via *The Diplomat* magazine (thank you!). Conservative-leaning commentators, MPs and Lords supported me in public during the long months of controversy. *The Times* carried a favourable editorial advising Dominic Raab to 'change tack and gracefully back down'. The paper wondered what the government's real purpose was, as I still wonder myself …

The agreement on my full ambassadorial recognition was sealed in May 2021, in the margins of a G7 foreign ministers' meeting at Lancaster House. Our own High Representative, Josep Borrell, and the then foreign secretary, Dominic Raab, concluded the deal in a bilateral meeting I also attended. It was the last bilateral after the final G7 plenary meeting and before all the ministers would gather for a cocktail reception in the presence of the prime minister. Our meeting was cut short as soon as an FCDO aide told Raab that Boris Johnson was already in the building.

In a beautiful late spring afternoon, ministers were ushered out of the building into the adjacent garden. The format was 'plus 1' and Borrell told me to join him. I stood behind, on the side, with the other 'plus 1' officials, mostly political directors, or junior ministers, as the foreign ministers took a few steps further, down towards the garden level. It was to my surprise and to the astonishment of Number 10 and FCDO officials that Boris Johnson, having spotted me on the left side of the platform as he stepped out of the building, came straight in my direction before joining the ministers and loudly saluted me: 'Welcome, João!' After a hug and a few words, he continued down the steps to join the ministers.

As if this unexpected gesture were not enough, before ending his short speech to the ministers he added: 'Before I conclude, let me say that I am happy to see my good friend João here as EU ambassador. We spent some time together at the European Commission in Brussels. Welcome to London, João.'

I can think of worse ways to put an end to a senseless dispute.

• • •

Now I could at last take the direction of the Palace.

My audience with HM Elizabeth II to formally present my diplomatic credentials as Ambassador of the European Union to the Court of Saint James's was finally scheduled for 19 October 2021, at 12.15 p.m. It was obviously the highlight of my stay in London, not only because it was so significant and had taken so long to happen, but also for a sad coincidence.

The whole ceremony was beautifully and carefully choreographed and timed – as only our British friends can do. It started and ended with a splendid horse and carriage taking my wife Maria Ana and me from Smith Square to Buckingham Palace and back. A gloriously sunny autumn day allowed us to move slowly through the streets of London while being kindly saluted by people on the pavements wondering who we were and surprised by the glamour of the convoy – but very happy somehow to be part of the event. Our instructions, elegantly transmitted by my good friend Alistair Harrison, the Marshall of the Diplomatic Corps (who had previously worked in Brussels as a British-seconded national expert) were precise and clear about how many steps we should take and where and how we were expected to bow to and interact with Her Majesty. Not to mention the need to feed carrots to the horses at the end of the ride ...

There was an understandable degree of anxiety on our side, but it totally vanished once the queen opened the conversation. We were watching her on a large screen from Windsor Castle. Since the beginning of the pandemic, Her Majesty had stopped (and never resumed) 'in-person' diplomatic audiences. Friendly, smiling, well briefed and showing a detailed memory of past events, the queen was wearing a beautiful dark-blue dress (we were tempted to believe it had been a deliberate choice of colour) and made us forget the solemnity of the occasion. We will always remain grateful for her kindness and hospitality and will remember our meeting fondly.

At the end of the audience, Her Majesty mentioned that she would travel to Northern Ireland the following day. She never did. That same evening, we were shocked: as we sat down in front of the television after a nice dinner at the beautiful French Residence, kindly hosted by my good colleague and friend Catherine Colonna (who would a few months later become President Macron's minister of foreign affairs), the BBC presenter announced that Her Majesty had been taken to hospital and doctors had advised her to take a pause to rest. Her trip to Belfast had to be cancelled. It was the first public sign of the deterioration in the queen's health, eleven months before her sad passing and just a few hours after our audience at Buckingham Palace.

All About BJ

Back to Number 10. I had known Boris Johnson since 1989, in Brussels, when I became a European Commission spokesman at the time of Jacques Delors' presidency, and he took a job as correspondent for the *Daily Telegraph*. Reconnecting with him thirty years later in our totally different new jobs was an intriguing prospect on coming to London. Chris Hope, then at the *Daily Telegraph* himself, unsuspicious of any closeness to the EU and later a good friend, was surprised by it when he interviewed me soon after my arrival. 'EU's new envoy has special relationship with PM' was the (clearly exaggerated) six-column headline that his even more surprised editor chose for Chris's interview.

The fact is that for a few years in Brussels, in the late 1980s and early '90s, I met this ebullient, atypical but nevertheless very bright journalist almost every day at noon when spokespeople faced a crowded press room for the Commission's daily briefing, in the iconic Berlaymont building. More often than I would have liked as a young spokesperson (I was in my early thirties at the time, he was a couple of years younger), I did my best to reply to his tough and convoluted questions. Both of us and everyone else in the press room were forced to use French, the only working language in daily briefings until the 1995 enlargement, which added a picturesque dimension to the dialogue. (I will refrain from characterising our accents talking in French about bananas and cucumbers and other equally unexpected items on Boris's agenda.)

We never really knew what was behind each of Boris's questions and even less so what would be the final editorial impact of our replies (if any), but we had to remain professional in our behaviour. He clearly was the *enfant terrible* of the Berlaymont press room, but also the darling of all those who wanted to have a good entertaining hour or so before pre-lunch drinks. For us, official spokespeople, British journalists in general and Boris Johnson in particular had at least one merit: to keep us on our toes. I could not have imagined at the time how the endurance and agility I acquired as a spokesperson facing Boris, the journalist, would help me as an ambassador to a country run by Boris, the prime minister.

The star-shaped Berlaymont was (and still is) the only EU building recognisable outside Brussels. But it had a major liability: it was stuffed with asbestos and had to be urgently abandoned to allow for major repair and refurbishment. I oversaw the file as spokesperson and briefed journalists on the first findings and their potential future impact. Speculation was rife regarding solutions to the problem. It was not without interest that I read Boris Johnson's piece announcing that the building would be imploded.

It was a tempting and wishful allegory for a much bigger downfall that he simply could not resist using.

The reality proved to be much more prosaic – the emptying of the Berlaymont to allow for a complex extraction of asbestos triggered an unspectacular, but still challenging, removal and relocation of thousands of officials into several alternative buildings. The press room moved to another location, the unremarkable Breydel building, a few blocks away. The withdrawal from the Berlaymont was a logistical nightmare that led some of us, in the darker hours of the transfer, to admit that Boris's suggestion, as detached from reality as it was, might have been a better solution.

The Commission would only return to the Berlaymont eleven years later. Curiously enough, I had to again deal with the same transfer, albeit in a reverse direction and in a different capacity, this time as chief of staff of the recently appointed new Commission president, José Manuel Barroso, as we inaugurated and reoccupied an asbestos-free Berlaymont.

Boris was no longer there to report that, contrary to his prediction or secret wish, neither the building nor the EU had imploded. He was then the editor of *The Spectator* but also an MP and was about to be excluded from the Tories' front bench for the way he handled, in Parliament, issues of his private life. *The Guardian* predicted this would be the end of his political career. Boris and *The Guardian* were both wrong.

I must say I personally enjoyed Boris Johnson's irreverent style as a journalist and his witty intelligence, but I cannot but regret – and was often forced to take the floor to challenge – his creative relationship with facts and sources and his almost obsessive bias against 'Brussels'. It is an established fact that anti-EU coverage in large-circulation British media over the years contributed to gradually shaping a negative perception of our Union in British public opinion. It was far from being the only factor impacting the outcome of the referendum, as I will discuss later, but it cannot be underestimated. Boris played a part in that as a journalist, and I was not as surprised as others to see him aligned with the 'Leave' camp as a politician.

Some kind of professional friendship grew nevertheless throughout our time together at the press room and in the corridors of EU buildings in Brussels' *quartier européen*. Our young families once briefly crossed each other sailing in tiny boats off the coast of some Greek island in the early 1990s. While our boats were still at some distance, I saw someone gesticulating and shouting my name. As soon as I detected a dishevelled blond head of hair between raised arms, I knew who was approaching. We had fun sharing navigation adventures, albeit in much shallower and calmer waters than those in which we would find ourselves decades later in London.

The next time I saw BJ was in New York some twenty-five years later, when, as EU Ambassador to the United Nations, I hosted a meeting of EU foreign ministers at our offices on 666 Third Avenue.

'What are you doing here, João?' he asked me as he stepped out of the lift, and I welcomed him.

'Well, I am hosting you, Foreign Secretary.'

Robert Peston was aware of our previous contacts when he interviewed me live for his excellent political show on ITV. After the usual questions on disputes and disagreements and on the Northern Ireland Protocol, at the right moment towards the end of the interview, when interviewers expect guests to be more relaxed and vulnerable, he fired: 'Ambassador, you knew the PM many years ago as a journalist in Brussels: did you ever think then that he would one day become prime minister?'

My reply came spontaneously quick and sincere, and was unmistakably clear: 'No!' I immediately realised this could be potentially undiplomatic and added in a rush: 'But I don't think he ever expected me to become the EU ambassador to his country either.' Peston laughed and I was relieved.

Something else neither I nor the future prime minister would have imagined back in Brussels is that we would both face the impact of the pandemic of our lifetime separated by a few miles, in the same city, and even less that a compatriot of mine would help save his life from the infecting virus.

This could be the story of 'the English patient and the Portuguese nurse'.

Covid's impact on Boris was, of course, far greater than on me, not only because of his larger duties as prime minister in managing his country's reaction to the pandemic, but also as far as his own health was concerned. The whole country was in shock and showed genuine sympathy towards the prime minister when he was rushed to St Thomas' Hospital in early April 2020. His was a life-threatening infection that took a few weeks to reverse. When he came out of hospital, he was keen to thank two nurses who had been at his side. One of them was nurse Luís Pitarma, from Aveiro, in northern Portugal, one of many hundreds of Portuguese nurses who had migrated to the UK. The first thing Luis asked Boris Johnson was how he would like to be addressed. According to the nurse, quoted by the National Health Service (NHS) website, 'He said to call him Boris.'

Highly appreciated by the NHS, Luis and his Portuguese colleagues illustrate the role of free movement of people inside the EU's single market in adjusting labour force supply to the needs of the different national economies. The UK benefited greatly from it. The severe crisis that was beginning to impact the NHS by mid-2022 would reveal serious staff shortages largely resulting from the end of free movement of the labour force originating in EU member states: no more visa-free, high-quality Portuguese nurses for the English patients.

Hasta la Vista

Beyond the Lancaster House welcoming hug, I came across the prime minister on several other occasions during my time in London. We chatted and had an informal photo taken backstage at the G7 summit he hosted in Cornwall, in June 2021, while he was touring facilities ahead of the meeting, shaking hands with every waiter and door attendant (proving again that BJ never stops campaigning). The following day, I sat across from him during his tense bilateral meeting on the Northern Ireland Protocol with

Charles Michel and Ursula von der Leyen, overlooking Carbis Bay beach. He reckoned that they should be talking about more global and relevant issues but still insisted on the protocol, clearly in a bad mood after equally tense, consecutive bilateral sessions earlier in the morning with President Macron and Chancellor Merkel.

The G7 summit – the first physical one in two years because of Covid – was in my view a partly wasted opportunity for the prime minister. Instead of making it a rare and especially useful occasion to project his image as a world leader with a vision for the future, hosting the recently elected Joe Biden for his first G7, he allowed the media agenda to be partly dominated by Brexit, by insisting again on a confrontational mode with Europeans regarding the Northern Ireland Protocol. It was neither the first nor the last time I was astonished by his focus on Brexit and on the EU to the detriment of other, certainly broader and more relevant political goals.

There was another brief exchange in the margins of the City's Lord Mayor's annual gala banquet, a lavish and glamorous medieval event bringing together almost 650 high-level guests from all City financial firms and from the political and diplomatic worlds. It is an unmissable occasion for the limited number of ambassadors who get an invitation. Before taking our seats and listening to the Archbishop of Canterbury, the Lord Mayor and the prime minister, ambassadors were lined up in our white ties to shake hands with Boris Johnson. When my turn came, after a Japanese colleague, he warmly saluted me and, as he always likes to do, immediately 'attacked'. Half-jokingly, smiling, but in a slightly provocative tone, he accused the EU of letting the UK down at the UN climate change conference, COP26, in Glasgow a few days earlier.

I politely contested and firmly denied. His point was that we had allegedly not supported the UK in resisting a last-minute diluting move from India and China, whereas our attitude in fact had prevented a total collapse of COP26 and saved the essence of the Glasgow compromise. After a critical reference to the Northern Ireland Protocol ('It has to go!'), he moved on to chat with the American chargé.

In the same vein, at a Foreign Office gathering after the Russian invasion, well before the EU decided to accept Ukraine's candidacy, he suggested: 'João, you should let Ukraine into the EU. We have left some free space behind ...' Inimitable.

The last time I spoke with Boris Johnson as ambassador was just a few days before my departure. He was, of course, no longer prime minister – two months and two prime ministers had passed – his image was still tarnished by his eviction from Downing Street and many people in Westminster wanted to avoid being seen in his company. He was climbing the stairs of Westminster Hall, accompanied only by security, and I was on my way out of the House of Commons where I had intervened in the first meeting of the joint Partnership Parliamentary Assembly created by our Trade and Co-operation Agreement. After another energetic shake of the hands and half a hug, I introduced him to the colleague accompanying me.

Johnson shook his hand and said: 'Hi, I am Boris Johnson.' As if my colleague had any doubt of who he was. As if he was again campaigning door to door ...

I said I hoped his life was calmer now after his hectic tenure at Number 10.

'Yes, but I am still very busy,' he immediately replied as if to reject any premature hint of 'has-been' idleness. He wished me the best for my future academic activities. I reciprocated.

As he dashed away followed by his security detail, I could not refrain from saying to myself: 'I am sure I will hear from him again ...'

Hasta la vista, Boris.

NARRATIVES AND TRUST

The Useful Enemy

When I arrived at St Pancras in early 2020, the most optimistic expectations for the EU–UK relationship – which I must confess I did not share – were that after some months of transition and adaptation, we would naturally start implementing the agreed bilateral treaties and a new phase would smoothly start. That was not to be.

The EU and the UK had initially negotiated, signed and ratified the Withdrawal Agreement, which contained important initial provisions ensuring an 'orderly withdrawal', mainly regarding a financial settlement, citizens' rights and an Ireland and Northern Ireland Protocol to address the consequences of Brexit for Northern Ireland. It entered into force on the first day of Brexit, 1 February 2020.

In that same year we negotiated and signed, just before Christmas, the Trade and Co-operation Agreement (TCA), setting out the terms of our future trade and economic relationship.

This sequence was necessary in order to guarantee a clear separation between an 'orderly withdrawal', with each side assuming its respective responsibilities linked to the separation (like a divorce settlement agreement), and the terms of the future relationship framework, covered by a separate treaty.

The TCA negotiations were as complex and agitated as the previous ones related to the Withdrawal Agreement. Moreover, they were negatively impacted by Covid and affected by internal domestic volatility and by the initial tensions associated with the first months of implementation of the Northern Ireland Protocol and the 'settled status' registration of our citizens.

Once the TCA was signed and entered into force in early 2021, the previously agreed treaty – the Withdrawal Agreement – and particularly its protocol on Ireland and Northern Ireland became the centre stage of our diplomatic and political acrimony. Brexit had created a totally new situation for Northern Ireland. For the government and most Conservatives and Unionists, Brexit was the solution for the relationship between Northern Ireland and the EU, and the protocol was the problem; for us and many in Great Britain and Northern Ireland, Brexit was the problem and the protocol was the solution to the problems created by it. That fundamental equation remained valid for the rest of my tenure, throughout 2021 and 2022. And with it came turbulence.

All signs pointed to the government wanting to weaponise the Northern Ireland Protocol. There is speculation that Boris Johnson had made a choice from the start: the fact that the negotiations were over, and the treaties had been signed and ratified and had entered into force, should not change the government's bellicose approach towards the EU. The 'Leave' coalition should be preserved, and the EU should continue to be its catalyst. More: everything possible should be done to *de facto* pursue the negotiation beyond the negotiation and, if possible, renegotiate the Northern Ireland Protocol. According to the well-placed Dominic Cummings' own words,[3] the intention had never been to implement it as signed.

The Cutty Sark Narrative

The prime minister's attitude towards Brexit and the EU had been visible since day one. And I mean day one.

On my very first working day in my new job – also the first working day of Brexit, Monday, 3 February 2020 – I had my initial direct contact with a narrative to which I would become accustomed. Boris Johnson had allegedly sought to deliver his first speech after Brexit from aboard the iconic *Cutty Sark* clipper ship, shored near Greenwich, as the symbolic backdrop for the launching of 'Global Britain'. The location was changed because of television coverage constraints, but not the intention. The speech took place at the beautiful Painted Hall in the adjacent Old Naval College, in the presence of several Cabinet members, MPs, Lords, business people, media representatives and ambassadors – including myself for my very first public event.

The Painted Room is known as the British Sistine Chapel, and it glorifies the country's past. Main implicit (and explicit) message from the location (and the speech): the UK is the champion of free trade and will once again send out many *Cutty Sarks* around the world, well beyond the narrow channel that separates it from the European continent. It was the launching of Global Britain.

The question in my mind then (and now): if you are so keen on free trade – and that is a good principle – why then abandon the largest free trade area in the world, a pillar of the WTO and a big promoter of the rule of law and of values-based standards and norms? A free trade area that happens to be your main trading partner, by far? Just a few miles away from your shores ...

Apart from some elaborate allegories, the speech contained undisguised attacks on alleged EU protectionism and flatly rejected the level playing field concept and the role of the European Court of Justice, both key elements of dispute in the forthcoming negotiation of the TCA. Minimising and dismissing the relevance of the EU and of the UK's withdrawal from it, the prime minister magnified the meaning of opening up to the world. Well briefed in advance, the *Sunday Times* had anticipated the speech over the weekend with a headline I took good note of: 'UK diplomats told to spurn old EU allies'.

This was the first illustration of the narrative that would be developed and refined in the following months and years, and that would gradually but systematically erode the political and personal trust in EU capitals towards the UK and its leadership. The rhetoric was particularly impactful because its main performer and instigator was the same prime minister who had just recently negotiated – and formally signed – the terms of divorce with his counterparts in the EU. The first speech after Brexit – the '*Cutty Sark* speech' that was not – did not bode well either for my tenure in London or for cross-Channel levels of trust.

Permafrost

The prime minister's approach vis-à-vis the EU was initially spearheaded by David Frost, his chief negotiator. He took centre stage soon after my arrival, becoming Boris's messenger and trusted extension (it is important to note that there was no minister between him and the prime minister, a fact that David constantly reminded us of).

David was made a lord in September 2020 and promoted to the Cabinet in March 2021, and he soon became the ideologue of hard Brexit. However, probably frustrated by his incapacity to take his more radical agenda fully forward, he left government a few months after joining it, just before Christmas of that same year. On the protocol, he had wished that the government would use unilateral action and its 'nuclear weapon' (Article 16) in a systematic way as part of a hard-power agenda against the EU, regardless of any collateral consequences. This was in line, as later became clear, with his overall hawkish concept of a Brexit Britain, reflected inter alia in his endorsement, in its initial stages at least, of Liz Truss's 'Trussonomics'.

Frost's ideas were outlined in a few highly political speeches that some considered somewhat pretentious coming from a civil servant – or a civil servant recently turned politician – and which took many observers and some of his colleagues by surprise. He made a point of delivering them outside the UK, in 'enemy territory'. Most relevant were those delivered in Brussels and in Lisbon (while the choice of the Belgian capital seems obvious, the reason for the choice of my hometown as a delivery location, to which he travelled for that single purpose, remains a mystery to me).

In those speeches, David Frost revealed a vision for Brexit that had little consistency with the actual content of the treaties and the political declaration he had negotiated on behalf of his prime minister. They reflected an outlandish interpretation of the Brexit texts that would become even more ideologically baroque as time went on and he started writing a column in the *Daily Telegraph*. It came as no real surprise to me that he had to leave government. He was moving away from the centre of gravity of the Cabinet's thinking (even if allegedly, in private conversations, he confided that he was a moderate voice in Number 10).

Reliable sources claim Rishi Sunak, then chancellor, and his advisers at the Treasury were wary of the risks of a trade war with the EU, if Frost's plans went ahead. This eventually led David to conclude that it was best to leave, and to pursue his crusade elsewhere. Boris Johnson's EU/Brexit agenda was from then on implemented in close complicity with Liz Truss, who got the Brexit file back into the FCDO's remit, from which it had been taken to the benefit of the Cabinet Office.

Insult and Injury

Some in my camp rejoiced at Frost's departure, but the fact was that a lot of damage had already been inflicted upon UK–EU relations. Since Brexit day, instead of creating conditions for a normal and gradual implementation of the agreements as they entered into force, the government opted for an inflammatory rhetoric, as if erecting the EU as a unifying and useful enemy would facilitate keeping Conservative, pro-Brexit Labour and former Labour voters fully energised. The coalition that had brought Boris Johnson to power was in fact his political life insurance. Not for the first time, the EU was a tempting and convenient tool in the pursuit of domestic political endeavours.

All this materialised in unilateral action whenever we showed resistance – or the prime minister needed to score points with his hardline Conservatives – and was ultimately illustrated with particular political cynicism by the introduction of two bills that, if they became law, would allow the government to breach the terms of a treaty it had signed, ratified in Parliament and even successfully submitted to popular vote. In fact, this also meant that the government was ready to breach international commitments made on behalf of the country, or international law. As one minister candidly admitted in Parliament, while presenting one of them, it 'would break international law in a very specific and limited way'.

The first such initiative was the Internal Market Bill, whose content was changed before it became law thanks to clever work done at the end of 2020 by Michael Gove, the member of Cabinet in charge of Brexit at the time, and the Commission's vice-president, Maroš Šefčovič. The second, even more relevant and far reaching, was the infamous Northern Ireland Protocol Bill introduced by Liz Truss, early in the summer of 2022, just before the fall of Boris Johnson.

In between bills in Parliament, the government tactically used autonomously decided grace periods and other unilateral measures to undermine the implementation of the protocol, gain time and delay the impact of the obligations it had signed. Its domestic target audience: the hard Brexiteer wing of the party, 'Leave' voters in general and the Unionists in Northern Ireland in particular. Its strategic goal: to keep the winning coalition alive.

The best example of such practice is what David Frost did in only his second day in office as a new member of the Cabinet, in March 2021. Via his colleague Brandon Lewis, the Northern Ireland secretary, he announced in the Commons a series of unilateral decisions regarding trade between Northern Ireland and Great Britain that represented a clear breach of the letter and the spirit of the Withdrawal Agreement and the protocol. The announcement was made a few hours ahead of Frost's first meeting with Maroš Šefčovič, his new counterpart in the Commission, without any warning. Not the best way to make a good first impression ...

I was asked if I had been surprised by Frost's undiplomatic and antagonistic behaviour. I replied: disappointed yes, surprised no. This was the second time that the government had acted against the terms of the protocol and had done so via a unilateral approach, as opposed to trying to find common solutions in a concerted way. We had no other option but to launch legal action against the UK, which we did a few days later. As far as David was concerned, he was simply confirming the accuracy of his Foreign Office nickname: 'Frosty'.

The government added the insult of rhetoric to the injury of Brexit and in so doing seriously worsened cross-Channel relations. Its permanently aggressive discourse towards us was coupled with a dismissive attitude regarding the country's obligations under British, EU and international law, which had resulted from the UK's own choices. It was as if it was the EU that had expelled the UK and should be made responsible for finding solutions to the problems created, also on British territory, by the UK's decision to leave. As if somebody else had negotiated and signed the agreements on behalf of the UK. I remember once asking David Frost, in his office: 'David, how do you want me to convince my leaders that you and your prime minister are genuinely interested in moving this forward? How can I make them trust you if you keep behaving and talking publicly as if you did not put your signature to the texts?'

This came on top of a deteriorating bilateral economic landscape. The fact is that by late 2021 and early 2022, even before the impact of Putin's invasion of Ukraine, trade and economic co-operation were suffering across the board, investment had stalled, business people were unhappy, and researchers were disappointed with the collateral damage to their access to EU funding and partnerships. People's mobility was severely constrained and reduced, while immigration from outside Europe was growing faster than before Brexit to compensate for the new obstacles to the flows from the EU. Our enemies and adversaries were rejoicing at our open divisions, be it on the Northern Ireland Protocol, fisheries, Horizon Europe, immigration, citizens' rights or financial services. The only notable exceptions were climate change and our good common work on G7 and Iran, and later Ukraine, even if joint action on foreign policy and security matters suffered from the lack of a reliable structured framework, which the EU had offered but London had rejected.

Clouds were low across the Channel and there was no sign that London wanted to clear the skies.

A Political Virus

In addition to issues around the Northern Ireland Protocol, there was another topic in the political landscape that soon became 'weaponised' during those critical 1,000 days after Brexit, until the end of 2022: the Covid pandemic.

As elsewhere, Covid-19 had an enormous impact in the UK. It affected people, disrupted the economy and substantially complicated and reduced activity in many levels of society, including diplomacy. Not in politics. Political debate never quarantined during the pandemic and beyond. It remained invariably tense.

Notwithstanding an eighty-seat Conservative majority, there was never a 'sea of tranquillity' around Downing Street – or inside it – and the 'moon crash', largely triggered or at least strongly influenced by the pandemic, eventually happened in July 2022. Turbulence never really subsided. Seat belts were permanently fastened during Boris Johnson's premiership flight. It could have inspired a Hollywood aviation disaster movie.

All aspects of the management of the Covid crisis quickly became almost as toxic as the virus itself. Boris Johnson knows something about it: his premiership was prematurely ended thanks to the way he behaved during the pandemic.

Vaccines were a particularly sensitive topic, as soon as the first wave of the pandemic passed and people started focusing, obsessively and understandably, on finding a vaccine.

There was, however, a long way to go before vaccines became available. In the UK, it was not a straightforward road. It was quite convoluted. And it started with a certain degree of denial.

There is always this thing about the UK: being special. Not the kind of divinely inspired, pioneering and somehow excessive exceptionalism that I witnessed in the USA. What I found in the UK is rather a sense of uniqueness, founded on pride in eccentricity and creativity, and the primacy of individual freedom over rigid, written norms and expectations – even if British people are keen to establish elaborate rules for the use of their spare time, from cricket to drinking port wine. All this is combined with an amazing collective resilience in tough times, drawing from insular endurance and self-reliance. This is what has made the UK a great country, as the queen illustrated in her solemn address about the pandemic.

This mix was, however, not correctly balanced in the first weeks of the government's reaction to Covid-19. Feeling too 'special' and wanting to stress the country's post-EU regained 'sovereignty', Downing Street fell into condescension and self-sufficiency. To be frank, there was some rational, theoretical coherence in the 'herd immunity' approach, but its supporters underestimated the constraints. Two problems, at least, soon appeared: the potentially prohibitive cost in lives and the unsustainable feeling of being always behind the curve (and the infection curve was getting steeper by the day).

The government thus had to do a lot of catching up and, in the process, Boris Johnson wasted time and credibility and showed inconsistency, as he was forced to change gear and to do later what others had already done before. He eventually paid the price with his own infection. Not only him: ironically (and sadly) enough, one week in April 2020 started with all three government Covid front-benchers (the prime minister, the health secretary and England's chief medical officer) removed from action and isolated, joined by the ultimate insider, Dominic Cummings.

When interviewed by the BBC's *Today* programme, in early March, two weeks before the first lockdown, I suggested we should all be humbled by the Coronavirus crisis. For at least two reasons: the extent of its impact and the limits of national action to counter it, as no country alone could successfully find solutions to a pandemic. Downing Street reluctantly and gradually also realised it and its language, and body language, became humbler by the day.

Being humble was also recommended when assessing the potential impact of Covid-19 on the EU–UK negotiations and on the implementation of the Withdrawal Agreement. The only thing I knew was that hardly anything would remain unaffected by this health crisis, and that included our relationship. Apart from preventing negotiating teams from physically meeting, the first obvious consequence of the crisis was that Corona (as it was sometimes referred to at the beginning of the pandemic) removed EU-related issues from front pages and forced the government to switch attention and resources to the virus. The second major impact had to do with the calendar. There was growing speculation about a possible extension of the Brexit transition period[4] as people doubted that the negotiations on future trade conditions could be concluded before the end of the year. A third consequence concerned business and consumers. Would they take the disruption in supply chains and the empty supermarket shelves resulting from the pandemic as a vaccine for a no-deal cliff edge – avoiding a double blow to the economy and to consumption? Or rather as a softener, a factor making the 'Australian model' of very loose relations with the EU more palatable?

Social distancing became the new norm in the UK and elsewhere as a protecting factor against Covid. But Downing Street added EU distancing to its behaviour. From ventilators to aviation safety and crisis management, with the single exception of the repatriation of stranded tourists and citizens – and even then, reluctantly – the attitude was to create and promote distance from us, avoiding mentioning the EU even when it was obvious that it would make sense. As described earlier, London did not hesitate to use some Covid-related bilateral incidents to score political points.

In the meantime, a government reshuffle did not produce any junior Foreign Office minister in charge of the EU brief (the foreign secretary covers that file, we were told), and further down the ladder the EU was followed by a sub-department called Europe South. The foreign secretary, Dominic Raab, while leading a daily crisis press conference, talked about joint efforts with other countries to ensure British citizens' repatriation. Although the EU as such was playing a direct role in those operations, and we in the EU Delegation to the UK were liaising well with government departments, all we got was a reference to a few member states.

'Safe distance from the EU' seemed to be the new government's mantra.

In Liz We Trust?

After two years of intense squabbling, unproductive narrative wars and diminishing levels of mutual trust, the very first weeks of Foreign Secretary Liz Truss's assignment as our interlocutor, in January and February 2022, were rather promising.

I am sure some of us thought that anyone but David Frost would be welcome ... but still the first impression she made was positive. There was a breath of fresh air when we were kindly invited for meetings and an overnight stay at her official country residence at Chevening to launch discussions and play billiards. The atmosphere there was a clear improvement even if, on substance, we had to painfully revisit most of the issues covered during 2021, particularly regarding the Northern Ireland Protocol, and remind our interlocutors of the commitments their country had already made. There was no point in trying to start from scratch, we warned. It was a charm operation, and we knew it, but it was in any case a welcome change.

The Chevening overnight stay on 13–14 January started with a one-on-one long walk in the park. Up and down the huge lawn, Liz Truss and Maroš Šefčovič, the Commission vice-president in charge of Brexit in Brussels, had a first opportunity to get to know each other better ahead of seated exchanges with a few colleagues on either side.

As I sat across from her and next to the vice-president, I was wondering about the personality of our new counterpart. In the coming weeks and months, watching her in private meetings and in public performances, I was able to draw a clearer profile: I saw in Liz Truss a professional politician, energetic, thick-skinned, stubborn, led more by intuition and sheer will than by a detailed and rational control of substance, always trying to steer the process and her interlocutors. There was an element of taking a tactical fresh look at things that could be dangerously mistaken for naivety. We knew from the start that she deserved respect and concentration from our side even if, I felt, she expected that her task of bringing us closer to her positions would be easier than it turned out to be. That revealed a degree of excessive self-confidence that future events would confirm.

I thought at the time that Truss's purposeful and pragmatic approach (remember 'deliver, deliver'?) could inject dynamism into what had been moribund discussions under Frost. It was unfortunately a short-lived hope. With time she realised that what she could eventually extract from us would not be enough to convince those in the hard Brexit wing of her party whose support she needed.

In late March, the foreign secretary invited me to a private meeting in her office. We had a good conversation for almost an hour about Ukraine and what the UK and the EU could do together to confront Putin. She was happy – and so were we – with bilateral co-operation on Ukraine and Russia. In retrospect, I believe the United Kingdom's early and firm commitment to supporting Ukraine played a crucial role in shaping the West's response to Putin. We talked about the USA and the G7 – I shared my experience of both – and how to make like-minded co-operation work better. But when at the end of the conversation we talked about Brexit and the protocol, I understood we had reached the end of the road with her. This needed now to go one level up, to principals, she said, and I was tempted to agree.

From that moment on, there was in fact almost total radio silence from Liz Truss and her team on any issue of substance regarding relations with the EU until September, when her election as leader was consummated. Silence except for the bad news of the tabling, at her initiative, of the very hostile and unilaterally provocative Northern Ireland Protocol Bill. And for good reason.

Two months before the end of my almost three-year term as ambassador, Liz Truss started her much shorter one as prime minister. She did so after an internal change of guard for which the Conservative Party seems to hold the copyright.

There was hardly any trust left across the Channel when Truss replaced Johnson in September 2022, but she could not exclusively blame her predecessor.

A former 'remainer' and Liberal Democrat and allegedly also monarchy-critical – described as 'blunt, binary and assertive' by American officials quoted in the *Financial Times* after her first visit to Washington DC as foreign secretary – Truss had become a true Brexit believer and managed to galvanise the Tory Party members by successfully presenting herself as having solid Conservative and hard Brexit credentials. She had steadily and ably exploited Boris Johnson's self-inflicted wounds while staying publicly loyal to him until the end. In the process, with Johnson's support and ultimately very much in line with her predecessor David Frost, Truss was perceived by our capitals as having sacrificed the quality of relations with the EU on the altar of Brexit purism and to the detriment of Northern Ireland's stability.

The Northern Ireland Protocol Bill, which she personally initiated, signalled the lowest point of mutual trust in our relationship since Brexit, but it was the pinnacle of Liz Truss's strategy to gain the support of her party's hard Brexiteers. A winning strategy for an ambitious politician, but one with considerable negative impact on the cross-Channel climate.

All the bad vibes regarding the EU and her concessions to the party's Brexit hardliners as foreign secretary were, however, of little help to Truss in the next (maybe not the last) chapter of her political life. Her premiership lasted just forty-nine days and became the shortest in modern British history. It was marked by the most amazing sequence of events in just a few weeks, from her confirmation with the queen on 6 September, two days before Elizabeth II passed away, at Balmoral Castle, to her extremely short resignation speech on 25 October, in front of Number 10.

I watched Truss's farewell statement live. I did not detect any visible emotion, not a hint of Theresa May's tears, no sign of Boris Johnson's flamboyant '*Hasta la vista*, baby.' Liz Truss woke up from her long-sought but short-lived dream without much drama. A performance as flat as herself, someone remarked. Robotic, others commented. Self-controlled but lacking self-awareness, I would say, slightly more generously.

Better Mood Music

Rishi Sunak stepped in four days after Truss's departure as 'my' third prime minister, albeit just for my last three weeks in the job. We welcomed Sunak's arrival with some hope but, at the time, with limited illusions. It was clear for me by then that any substantial qualitative change in the EU–UK relationship was unlikely to happen before another general election. But we were adamant that the EU would be the last one to shut the door or turn off the lights on talks about our lingering dispute on the Northern Ireland Protocol – and would seize any opportunity to improve things on that front, albeit not at any price. We wanted to move on.

The first weeks of Sunak's tenure did bring a change of tone and the confirmed foreign secretary – James Cleverly, an extrovert and likeable, down-to-earth politician whom I had known as Europe minister – was the face of it, even if the last word was clearly with Number 10. Attitude and body language changed, public statements as well. But we were not yet seeing that translated into concrete change at the ongoing technical talks. The political contacts remained vague and declaratory in the first weeks. Tangible evidence of changed positions was indispensable if some trust was to be restored.

As I summarised in a valedictory interview with George Parker of the *Financial Times* three days before my departure, 'The mood music has changed, the melody is nicer, but we have not yet seen the words of the new British song.' Still, I was happy to leave London on a comparatively higher note than in most of my time there. Strategic patience seemed to have paid off. Maybe a new cycle was about to begin?

Asked by a colleague ambassador to assess the state of EU–UK relations at the end of my posting in November 2022, I said I was moderately optimistic in the long run but remained pessimistic about the short term. It could still take a while before the useful enemy became a useful partner.

THE LAST (MESSY) MILE

The last weeks before Rishi Sunak took office deserve a closer look.

My time as first EU envoy to Brexit Britain was about to end when I returned to grey London from the sunny Algarve in late August 2022 for my last few months in that position. As a new post-Boris/post-referendum cycle was beginning – with the appointment of a new prime minister (or rather, two) – it was time for me to start a new one as well. I was already mentally preparing for my retirement at the end of January 2023, one year later than foreseen by EU rules and expected by me and my family, concluding a forty-year-long career at the service of Europe. But I still had to endure, or enjoy, depending on the mood of the day, a hectic final stretch.

Johnson, Truss and Beyond
The *rentrée* of 2022, right after the summer break, was, to say the least, a short but eventful period.

The prime minister who had 'made Brexit happen' had not been able and/or was not allowed by his party to 'get Brexit done'. The promises and the dividends that he and all the 'leavers' had announced had failed to materialise and the toxic combination of Brexit, Covid and Putin had thrown the country into dire economic trouble with double-digit inflation not seen for a generation and the heaviest tax burden in decades. As Boris Johnson left power, consumer confidence had fallen to its lowest level since comparable records began almost fifty years before and people were enduring the largest drop in real wages for more than twenty years. Energy prices had skyrocketed and pressure was mounting across public services.

The internal party revolt against Boris Johnson's personal and political shortcomings resulted in the consecutive appointment of two prime ministers with a totally legitimate mandate from a parliamentary democracy point of view but lacking the key muscle that only a fresh popular national vote can provide, which is particularly relevant if the international and domestic context imposes hard choices, as was the case.

The UK was also left with a divided and weakened governing party increasingly vulnerable to electoral accidents, as the demographic profile, concerns and aspirations of rank-and-file members who had elected Liz Truss were far from matching those of the parliamentarians who replaced her with Rishi Sunak. Moreover, none of them seemed to match the sentiment of the general electorate. Across the aisle, the main opposition party was finally beginning to come out of a long Brexit tunnel, had concluded a significant leadership and ideological transformation and seemed ready to embark upon the last mile towards Downing Street.

A Week Like No Other

The post-Boris cycle formally started in September 2022, and its debut did not go unnoticed, far from it.

Liz Truss had taken the helm of the country just two days earlier when the sovereign who empowered her sadly passed away on 8 September. King Charles III became the new monarch. In a single week, the UK had two prime ministers and two sovereigns.

It was indeed a week like no other. On Monday, Elizabeth Truss becomes leader of the Conservative Party. On Tuesday, Elizabeth II appoints Elizabeth Truss as prime minister. On Thursday, Elizabeth II dies. On Friday, Elizabeth Truss has her first audience with the oldest son of Elizabeth II who succeeded her. On Saturday and beyond, a whole country mourns its longest and most revered monarch and hopes Elizabeth Truss will lead it through one of the most challenging times in its history. An era ended and a new political cycle began in a week of two Elizabeths.

The new prime minister's opening salvo – a far-reaching financial and energy package to prepare the country for a winter of hardship caused by Putin – was being presented late on Thursday morning in Parliament while the first disturbing news of the queen's health started appearing on my Twitter feed. I first read those tweets on my way to the station (St Pancras, of course) to fetch my wife, who was visiting from Brussels. 'I'm afraid the queen is really not well', I said when she entered the car. We immediately reminded ourselves of the unforgettable audience at Buckingham Palace a year earlier and became worried. Elizabeth II would die later in the afternoon of that Thursday, at Balmoral Castle, in the Scottish Highlands. Of 'old age', according to the official death certificate released a few days later. May Her Majesty rest in peace.

The country stopped in shock for the following ten days. Another layer of the national transition process had just been added. And a very significant one if we consider – as we should – Elizabeth II as a major unifying factor, a force of wisdom, serenity and continuity, who contributed immensely to what the United Kingdom of Great Britain and Northern Ireland is today. The national, largely consensual and impressive reaction to the passing of the queen should have reassured those who had doubts about the relevance of the monarchy for the sustainability of the Union.

Forty-Nine Mad Days

But suddenly, after the queen's departure, events took over. At a frenetic pace.

After the 19 September state funeral and the period of national mourning, Liz Truss and her chancellor and close friend Kwasi Kwarteng emerged from 'policy confinement' at Chequers (extending initial brainstorming in August at Chevening) with a radical libertarian agenda. Strongly influenced and intellectually supported by think tanks that had been behind the hard Brexit discourse – and, I am told, in the absence of any reliable counter-factual discussion outside a restricted group of like-minded people – they presented a 'mini budget' on 23 September that would ulti-mately determine their 'maxi fall'. Tax cuts (particularly for the wealthiest) not funded by new resources, and big spending, with no credible plan to absorb the corresponding increase in deficit and debt, could only result in a politically unfeasible equation.

'Why such a hurry?' asked Kwasi Kwarteng at one point.

Liz Truss explained: 'I've only got two years.'

To which he replied – as he told Tom Newton Dunn on Talk TV and in *The Times*: 'You will have two months if you carry on like this.' She had two weeks.

Markets went ballistic, the Bank of England was forced to act, and public opinion wondered what was happening. Conservative parliamentarians became extremely nervous about the prospect of losing their seats, members of the Cabinet resigned, the party and the country were in turmoil, Liz Truss lost control. On 20 October, Prime Minister Truss resigned and four days later Rishi Sunak took over. In the meantime, the British economy had taken a major hit and the hard Brexit, libertarian, Singapore-on-Thames model had basically collapsed. Truss had gambled and lost. Big time.

For us, apart from the fascination of watching, live, an amazing combination of the original British and the enhanced American versions of *House of Cards*, it meant holding all our cards, waiting for the dust to settle on the British political scene. We had witnessed months of unique turbulence inside the governing party and now it might stabilise at some point. I was hopeful that the new paradigm would be more appropriate for serious conversations on the way forward for our relationship. But who could guarantee that?

On 17 November, two days after my departure, Jeremy Hunt presented in Parliament a harsh package of tax rises and spending cuts. The UK was back to austerity, or rationality, depending on one's opinion. This was in any case paving the way for years of pain, as summarised by the *Financial Times*. Gone were the days of Keynesian Boris and libertarian Liz. Welcome austere and rational

Rishi. From September to November, the country had gone from a royal funeral to what could well, and soon, spell the Conservative Party's own demise. By December, only one thing was guaranteed: the UK was bracing for a harsh 2022–23 winter of discontent.

Less than two years later, in July 2024, the fourteen-year-long Conservative stewardship finally came to an end and Labour returned to power. The majority in Parliament changed colour. Number 10 changed tenant. Brexit, however, like Downing Street's 'Larry the cat', remained in place.

5

Breaking Up is Hard to Do

Looking closer at the 'mother of all divorces' is a useful exercise. It provides factual testimony to the downsides of separation between nations once closely linked by human, political, economic and regulatory 'common goods', and illustrates how difficult it is to identify the rationality of a looser relationship between neighbours, allies and friends.

In November 2022, when I left London, and despite a clear change in the government's body language (and real language) since the arrival of Rishi Sunak, it was no time to be complacent: Brexit was far from done and in times of geopolitical and geo-economic turmoil a lot was required from EU–UK co-operation, regardless of our recent divorce.

The full impact of that divorce was actually only beginning to be effectively measurable – first, because Covid had blurred the picture and masked Brexit's initial effects (as equally did the aftershocks of the invasion of Ukraine, which happened immediately after); second, because the provisions of both the Withdrawal Agreement and the TCA were far from being fully implemented as a result of the combined effect of British unpreparedness, the deliberate choice to postpone the negative impact of Brexit and the conflict around the Northern Ireland Protocol.

It was only in the last quarter of 2022 that the assessment of the impact of Brexit started leaving the restricted circle of think tanks and economic institutions to become a matter of public awareness. Every week brought new negative data and this trend would clearly accelerate at the beginning of 2023, intensifying throughout the year. It did not reflect the doomsday scenario that the

'Remain' campaign had anticipated, but it provided no evidence of net benefits either.

However, even when Brexit costs and the lack of obvious upsides became visible and quantifiable, politicians from both sides of the House did not show any readiness, let alone eagerness, to talk about its real impact in a meaningful way. Brexit, although always present in the background of political strategies, remained a taboo in the public party-political discourse and was never a substantial issue of discussion or argument. It was obviously too dangerous a territory for any of the main parties to dare entering. As with Covid, these parties had been vaccinated – and boosted – against the Brexit virus.

THE UK'S BREXIT LOCKDOWN

Upon my arrival in London, I quickly confirmed and found evidence of what I had suspected watching the British political scene from the other side of the Atlantic: the UK had been the object of a deep cleavage right before and right after the Brexit referendum. One cannot underestimate the significance of the 2016 vote. A senior British diplomat once told me: 'I witnessed two extraordinary events in my lifetime: a referendum to stay in the EU and a referendum to leave the EU.' A full cycle of wedding and separation in just a few decades.

The Brexit wounds in the UK are still far from healing. The division is transversal to British society, does not respect regional boundaries and cuts across friendships and families. That is particularly true for political parties, made even more relevant by the fact that both Conservative and Labour are 'broad church' or 'big tent' parties, bringing together different sensitivities of the right and left, respectively.

The Conservative camp is far from homogeneous regarding Europe, as we well know. I was able to witness that in many warm encounters with the Conservative European Forum, around David Liddington, and in my interaction with many Tories active in the European Movement or contributing to debates promoted by Bright Blue, the CER, UK in a Changing Europe, and Best for Britain, to mention just a few fora. However, the most interesting case of intra-party scission happened within the Labour Party.

Many Labour militants and voters, particularly in what became known as the 'red wall' of underprivileged communities in the north and north-east of England, had opted for Brexit in 2016 and even voted Conservative in 2019. It was hard for the new, post-Corbyn Labour leadership to assume a proactive and 'progressive' discourse on Europe, in line with the anti-Brexit majority of their members, if they wanted to bring back to their tent those pro-Brexit voters who were vital for any strong showing at the next elections. I witnessed that struggle to find the right balance as I closely observed and engaged with the main opposition party. It soon became clear that the last thing Keir Starmer wanted was for the next election to be fought on the previous one's dividing lines: in favour or against Brexit. It had to be about more than a decade of Conservative governments and the state in which they had left the economy.

My relations with Labour were always good, including on a personal level, at the initial stages mainly with the very engaged Lisa Nandy and with Jenny Chapman and Catherine West, sparsely with Emily Thornberry, and afterwards also with good friends David Lammy, Peter Kyle and Stephen Doughty, as well as later with Nick Thomas-Symonds. But Keir Starmer was clearly not in the mood to engage visibly on Europe and Brexit in the early days of my tenure. Our first meeting happened more than a year after my arrival. It was substantial and friendly, and signalled the beginning of an evolution in Starmer's exposure to the Brexit file. The degree of caution he deployed in my meeting would continue to mark his attitude throughout my term in London as he slowly progressed in his public discourse.

I was nevertheless happy to acknowledge a visible evolution between the 2021 and 2022 party conferences and the growing confidence shown by Starmer and his team in assuming clearer positions, although always short of questioning the decision taken in 2016. It was apparent to me at the time that Labour discourse and practice would fundamentally change – even perhaps to the point of reviewing the relationship format – only after winning an election, or maybe even two.

The Conservatives, in power well before Brexit – and after it with an even larger majority – need to address another set of questions, for which I must confess I did not get an answer while in London: What was the 'Leave' plan? What is the Conservative Brexit endgame? What is their vision for the UK–EU relationship? The most frequent reply I heard from the hardest supporters of Brexit within the party, particularly when it became easier to quantify the negative impact of Brexit, was the classic defensive line: Brexit is great, but Covid, Putin and other factors delayed its benefits. Or even, especially coming from the Truss, Frost and Rees-Mogg camps: we have not been allowed to implement Brexit properly yet.

Under renewed pressure from its right flank, with the surge in support for the Reform Party and facing newly elected MP Nigel Farage's continued activism, it will be even more difficult for Conservatives to escape clarification as they change sides in the Commons and prepare for the coming election battles.

Extreme cautiousness about Brexit was not exclusive to politicians. It was also visible in business circles in the early days of Brexit. Even those – the majority – who opposed Brexit were extremely shy in stating any opinion explicitly. This is partly explained by business people's traditional reluctance to enter the political arena, particularly if it implies criticising the government. But beyond that, the main reason for this attitude regarding Brexit was the same as in the main opposition parties: they did not want to reopen old wounds and risk dividing their camps.

As time went by, however, I noticed a growing dissatisfaction with the management of Brexit and its negative impact on business activities. Businesses did not detect the alleged upside of Brexit and were feeling the negative impact of all its downsides, from trade disruption to longer supply chains, not to mention labour shortages. Does this mean that they were calling for a divergence agenda? For Singapore-on-Thames?

In my frequent and numerous contacts with businesses in London and around the country, I was particularly interested to check whether there was any appetite for regulatory divergence or any room for manoeuvre to accept or request systematic deregulation. I found none of that. On the contrary. Every single business representative from the Confederation of British Industry, the Federation of Small Businesses and the Chambers of Commerce, and all the sectorial representatives of manufacturing, food and drink, and agriculture, replied 'no' to my blunt question: Do you want or need major divergence from EU rules and standards? And the reasons were pragmatically obvious: 'The EU is our biggest market and is likely to remain so for many years; why would we want to force upon ourselves the extra costs of producing for two regulatory universes – the domestic market and the single market?' For all these reasons, the negative reaction of business to Jacob Rees-Mogg's crusade to revoke EU-inspired laws (which Sunak eventually killed) did not surprise me.

The only area where I detected a potential appetite for divergence was in nascent technologies where people saw an interest in anticipating any EU framework, benefiting from a quicker decision-making process at national level to establish a first-mover competitive advantage in the regulatory and technological landscape. Artificial Intelligence came at the top of the list of such sectors, but even here more rational voices would warn about the limits of national regulation against the background of globalised markets.

Business dissatisfaction with Brexit grew as time went by and particularly once the Covid and Putin factors intervened to potentiate its negative impact on the British economy.

Covid lockdowns brought the British economy to a halt and made London a ghost town for lengthy periods of time. Putin's action in Ukraine added another layer, triggering strategic and economic uncertainty. Energy- and commodities-induced inflation increased Covid-related social tensions. A gloomy economic climate eventually emerged and strikes paralysed hospitals, railways and more.

The Covid and Putin factors were obviously relevant in explaining the country's struggles, but something deeper and more complex, something intrinsic to the country, was holding the UK back. Some sort of unresolved dilemma kept forcing the country to look backwards rather than forwards. Preventing it, for instance, from assuming, without guilt or shame or complexes, a normal relationship with its most important neighbour. That something was a recent traumatic divorce, a litigious separation whose scars were far from disappearing.

The real British lockdown in recent years has not, in fact, been the Covid lockdown; it has been the Brexit lockdown. It was used by some to cement the coalition of different political groupings in power and by others as justification for not presenting potentially divisive alternative models. The EU had moved on from the Brexit shock. We were out of Brexit confinement (we never really entered it). The UK was still 'locked in'.

As Jon Sopel from *The News Agents* noted: 'In the thirty-seven years from 1979 to 2016 there were just five prime ministers. In the six years since 2016 we have also had five PMs. Something pretty destabilising must have happened that year.'

During the tough times in 2022 when the negative impact of a pandemic combined with a war on the European continent, many in the British government argued that hardship was not exclusive to their country. Other countries, certainly within the EU, were feeling the same pain. That is correct, but an extra layer of pain was directly inflicted by Brexit and particularly the kind of Brexit that had been chosen: less trade, a smaller workforce, less investment, less public financial support for regional development, more rigidity at the border for people and goods, and a higher burden for business and consumers.

All this is relevant, but what I call the 'Brexit lockdown' is in fact not only strictly or technically about the UK's withdrawal from the EU or its economic impact. It encapsulates more than that. It has to do with the country's search for a path forward in the twenty-first century.

Being a member of the EU for forty-seven years was part of the process of digesting and absorbing the end of a vast empire and adapting to the return to the country's core dimensions and its role in a rapidly changing and volatile world. Leaving the EU forced the country to accelerate that trajectory.

The impact of Brexit is not restricted to trade and labour flows and other economic factors. It touches also upon some fundamental features of the UK as a country and as a union. The EU's policies, its financial instruments and its vast normative framework had placed the different components of the UK under a wider 'common house'. Leaving that 'common house' meant revisiting the country's own house – deciding how to reorganise it, how to find the right 'subsidiarity' balance between central and regional and between regional and local powers, and what to do with the legislative and normative inheritance from almost fifty years of European integration (the debate triggered by Jacob Rees-Mogg and Boris Johnson about the scrapping of EU laws was symptomatic).

Such a 'structural' impact would necessarily trigger tensions within the kingdom, between England and the administrations of Scotland and Wales and, albeit differently, Northern Ireland. How were authority, competences, wealth and wellbeing to be rebalanced and redistributed now that the EU norms and rules no longer prevailed? Answering these questions involves, for instance, recreating an 'internal' single market and redesigning internal budgetary transfers. I had vivid evidence of growing internal tensions during my several visits to Scotland, Wales and Northern Ireland. This new context has also given new prominence to the issue of 'levelling up' within England itself, between London and the south-east and less privileged regions in the north.

Even more significantly, Brexit has magnified the debate about the cohesion of a multi-nation country if one considers the potential for Scotland's independence and Ireland's unification, both boosted by a hard version of Brexit, even if the Scottish case has been weakened by self-inflicted wounds within the independence camp.

Having 'taken back control' of its borders and trade policies, the country was also – and still is – grappling with the harsh realities

of the limits of traditional national sovereignty in times of globalised interconnection and interdependence – and now hard
power rivalry and confrontation.

The initial vague concept of 'Global Britain' (see the *Cutty Sark*
episode in Chapter 4) and the advocacy of free trade are hardly
compatible – in my view, they are contradictory – with the decision to give away the influence and power that a country benefits
from as part of the biggest trading bloc in the world, which is
able to use its continental scale and its vast and dense regulatory
arsenal. Some thought it possible that the USA could somehow
be an alternative to the EU, that it would be willing to make the
trade and regulatory concessions to a market of 67 million people
that it had denied to a market worth half a billion consumers.
Having launched as EU ambassador in Washington an attempt
that ultimately failed to establish a trade and regulatory common
space across the Atlantic (the Transatlantic Trade and Investment
Partnership, or TTIP), I was well placed to judge the likelihood of
success of the British endeavour. When people claimed to me that
a post-Brexit UK–US trade deal would be 'a piece of cake', I simply
replied: 'Good luck with your cake ...'

Opting for Brexit, the UK chose to dispense with the 'Brussels
effect' and now needs to prove it can succeed globally in the
absence of that leverage. The UK is still searching for its own
alternative (a 'London effect'?), but it is likely to realise that in
today's globalised and competitive economy it is not easy to be
a lone knight.

'Global Britain', as I have mentioned, was Boris Johnson's early
mantra. It never really materialised and Rishi Sunak realised that
a shrunken rehash of EU trade deals at national level would not
bring substantial additional benefits and, in the urgency of showing results, could even produce costs. Then some envisaged moving
towards a privileged relationship with a group of emerging powers
and markets, assuming a long-term perspective, as if it could somehow provide an alternative to a close relationship with the 'big
neighbour'. None of these options seems to pass the test of scale
and credibility as a real alternative to the pre-Brexit situation.

The fact is that Brexit has consequences for the UK's place in the world, which, while not being existential, are still consequential enough to require thoughtful handling.

Peter Mandelson, always bold and unconventional, says the post-Brexit UK is 'an offshore power'. 'Brexit has cost the UK in both trade and investment but it is important that Britain is not defined by Brexit,' he says. 'This is equally the case internationally. In leaving the EU, Britain has lost its foreign policy multiplier and now has to restore its footing and top up its influence around the world. This is possible – we remain important members of the UNSC and the G7 – but we cannot do it without rebuilding our relationship with the EU while remaining close to the US.'[1]

Stefanie Bolzen, who corresponded for many years from London to the influential German newspaper *Die Welt* and is now their envoy in Washington, has no doubts that 'Brexit has damaged the UK's standing in the US'. For her, despite Donald Trump's initial welcome of Brexit, 'the US administration understood that their "special relationship" had now lost special influence on the European Continent'.[2]

A leading ambassador to the UK, who wished not to be identified for diplomatic reasons, is more pessimistic and even admits a daring scenario: 'It could soon no longer be a taboo to propose that the UK should no longer be a member of the P5', the group of permanent members of the UN Security Council.

Peter Ricketts, now a lord but formerly the National Security Adviser to David Cameron and ambassador to France, wrote in his recent book *Hard Choices* that 'outside the EU, Britain is more dependent on its strategic partnership with the US, but less useful to Washington given its lack of leverage in Europe'.[3]

Stefanie Bolzen recognises that beyond Brexit other British links with the US remain vitally relevant: 'The most important ones are military and intelligence' (the 'five eyes' partnership among US, UK, Australia, Canada and New Zealand, in particular, and also AUKUS, a key element for America's Indo-Pacific strategy).

Kim Darroch, who represented the UK abroad at the height of its global influence but also witnessed the external reputational impact of Brexit, asks, anxiously: 'Can we settle for a future of decline and irrelevance which is what characterises being a middle-power outside a major bloc?'[4]

Antonio Patriota, the Brazilian Ambassador to the United Kingdom and former foreign minister, accepts that the UK 'needs to find a new profile' but is less negative about the current status of the country, underlining the significance of both its soft and military power. 'British attractiveness is still there,' he adds.[5]

Dean Acheson, former US Secretary of State, certainly overstated it when he famously said, at the West Point Academy in 1962, that 'Britain lost an empire and failed to find a role.' However, after Brexit, his words, even if exaggerated and taken out of context, should sound a friendly warning and act as a wise invitation for serious reflection.

• • •

It may be useful for such reflection to start with a rather down-to-earth question: how and why did Brexit happen?

Fast backwards: it is now obvious that, in the run-up to the referendum, 'leavers' had no post-Brexit plan and 'remainers' were excessively confident about the rationality and self-explanatory nature of the benefits of membership ('a wall of facts', as a close observer described the anti-Brexit campaign).

'Leavers' had no plan at all – except to leave – but played on emotions and won. 'Remainers' had a simple plan – to remain – but they were not able to put emotion into it and lost.

In EU capitals, the run-up to the referendum was followed with concern, of course, but also with intellectual and political curiosity – and some degree of perplexity. The merits of what the UK had obtained after a continuous fight for specificity inside the Union, in all its different iterations, treaty after treaty, opt-out after opt-out, exception after exception, seemed to be undervalued and underestimated in the context of a highly polarised confrontation of two camps. Had this not been the case, maybe people would have realised that the UK's terms of engagement with the EU were a wise combination of virtually all the benefits of membership and a series of sweeteners that addressed most of its downsides. Were British voters overlooking and discarding the best of both worlds?

The reality in the UK was, however, more complex than the way some perceived it on the European continent. Doubts about membership and objective and subjective conditions for exit had been building up long before 2016. Brexit had deep roots.

It may all have started with the narrative that led to accession in the 1970s: an economic case, rational and cold. The European Community, the Common Market, was seen as economically favourable to the UK, then 'the sick man of Europe'. The country would benefit from access to a vast market that it would help develop even further, thanks to an unexpected alliance between Margaret Thatcher, Lord Cockfield (British Commissioner in charge of the single market in Brussels) and Jacques Delors, the President of the European Commission at the time. In areas where it felt less concerned, or that were less interesting for the UK, like the Common Agricultural Policy, it would try to change the EU from inside or prevent it from moving forward. It was a clearly pragmatic approach to European integration. Moreover, at the time there were no signs of a political union, no grandiose plans yet in Brussels that would trigger resistance from islanders keen on their specificity and sovereignty.

For David Rennie of *The Economist*, this was 'a cursed beginning'.[6] In fact, every time the economic case became less obvious because of Europe's underperformance – or because of the downsides of globalisation, closely associated with a 'globalist' EU – public support for membership suffered.

For Ivan Rogers, former Downing Street sherpa and UK Ambassador to the EU in Brussels,[7] one of the most knowledgeable voices on Brexit, what Brussels saw as a 'best of both worlds' package of opt-outs, carve-outs and special deals had in fact a perverse impact on the UK's approach to Europe. It increasingly created 'an anxiety that this right to opt out of further integration will be under constant attack or that the interests of the majority of member states that choose to go further will erode and override the interests of those who choose not to'. That became particularly visible when the interests of the euro area countries were seen as diverging from those who remained out.

The exit from the Exchange Rate Mechanism and the opt-out from the European Monetary Union (EMU) in the 1990s had been 'the first signals of the parting of the ways', says Ivan Rogers. 'For Britain, the single market was an end in itself and made a lot of sense. For Delors and most of the other member states, the EMU was a further stage of integration without which the single market would not survive,' adds Rogers. As time would confirm, it was also a step towards a political union.

The gap was indeed opening up across the Channel in parallel with the EU's own progress towards further integration from the Maastricht to Lisbon treaties. Gordon Brown famously made sure he would arrive later than other leaders to my hometown in order not to be part of the ceremony of collective signing of the new treaty – a clear indication that the British heart was not in 'an ever closer union'.

Back home in the UK, there was in fact not enough of an emotional or political cushion – and no media sympathy either – for the overall European project, which could soften the impact of EU economic shocks on British public opinion's image of Europe as a good 'economic' option. That became particularly evident during the euro area sovereign debt crisis of 2010–12, maybe the last nail in the coffin of positive perceptions. 'If you never liked the club and only stayed because it was a route to prosperity, once you decide the club is for economic losers, there was no reason to stay,' David Rennie believes.

Then there was immigration and border control. As in other European countries, the debate in the UK about the arrival of foreigners grew in intensity at the turn of the century and was made more serious with the 2004 enlargement to include eight central and eastern European countries, together with Malta and Cyprus. The revenue gap between the UK and the countries previously behind the Iron Curtain, and Tony Blair's generous decision to allow free movement of people from day one, triggered considerable flows of workers ('Polish plumbers' as some Eurosceptic media would refer to them). Asked to identify a single factor behind Brexit, Stefanie Bolzen, from *Die Welt*, had no hesitation: 'Migration!'

'Remainers' and mainstream politicians, as in other European countries, had difficulty in handling immigration as a consequential political phenomenon, even when the 2015 migration crisis hit Europe. All this allowed populists gradually to put together an explosive cocktail of immigration, money (the British budget contribution), borders (lack of control) and Europe (presented as an economic failure and a 'bureaucratic lunacy'), in preparation for 2016.

In 2011, during the worst of the euro area crisis, one last event contributed to the decision to call a referendum on Brexit. When EU leaders were trying to save Greece, the euro and actually the Union itself from collapse, David Cameron tried to extract from them concessions to the UK on financial services and on the relationship between 'ins' and 'outs' of the euro area. The prime minister tried to use the vulnerability of his colleagues to the UK's advantage – at least, that was how it was perceived in Paris, Brussels and Berlin. His colleagues strongly resented the move and flatly rejected it.

Returning home, Cameron must have concluded that he could no longer bear the pressure from inside his party and something radical had to be tried at last to put to rest the dispute over Europe. And the rest is history ...

STANDING THE EU GROUND OR THE COOLNESS DIVIDEND

On the EU side, Brexit represented the very first (and hopefully last) time that a member state decided to leave. It was an event of historic proportions in the relatively short life of European integration. There was no alternative: we had to make it right for existential reasons. It was far from being an easy task, but at the end of the day, the EU's positive management of the fallout from Brexit surprised more than one observer.

On the continent, the EU focused initially on assessing the impact of the British decision and containing its negative effects. Internally, the primary concerns were keeping a united position and avoiding contagion. Rewarding withdrawal should be excluded and fair treatment of both sides' interests should be guaranteed. These principles guided the EU's approach.

The first step was to identify the EU's key interests and priorities – as well as the right sequence of post-referendum steps. First the divorce settlement and only then the future relationship. Clear-mindedness on the EU side was met by surprising improvisation among the British camp, partly explained by domestic political volatility, particularly inside the Conservative party. Evidence of this was provided by the UK's decision to rush to invoke Article 50, which implied a strict and short calendar of decisions and deadlines, without prior proper reflection and consideration of what it wanted to achieve.

The EU remarkably kept its unity of purpose and tactics throughout the often dramatic – and overall traumatic – negotiations of the terms of divorce and of the future relationship. Against all odds, contagion inside the EU was avoided and support for the EU sustainably increased among our public opinion, as the downsides and shortcomings of the British withdrawal became visible, and as people realised that the EU and what it represented could not and should not be taken for granted. With time, the EU even managed to progress on files that would otherwise have been slowed down by the UK if it had remained a member, like new financial and budgetary tools and a boost to the defence and security agenda.

In post-Brexit London, I tried to keep calm and carry on, with no arrogance but with no naivety either. If such a comparison makes sense, I would say that where, later in the process, Rishi Sunak scored points with his 'dullness dividend', we, from the very start, capitalised on a 'coolness dividend'. In exactly 1,020 days, by the time I left, the brand-new EU mission we had put together from scratch had managed to 'exist' and be respected within British political, media, business and diplomatic circles from London to Edinburgh and from Cardiff to Belfast.

This was done against all odds, including the initial refusal by the government to grant us full diplomatic status, as described above, the worst pandemics of our lifetime and geopolitical and economic turmoil created by Vladimir Putin, not to mention historically important levels of agitation and unpredictability in British politics. Thanks go to my wonderful team at Smith Square, starting with my efficient deputy Nicole Mannion (and, before her, the acting one, Adebayo Babajide), and to all my fellow ambassadors and respective teams in the twenty-seven embassies of our member states.

From Smith Square, we promoted a new culture of co-operation, firstly within the EU's diplomatic family: we chaired and hosted regular co-ordination meetings and systematically shared intelligence and 'lines to take' with all the member states' embassies. I established a functional and friendly relationship with member states' ambassadors, most of them belonging to the top tier of their diplomacies, whom I hosted for co-ordination meetings every other week. Regularly, I would be asked to brief visiting EU member states' ministers – and a few prime ministers – ahead of their meetings at Downing Street or the Foreign Office.

Co-ordination among the EU diplomatic family in any capital of the world under the leadership of the EU ambassador and his colleagues at the EU Delegation is one of the major innovations of the Treaty of Lisbon. It allows the Union to project its image and enhance its presence and influence in a way that was not possible under the system of rotating presidencies. Continuity, coherence and visibility are key outputs of the new system, which I experienced in its launching stage in Washington in 2010–14, which matured during my time at the UN, in New York, and which became fully established in the last few years. In London, we had to start from scratch as there was obviously no EU diplomatic mission in the UK before Brexit because we were not operating then in a third country. It was a smooth process and very soon we were as operational as in any other capital, despite all the constraints.

Outside Smith Square, our network of friends, acquaintances and sources grew rapidly. Our caution regarding interference in the domestic debate about Europe did not prevent us from gradually assuming an active role in discussing in public the state of our bilateral relationship and matters of common interest. I had identified to my team several circles of interaction that should be our targets: government, parliament and other political actors, business, academia, media and think tanks. We pursued all of these in parallel.

In Parliament, the House of Lords produced the best work on Brexit and on the Northern Ireland Protocol. I had particular pleasure in engaging with Lords Kinnoull and Jay, who admirably managed the European Affairs Committee and the Northern Ireland subcommittee. Real quality work by two cross-bench Lords.

We were helped in our work by the degree of interest in public affairs, politics and foreign policy that we encountered in London and the rest of the UK. Think tanks play a relevant role. I knew that, alongside Washington, where I had had direct experience of a vibrant thinktank scene, London was the other global thinktank capital. This was fully confirmed in the field with a solid relationship with Chatham House, CER, UK in a Changing Europe, Ditchley, Royal United Services Institute, Bright Blue, Aspen UK, Keeping Channels Open and many more, all keen to engage. We worked well with other more politically minded structures like the European Movement, the Conservative European Forum and Best for Britain. Our red line here as in other settings remained clear: debating and informing, yes, campaigning or being perceived as campaigning, no.

A major consequence of the Brexit divorce was to be felt by EU citizens in the UK and British citizens in our member states. Our responsibility as the newly created EU diplomatic mission was, of course, to interact with the former and be concerned by the extent to which they would be affected by Brexit. Our main purpose was to make sure that their rights would be upheld and that they could benefit from the provisions in the Withdrawal Agreement relating to their post-Brexit situation. They were somehow the children of the divorced couple.

My first question upon arrival was an obvious one: how many are we, the EU citizens in the UK? There was some embarrassment among my colleagues and other interlocutors, but the answer eventually came: we don't really know. Three million was the working hypothesis, which led some of the most active militants of the noble cause to create a non-profit organisation called '3 Million'. It turned out that this estimate was largely inaccurate, for reasons that have to do with the absence of mandatory registration either at consulates or with the British authorities. After a very intense campaign throughout the country, in good cooperation with our member states' consular network and with the support of highly dedicated civil society organisations, we actively contributed to the registration of more than 6 million EU citizens to provide them with pre-settled or settled status. It was roughly double the original estimate, and counting, as late applications were still being considered when I left.

Work in this domain required a triple-track approach: first, establishing mutual trust and complicity within the EU family in a policy area that member states normally see as closer to their specific competence than the EU's; second, acting as a solid team in our relationship with the Home Office and other government departments; and last but not least, relying on grassroots organisations to become more aware of everyday problems and concerns, and to create a direct link with our citizens scattered around the country, for the sake of information provision and two-way communication.

I realised not only how impressive our community was in numbers and in contribution to British society, but also how so many of them were unaware of the impact of Brexit on their individual and family lives. We launched an ambitious information campaign and provided legal counselling. I made a point of meeting EU member states' consuls where they existed and always include citizens' NGOs in my list of contacts when travelling around the country. Those opportunities of human contact were among the most rewarding moments of my stay in the UK.

The Home Office was our main interlocutor on the official side. It took some time to create the conditions for a sound dialogue, which eventually worked – not without divergence of views, but I must say, for most of the time, with a mutual focus on concluding the process in an efficient way. Their output was negatively impacted by the overall political climate but also by the competitive effort required from their teams regarding three emergency situations: people arriving from Afghanistan, Hong Kong and Ukraine.

INSIDE THE LION'S DEN

I knew from my arrival that a lot would be played out in public, and the media would be a crucial element in our success or failure in managing the first couple of years after divorce. I was particularly aware that my team and I would be observed, and if ever we took the wrong steps or made clumsy mistakes, the media would not spare us. Obama's first commandment on foreign policy became mine: 'don't do stupid shit'.

The next step was gradually to reassure British interlocutors and the public in general about our genuine wish to respect the referendum outcome, even if we regretted it, and to contribute to a balanced relationship within the new paradigm. My agenda was not to challenge the UK's departure and, of course, even less to campaign for rejoining, but rather to implement what we had agreed upon, rigorously but in a co-operative way. I had to say it and mean it from the very start.

The media were the most obvious conveyors of the message and for that purpose I needed to be willing to engage openly, even if it implied countering the government's positions and stretching my own room for manoeuvre vis-à-vis Brussels. This approach, which was, of course, not free from risks, was in line with my firm belief that modern ambassadors need to be ready to use public diplomacy as a necessary tool in their interaction with the country of posting. It proved to be the right way to proceed, even if it implied great investment from me and my excellent media section, led by Federico Bianchi, a charismatic Italian national diplomat who was part of my team from day one.

One initiative, in particular, turned out to be a milestone in my journey engaging with the British media: an on-the-record lunch with the 'lobby' (I was told, but was never able to confirm, that I had been the first ambassador to be invited, or at least to have accepted). The lunch took place in May 2022 in the catering area of the House of Commons in the presence of dozens of political editors and Westminster reporters of major British media, the members of the so-called 'lobby' (because the famous lobby of the Houses of Parliament is their daily 'arena'). We all know it is more dangerous to face a wolf pack than a lone one and particularly on their own turf … but I still did it, even if some friends advised against.

I realised when I entered the room that the participants were not only journalists. The lobby members were allowed to invite guests from the two Houses of Parliament. Glancing around the spacious room and its several tables, I immediately spotted two in particular: David Davis and Steve Baker. They were staunch Brexiteers and members of the European Research Group, the powerful pro-Brexit lobby inside the Conservative Party. I prepared psychologically for a fierce battle. The good thing is that guests are not allowed to ask questions, even if I had no doubts that some would be able to plant their own queries via their neighbours at the table. At the end of the long question-and-answer session, David and Steve joined me, we laughed and took a nice picture, which I kept as a symbol of my ecumenism.

The conversation with the lobby members centred, as expected, on the Northern Ireland Protocol and the overall state of our relationship – not good at all, at the time – and my messages were aimed at the journalists there as much as at the government.

'New season, same plot' was my main headline. In these words or similar ones (I spoke without notes and my memory may fail me), here are the messages I conveyed to the 'lobby':

- The new season of the Brexit saga looks worryingly like previous ones. The plot does not change. We will have an internal market bill 2.0. The UK will again try to override an international treaty with unilateral measures that do not solve any problems and risk creating many more. I am sincerely hoping for more creativity. And ultimately a happy ending … but I do not see it yet.

- Brexit ratings are already very low in Europe and they risk going down further. EU leaders simply want to move on and focus on what we have in common – look at our excellent co-operation on Ukraine – and on the challenges we both face – think of Russia, China, climate change or inflation. There is life beyond Brexit. Let us make it work for our citizens and our business.
- The British government says the EU negotiators should get a new mandate on the Northern Ireland Protocol. Well, the message we are getting from our member states is loud and clear. They tell us: you do not need a new mandate and even if you asked for one, we would not give it to you.
- We recognise that there are issues in implementing the protocol and issues in the perception of the protocol by some in Northern Ireland. We have been working together on those for more than a year. We made far-reaching, practical proposals, but we are frustrated that all that seems to be ignored by the government. There is still untapped potential in our proposals. Let us dig deeper into them and look for joint solutions instead of risking an all-out confrontation. Who would benefit from that? I can only think of our adversaries.
- We are always ready to talk, we will be the last ones to turn the lights off and we hope there is a clear commitment from the British side to find solutions. But we are also very clear that unilateral action will require reaction. We would very much prefer to engage in bilateral action. But we will not hesitate to match any unacceptable British unilateral behaviour with a graduated but firm response from our side.
- The protocol is not an invention of the EU. It is the jointly agreed solution to deal with the grave consequences for Northern Ireland of the kind of Brexit the British government has chosen. There was and there is no alternative to it.
- Blocking the protocol is preventing Northern Ireland from fully reaping its benefits. Northern Ireland's economy is already performing better than the rest of UK, largely thanks to the protocol and the access it provides to both the British

and the EU markets for goods. If investors are given certainty and predictability about the implementation of the protocol, they will open their wallets and Northern Ireland's economic performance will be even better. Blocking the protocol is blocking Northern Ireland's prosperity.

With hindsight it was remarkable to see Prime Minister Sunak, almost a year later, in March 2023, use some of the above-mentioned arguments when he presented his Windsor Framework to the doubters in his party. I was happy to see some reason return to the political scene. One note on the Windsor Framework: while it played a relevant role in calming down spirits and in allowing Unionists to return to the Northern Ireland executive, its content is not far from what the EU was ready to agree within its proposed adaptations to the protocol. The art of politics ...

Back to the 'lobby' lunch: I came out of the Houses of Parliament tired but relieved after this 'act of initiation'. I had survived an incursion into the lion's den. I did not expect to have convinced all the attendants and maybe not even a single one. But at least our arguments could not be ignored by the 'lobby'. And I felt that the lion had appreciated the gesture of a visit to its sanctuary.

I insisted on accepting the lunch invitation for all the reasons above but also because – I must confess – I do not mind the adrenaline of political confrontation and risk taking. That is also why I never really hesitated to engage with the toughest political reporters and commentators. Dozens of live interviews and background conversations allowed us to have the EU's point of view made available to the British public, without any filter but with a sense of measure and, most importantly, with respect for the choices made regarding the EU.

This degree of intense engagement started from the very first days with a short introductory interview to Catherine Philp from *The Times* followed by a podcast conversation (summarised in the printed edition) with the *Daily Telegraph*'s Chris Hope and later with the Radio 4 *Today* programme. It continued throughout my term and concluded with interviews with Tom Newton

Dunn for Talk TV and George Parker for the *Financial Times*. Informal small gatherings in London restaurants or clubs, at our offices or on the margins of party conferences and other events were very agreeable occasions to discuss issues 'off the record' and understand better the deep feelings in the media and public opinion. I learned a lot from the journalists I met and hopefully improved their understanding of our positions and the reasons behind them.

Once Covid allowed (even if still under a strict 'six people rule'), Federico Bianchi hosted at his Chelsea home a first intimate dinner with top political journalists. Over great Italian food and Portuguese wine, I made my 'debut' with Laura Kuenssberg, Tom Newton-Dunn, Beth Rigby and Fraser Nelson. On the margins of the annual party conferences, I made a point of always having a dinner reserved for a selected media group. I remember, for instance, the well-attended occasion in Birmingham during the 2022 Conservative Party conference that confirmed Liz Truss as leader. It was a very lively and political dinner, supplemented by a good amount of inevitable gossip. Chris Hope was very vocal in defence of Boris and Boris's sister Rachel was very direct in her remarks about Boris the politician, but at the same time genuinely touching in exchanging views with me, in private, on Boris the brother and the journalist.

From George Parker, Chris Mason, Pippa Crerar, Emily Maitlis and other elite political editors and anchors around the table, the comments were very frank about BJ, his successor and the overall situation inside the Conservative Party. On these occasions, the best thing for the host to do is to create a relaxed atmosphere, invite journalists to tell their side of the story and allow them to chat among themselves. I always learned more when I managed to escape being the sole target of the journalists' curiosity and was able to listen to their comments and discussions. This dinner was no exception.

Of course, there were tough moments of intense questioning in a way that only British journalists dare to do. Radio is particularly challenging because you must be short and sharp, and in contrast to television, you cannot use body language to support your points. This is especially important if you are not expressing yourself in your mother tongue, as was my case. The *Today* programme on BBC Radio 4 always treated me well, but my levels of concentration were at the top every time I was invited there. I knew I would be listened to by the elite of the country, in more definitions than one. Mishal Husain was my first questioner there, in my early days in London, early in the morning, after a warm welcome from the then *Today* editor, Sarah Sands. I could not think of a smoother interrogator than Mishal, extremely professional and tough when needed – someone I learned to admire. *Newsnight*, where Emily Maitlis and her colleagues interviewed me several times, was a must for its capacity to go behind the story and ask frontal questions, while allowing you more time than usual to make your point. I also enjoyed Robert Peston's irreverence and sharpness on ITV and Trevor Philips' calm and focus and Beth Rigby's energy on Sky News. Channel 4, Bloomberg TV and Talk TV completed my regular presence on television shows, trying to complement the reporting and commentary with an understanding of the EU's approach.

The British written press is, of course, different from media in other countries in being truly relevant in shaping public perceptions. My approach there was very Obama-like (see above) because you are never in full control of the message, contrary to live audiovisual stints. I was very keen to engage not only with those that were expected to be more sympathetic to our message, such as *The Guardian* and the *Financial Times*, but particularly with the likes of the *Daily Telegraph* and *The Times*. I must say I did not regret that investment, particularly with the *Telegraph*, which always treated me decently. *The Times* had excellent editorial pieces and good reporting by Catherine Philp, among others. I had, however, two incidents there. A small one related to a slightly abusive headline and another more important one related to an interview that I gave to the *Sunday Times* but which was never published. It's still a mystery to me.

As an EU ambassador, I felt a deep sense of duty and an obligation towards our own citizens and member states. On the press side, this led me to meet regularly with EU correspondents in London and to give interviews to leading newspapers and television stations from several countries, including Germany, Italy, France, Spain and, of course Portugal. It was important for us also to relay our messages to our own capitals. A matter of transparency and accountability.

I kept up high-intensity media activity throughout my tenure. Some of my ambassadorial colleagues wondered how I coped with that level of exposure and risk (with just a few valuable exceptions, they chose to be largely absent from the media). 'You have to like it,' I replied. 'Don't try it if you don't enjoy it. You risk regretting it.'

SCHMOOZE POLITICS

Managing divorce in the UK involved another dimension of public diplomacy, albeit a more traditional one: receptions or 'events'. They play a particular role and are always watched attentively and judged on their merits and meaning – and on the gossip level as well, of course. In parallel, meeting politicians individually in relatively informal contexts is an irreplaceable opportunity to enhance proximity.

Welcome and farewell receptions are often among the best indicators of the state of relations with the domestic authorities. Three such occasions during my stay in London are worth mentioning for that reason.

At the time of arrival, I insisted with my then very small team that we should host a short reception right after presenting the copy of my credentials, which we did in the evening of Monday, 3 February 2020, my very first working day in office (which had started close to the *Cutty Sark*). I invited my fellow EU member states' ambassadors and senior officials from the Foreign Office. The permanent undersecretary (PUS), the highest-ranked Foreign Office official, accepted and said a few words of warm welcome. We all lined up for a Twitter photo, providing the material evidence of my arrival, in front of a new plaque on the façade of Europe House. A couple of hours earlier,

I had presented an official copy of my credentials signed by presidents Charles Michel and Ursula von der Leyen to the Foreign Office minister in charge of Europe.

It is curious to note that Sir Simon MacDonald, the PUS at the time, and Chris Pincher MP, the then minister for Europe – who were, by the way, extremely nice – became famous two and a half years later, during the days and hours preceding Boris Johnson's fall from power. As an MP, Pincher was the subject of a sex-related scandal that was the 'last straw' that eventually brought down the PM. MacDonald was instrumental in publicly confirming – the very morning of BJ's resignation – that, as foreign secretary, Boris Johnson had been made aware of the allegations against Pincher but still went ahead and appointed him as minister and later as a parliamentary whip. My arrival and Boris's departure shared the same supporting actors.

Eighteen months later, I stepped out of the royal carriage to host a traditional *vin d'honneur* at our offices at Smith Square, immediately after presenting my credentials to the queen. It was a larger crowd with ambassadors, Lords, MPs and representatives from different walks of life, including many journalists. David Frost, then a member of Cabinet in charge of EU negotiations, had promised me that he would join us and make a short speech. He did not because of sudden illness. Alistair Harrison, the Marshall of the Diplomatic Corps, as is customary, said a few words of welcome and I made my speech. Frost was replaced by a senior official, which meant that the government was not represented at political level. It was well noted.

Things were quite different a year later when I hosted my farewell party at my favourite London club, the Athenaeum. James Cleverly, the foreign secretary, together with his lovely wife Susan, was keen to join us and delivered a warm farewell speech. Other members of Cabinet attended as well, including Therese Coffey and Chris Heaton-Harris, amidst a large and high-level group of diplomats, Labour Shadow Cabinet members, other MPs, Lords and other politicians, academics, and business and media representatives. The difference of government treatment was again well noted. Positively.

This is how Chris Hope, from the *Daily Telegraph*, reported it:

London's diplo-corp squeezed into the Athenaeum Club on Pall Mall for EU ambassador João Vale de Almeida's leaving do last night. Vale de Almeida is an absolute class act, who will be much missed, and who I interviewed for the *Telegraph*. He told guests including Labour's Lord Mandelson and Peter Kyle that he had arrived in London the day before Brexit Day (Jan 31, 2020) and was told to set up a mission 'without a users' guide'. He said he hoped that this 'new cycle in British politics would lead to a new cycle in EU relations' as James Cleverly, the Foreign Secretary, and Chris Heaton-Harris, Northern Ireland Secretary, looked on. 'Let's make it happen. This relationship deserves that it moves on. That's my hope for the future,' he said to warm applause. I hope he's right.

Annual party conferences are a must in the British political and diplomatic calendar. In 2020 I had been deprived of my inaugural party conferences because Covid had cancelled them, and as a consequence I was very much looking forward to my very first one: the Labour gathering in Brighton, in 2021. I knew how relevant these rendezvous were in British political culture as a key moment of stocktaking, mobilisation of troops or otherwise great drama inside each party. I am not aware of any other country where such an annual event has such great importance.

A huge storm welcomed us to Brighton where Labour was meeting. I got to the hotel considerably wet from heavy rain and strong winds. Inside the conference the atmosphere was definitely warmer, but I soon detected some 'wind' of opposition. This was the first formal moment for Labour's new leader, elected just a year before in the midst of Covid, to measure his support and the degree of remaining 'Corbynite' resistance. Starmer did not seem totally at ease yet in his role, and a few left-wing hecklers in the room constantly reminded him that his position was at least being critically observed. The whole ambiance reminded me more of university or NGO gatherings than a traditional party congress. It was a tale of 'Starmer at stormy Brighton'.

I went there with a small team from our mission and was joined by several colleague ambassadors from our member states, as I would consistently do in other party conferences that followed. I had several bilateral meetings with senior Labour delegates and leaders and business and trade unions representatives, talked to a few journalists and attended a few receptions, including of course our own. I had invited Lisa Nandy, whom I sympathised with and who was then the shadow foreign secretary, to say a few words. Several colleague ambassadors lined up in the first public demonstration in Labour territory of the new EU post-Brexit diplomatic family in the UK. The atmosphere could not have been warmer. Very different from the real world of stormy Brighton (and Britain) outside.

A few weeks later, in Manchester, I hosted one of the most memorable political receptions of my term in London, in 'hostile' territory. Conservatives were gathering under Boris Johnson, at the height of his tenure as leader, for their annual party conference. I had made the point of marking it with a formal reception, as in Brighton. There was no difference in treatment, despite significant tensions across the Channel with the Conservative government.

Wendy Morton, Foreign Office minister for Europe at the time, was invited and charged with responding to my speech. In my brief address to a packed room of party delegates, EU member states' ambassadors, journalists and other guests, I chose to underline how much Conservatives had contributed to what the EU is today, from Margaret Thatcher and Lord Cockfield's impetus to the single market, to Sir Leon Brittan's role in shaping trade and competition policies, and many distinguished Members of the European Parliament (MEPs) for their parliamentary work (some were in the room). The point was well taken, even if some were a bit puzzled by the timing of my historical, although totally accurate, reference to the party's past constructive engagement in European affairs. David Frost had promised to come and this time he did come. I shared a few beers with him and we chatted in a relaxed atmosphere, together with a couple of German MEPs from the Bavarian Christian-democratic party, the CSU, invited by the Conservatives. It was one of the few de-Frost moments of my entire mandate ...

THERE IS LIFE AFTER BREXIT

Back to the future, or rather the present.

Now that new political cycles are starting, fixing the post-Brexit EU–UK relationship should be a concern, if not a priority, for leaders on both sides of the Channel. Given the current regional and international context, none of the twenty-eight countries can afford to ignore the relevance of this 'couple', even if they all realise that it will take time to rebuild what Brexit has shattered.

In the UK, Brexit wounds have not healed yet and the long-term direction of travel of Brexit Britain is still not clear. Time, the new majority in Parliament and material evidence of the impact of the withdrawal will play a key role in defining the new balance in public opinion, in business and ultimately at the polls – and that will determine the future trajectory of the country.

The terms of engagement between the UK and the EU will thus still take some time to stabilise and even longer to evolve substantially. Despite late positive developments like the Windsor Framework and the return to Horizon Europe, no fundamental evolution has happened since Brexit under three Conservative prime ministers. The new government will need time fully to articulate and then to consolidate its approach. Comparing the pre-Brexit and the post-Brexit realities with the prospects of the future relationship will emerge as a key element of discussion. I can only hope it will be a (relatively) rational one. Ultimately, Brexit will only be 'done' when the UK replies to the question which it has not really been able to address since 2016: 'what do we want to do with this Brexit?'

On the other side of the Channel, the scope for evolution in relations with the UK will depend upon two main factors: first, political will and the level of consensus among member states; and second, the evolution of the EU's institutional design and its attitude towards its closest neighbours.

Starting with the 'political will' factor, openness and commitment from EU leaders to a rebounding of the relationship will depend upon three major conditions: available space in the political attention bandwidth, sufficiently high levels of trust between EU and British leaders and the attractiveness of the British 'offer'.

Attention bandwidth: it is crowded and the existing slots are narrowing down. The EU is confronted with pressing challenges that require full engagement from leaders, from domestic to geo-strategic, some of them existential. Investment in cross-Channel relations is not at the top of the priorities list, and the trauma created by the long and convoluted Brexit negotiations has created no appetite for 'more of the same'. For leaders to engage, there will have to be positive inputs from the two other conditions.

Trust: by this I mean two kinds of political trust. The short-term trust has to do with the relationship with the new UK prime minister, Keir Starmer, and how much the first months and years produce a sound basis for future co-operation. In principle, if well managed, it should not be too difficult to draw a distinction with the recent past and put the relationship on a healthy, trustful basis in the first twelve months of the new British parliament. The second and even more important kind of trust is the long-term one, what I would call the 'structural trust'. It has more to do with the country itself and its political actors in general, and less to do with a particular party or even less a particular government. The EU and its member states would need guarantees that there will be sustainability in the engagement on the British side to justify investment from European capitals, and that they would not be faced with quick turnarounds or an excessively transactional and short-term agenda. The return of Nigel Farage to the political arena and the possible return of other political figures linked to the 'dark' Brexit period as potential leaders of the opposition, with a natural expectation of reaching power sooner or later, are not conducive to creating confidence. The re-election of a pro-European leader or even a generational change of political class may be needed for that kind of sustainable, long-term trust to materialise.

Attractiveness of the British 'offer': the Brexit agreements are not ideal for either side, but they have proved to be more palatable for the EU as they delivered on its main asks and safeguarded its fundamental concerns. Exchanging them for an alternative requires the new 'offer' to be substantially more interesting and sustainable in its positive effects, partly because it would need unanimous support within the EU member states. A British wishlist that amounts to picking and choosing on the basis of what the UK did not obtain in the initial negotiation, without changing its red lines, will be received with suspicion and produce a very defensive reaction. 'Super cherry picking' is not the way forward and will stall progress in the relationship.

On the second factor, the future of the EU, some questions are still open. Will enlargement take place, and if so, when and how? Will there be a 'concentric circles' EU (groups of countries within the EU that agree and are allowed to move faster than others in their process of integrating policies)? If so, will it allow for new room for manoeuvre with the UK? How will the concept of European Political Community evolve and what will be the position of the UK within it? In the current geopolitical context, the least we can say is that the long-term future is very uncertain. What we would need to look for is possibilities for the UK to engage more substantially with the EU short of rejoining, making use of possible future opportunities. This is very much an open platform for further discussion.

At this stage, speculation around future scenarios may be tempting but it cannot ignore the reality: under current status and binding international treaties governing our relationship – which reflect the red lines established by the Conservatives and confirmed by Labour – the margin for evolution in the short term is relatively limited, and even that requires beforehand that sufficient levels of trust are re-established among leaders and also among public opinions across the Channel, as mentioned above.

What could happen in the near future if red lines do not change? This discussion, which will certainly increase in intensity within the new political cycle, has so far largely underestimated, voluntarily or involuntarily, two aspects.

The first is passive divergence. The most immediate cost of any separation is, of course, the 'loss of intimacy', a growing gap between former partners. In this particular case, the natural evolution will be that even if there is no active pursuit of regulatory or other type of divergence, the simple dynamics on each side of the Channel will naturally produce distinct rules and legislative frameworks. This with time will trigger additional tension at the borders and place a heavier burden on businesses and citizens, making constructive and facilitating changes more difficult within the existing framework.

The second overlooked aspect is what I would call the 'pregnancy test' as applied to the single market and the customs union. You are either pregnant or not. There is no middle ground. That is valid for the single market: either you are in or you are out. Measures aimed at softening the impact of this reality can only have very limited effect, particularly if we keep in mind the previous reference to passive divergence. There is only so much that you can achieve with voluntaristic attitudes. Sooner or later you are faced with the wall of British red lines. Unless you are ready to move the wall ...

That being said, this relationship is so relevant for both sides, and the geopolitical context is so equally challenging, that it deserves, and requires, sufficient investment and attention – and creativity. This implies first and foremost the personal investment of leaders and symbolic and substantial new moments of co-operation and convergence. It also requires a high degree of honesty and realism – the opposite of what led to Brexit.

Security, defence and geostrategic issues are the most promising areas to kickstart this joint effort, aligned as our countries are in fighting back against Russian aggression and countering Chinese economic and technological competition, as well as dealing with an evolving USA. Here, we should begin by filling the gap created by the British opposition, during the Brexit negotiations, to the inclusion of provisions on security and defence to create a solid basis for common work. On that foundation, the next stages could aim at improving existing provisions where possible and, even more important, investing in other issues not covered in the current bilateral treaties. Adding rather than changing could be a good guiding principle – a pragmatic approach, non-politicised wherever possible. Again, this is quite the opposite to what happened in the early post-Brexit years.

There is life after Brexit for the EU–UK relationship. Both sides need it to be constructive, friendly and productive. Both sides would be well advised to invest in it if we want to limit, and even possibly reverse, the negative consequences of cross-Channel divorce.

6

Swimming Against the Tide

It is too easy to criticise a break-up like Brexit and denounce a global trend towards polarisation and confrontation within and among nations, and not acknowledge in the same breath how difficult it is to do the opposite: to bring nations together. This is particularly true in times of change and disruption, like the current ones. Hence the relevance of looking into the EU as a successful case of 'ever closer union' and international co-operation, and at some of those who have, in different ways, been its faces and voices during the first quarter of this century.

THE EU: A LONG AND WINDING ROAD

History is sadly made not of glorious *ententes* but of devastating wars and conflicts. Geography and borders, ethnicity and tribes, religion and culture, trade and technological competition, greed and rivalry, and the prevalence of strong men and narcissistic egos have been driving factors in international relations. History seldom registers peace and reconciliation, not to mention pro-active integration of countries and nations, as key landmarks in mankind's trajectory. Because they do not abound.

That is why the European Union will certainly be recognised by the historians of the twentieth and twenty-first centuries as a noble example of the willingness of states and nations – and peoples – to share their sovereignty in order to forge a voluntary political union around common values and interests. A union that has been hard fought, incrementally and painstakingly built, over the last seventy years. A union that first focused on healing the wounds of European civil war and now aims at counting as a force for good in a world where evil instincts tend to prevail. A union that often found itself swimming against the tide of history and now stands – in spite of all its difficulties – as the most promising co-operative, anti-divorce project of the twenty-first century.

The EU began this century with high ambitions and a great deal of optimism. The 1990s had been productive and positive, and its fifteen member states had just established a single market. The plan was to make it, by 2010, the basis for the most advanced, competitive and sophisticated knowledge economy in the world – under the banner of the 'Lisbon agenda', a tribute to my hometown, again – supported by a single currency and reinforced by a historic enlargement to countries previously behind the Iron Curtain.

Throughout the first quarter of the twenty-first century, the EU almost doubled its membership. Even if the economic prospects for 2010 did not really materialise for a number of reasons, the Union successfully overcame the rejection of a draft Constitution and the impact of the financial and sovereign debt crises, and survived Brexit and Covid with unexpected flying colours and one 'Hamiltonian' moment. The EU consolidated the euro as a global currency, second only to the US dollar, while enlarging its membership. It led the international community in an existential fight against climate change and positioned its market of half a billion people as a serious competitor of the American and Chinese powerhouses, with the comparative advantage of its social market economy model. More mature and tested by hard times, the EU even ventured, albeit cautiously, into the previously uncharted territory of foreign policy, security and defence.

Not all was perfect, not all was swift and proper. There were internal tensions, the rise of populism, some major disagreements and long nights of endless negotiations, but progress happened and citizens welcomed it. Levels of public support at the end of the first quarter-century are remarkably high.[1]

The strongest headwinds came curiously from outside, and particularly from the east. From the middle of the quarter onwards, the EU was gradually forced to abandon its comfort zone under the threat of increased Russian aggressive behaviour and Chinese competition. From the west, the spectre of American regional and global disengagement and the election of a populist US president did not help. War-induced inflation and migratory pressure from the eastern and southern flanks, not to mention instability in the Middle East and Sahel, completed a set of major exogenous challenges.

The EU ends the quarter-century less optimistic about the future than at its dawn. It is tormented by new existential questions, with wars ravaging its neighbourhood, a serious deterioration of the overall international context and the pressure of another enlargement. Domestically, populist forces are becoming stronger and governments weaker in some member states. The recently elected European Parliament and many national parliaments will be more challenging to manage. Politics is back to centre stage in the EU.

That being said, I believe the EU should have no reason for depression. Here's why.

- The history of what is now known as the EU is one of crises and responses to crises.
- The secret of its success is that those responses enabled it to deepen its economic and political integration, extend its geographic scope and increase the sophistication of its apparatus, in spite of the crises.
- The challenge to its sustainability is to make sure that this path towards an 'ever closer union' continues to gather the support of its citizens (so far it does!).
- The condition for its survival is peace, now no longer only among its members but, most importantly, also in its neighbourhood.
- The guarantee of its prosperity is the combined effect of the deepening of its single market, the vitality of its 'four freedoms' (free movement of people, goods, capital and services), the creativity of its scientists and artists, the dynamism of its entrepreneurs and workers, and the competitiveness of its economy.

- The new frontier for its dream is three-fold: enlargement to the other countries on the continent that deserve and aspire to join – providing continental scale while allowing an inner core voluntarily to integrate further – the security of its borders and the protection of its citizens from regional and global threats.

The EU has travelled a 'long and winding road' since its creation, and particularly in the last twenty-five years. It enlarged, matured and became denser internally, and at the same time opened up to the world, gained scale and clout. There were bumps, sometimes severe ones, on its trajectory. The destination itself was not always clear, but that is part of its nature: incremental rather that predetermined. There were depressing moments – it had to abandon some perhaps excessively ambitious projects – and exciting times. It was a road full of twists and turns, and not short of conflicting emotions, as if wanting to pay tribute to the wonderful Beatles song. But the project – in reality, the dream – was kept alive, defying all Cassandras. Lennon and McCartney put it better than anyone when they said that the road would never vanish.

BARROSO AND A WINDOW ON THE WORLD

I travelled on this road for more than forty years. Halfway through it, in 2004, I was in charge of deepening EU action and co-operation among EU member states on issues relevant to our young people. As a relatively young director, the second highest level in the European Commission's managerial hierarchy, I was aware of how much Europe's future depended upon younger generations understanding and committing to the European dream. Action was needed in Brussels and other capitals to support that goal. After experiencing the Commission's political circles as spokesman and deputy chief spokesman directly under the authority of presidents Jacques Delors and Jacques Santer, after managing the Commission's network of representations in member states' capitals and after being part of President Prodi's transition team, I was enjoying working at grassroots level, energised by the dynamism of younger Europeans.

I had obviously followed with great interest and patriotic excitement the news that my fellow countryman José Manuel Durão Barroso, Prime Minister of Portugal since 2002, was being considered as the next President of the Commission, but his invitation to a meeting on that warm afternoon of summer 2004 still came as a great surprise. He had just been chosen by his fellow members of the European Council as the successor to Romano Prodi, from Italy, as President of the European Commission, and had been elected as such by the European Parliament. He had now to prepare for the long battle of selection of his college of commissioners and its final confirmation by the European Parliament. He was looking for someone to help him do all that and maybe more.

We had never met before, even if we were from the same generation and we had been born and raised in Lisbon. We had both been privileged, as politically aware teenagers, to live through the magic of the Portuguese Carnation Revolution of 25 April 1974, but our paths had never crossed.

A forty-five-minute 'getting to know you' conversation at the Portuguese diplomatic representation to the EU in Brussels revealed enough common ground and personal chemistry. That, combined with kind endorsement and encouragement from common friends, led Barroso to invite me to put together a small team to help him steer through the process of his full and final confirmation by the recently elected European Parliament.

The final passage through the parliament would be more dramatic and stressful than the experience at the European Council, but Barroso eventually obtained a strong majority in support, a few months later. It was a remarkable achievement for a committed and enthusiastic supporter of European integration, who saw the future of his country inexorably intertwined with the EU and would now lead its most relevant institution.

It was then my turn to be confirmed by the new President of the European Commission as his *chef de cabinet* (chief of staff and main adviser) and to start a unique new adventure. Our 'blind date' had opened the door for what would be five years of highly intense and productive co-operation and many more of mutual friendship (and of my personal admiration and gratitude).

My job with Barroso for the incoming five years would imply multitasking, as for any top leader's chief of staff.

The first task was to help the president manage a college of twenty-five commissioners (twenty-seven from 2007), the largest ever, comprising top national politicians, some of them former prime ministers like him – and a huge machinery of dozens of services, staffed with more than 30,000 Commission officials. I was asked, together with the secretary-general (two Irish friends followed each other in that post, David O'Sullivan and Catherine Day) and the great colleagues in my Cabinet team, to make sure that this enormous, highly professional and technically competent apparatus would deliver a coherent policy agenda in line with the president's programme, with a maximum of efficiency and effectiveness and a minimum of disturbing noise.

Next came the even more political role of liaising with the private offices of the heads of state and government of the EU member states and of the political leaders and top officials of the other European institutions – particularly of the European Parliament and the European Council – in order to anticipate problems, manage crises and ensure convergence and support for our agenda. My rule of thumb was: the EU only makes sense if it serves its citizens and the best way to achieve that goal is to be in concertation with their elected representatives, via parliaments and governments. In doing so, I set myself another objective, only shared with the president: to create conditions for Barroso to be re-elected to a second term, with the support of the European Parliament and the member states, thus becoming the first President of the Commission since Jacques Delors to do so (he was re-elected in 2009, immediately before I moved on to become the European Commission's Director-General for External Relations).

Last but not least, my job involved a crucial international dimension: being the European Union's 'sherpa' to international summits of the G8 and, starting in 2008, also of the G20, as well as to bilateral summits with our key partners, and liaising with my colleagues in the respective leaders' offices. There had been in the past, and after I left, different options for the choice of a personal representative in these fora. My model, fully endorsed by Barroso, was Pascal Lamy's amalgamation of both jobs – chief of staff and sherpa – during the presidency of Jacques Delors, which I had closely watched and learned a lot from.

I could confirm during five years in both functions that the choice made was indeed the best option. Even if an internal/external job description implied an extremely heavy work and travel load, it provided the necessary 'clout' for the EU representative, for two reasons: the personal closeness to the leader (direct access is an indispensable and highly valuable asset in international diplomacy) and the horizontal knowledge of all the relevant files covered in global summits (which were virtually all part of the Commission president's agenda). Internally, it facilitated incorporating the international dimension into the proceedings and the agenda of the Commission, which is sometimes tempted to turn too much inwards.

My task list would, however, not be complete without the most important role of any chief of staff: to be the first port of call for advice and the last resort of arbitration within the inner circle of a leader and, most importantly, the sole trusted professional partner in his most solitary moments (of which there are too many in politics), at whatever time of the day or night, at whatever latitude or longitude.

President Barroso's job was to steer an enlarged Commission and an enlarged Union through bad seas and still keep the European vessel afloat and on the right trajectory, and its crew united and focused, in spite of the storms on the horizon. That is what Barroso did for ten years, on a daily basis, relentlessly, with unending travels, sparing no effort, neglecting nobody, avoiding unnecessary friction and always looking for the highest possible level of European consensus. He had to juggle many balls at any given time. The task of 'herding cats' or, more nobly put, of bringing leaders together around common positions in spite of their differences and incompatibilities, is absolutely central to the role and he was a master at doing it, as his re-election proved. Already then, avoiding divorce was the name of the game ...

An office on the top floor of the star-shaped Berlaymont building, the headquarters of the European Commission, next to its president, overlooking the *quartier européen* of Brussels, is 'probably the best place in the world' (to paraphrase the advert for a famous European beer) to watch the EU and its member states. The Commission is the geometrical centre of the EU's decision-making process. It is the sole initiator of legislation and the main entity in charge of its implementation, as both an administration and the legal guardian of the treaties. It interacts with national governments, social partners and other stakeholders in the twenty-seven member states and operates in close contact with the two co-legislators, the European Parliament and the Council of Ministers. At presidential level, the Commission is a member of the European Council and represents the Union externally for all matters with the exception of the Common Foreign and Security Policy, including as a member of G7 and G20.

Chris Patten, member of the House of Lords, former EU commissioner and last Governor of Hong Kong, once said that presiding over the European Commission is the toughest job in the Western world.[2] Others would say it is an impossible job. From experience, I can guarantee that this is not an exaggeration. I could not have been more honoured to help José Manuel Barroso successfully handle such a challenge, and could not have enjoyed it more.

Like the Berlaymont in regard to EU affairs, it is hard to think of better places to observe the world than an office at the corner of Pennsylvania Avenue, a few blocks away from the White House, a residence on New York's 1st Avenue with a scenic view of the UN headquarters, and a building that was once occupied by Margaret Thatcher, at the heart of London's Westminster borough. I was lucky and privileged enough to be able to contemplate the first quarter of this century from those watchtowers, but it was my role in Brussels as Barroso's chief of staff and EU sherpa for international summits that provided the first glimpse of the complexity of global governance in times of paradigm change. Berlaymont's thirteenth floor was my first real window on the world, just at the start of the new century.

Barroso's personal interaction with EU national leaders, as well as with international partners in the USA, China and Russia, not to mention many other countries around the world, was definitely the most fascinating aspect of his job for me to support and observe. He was a master in it and created an impressive network of personal contacts with leaders in all continents that enhanced our global influence and set the basis for the EU's future investment on the international stage.

In politics, national or international, personal investment pays. There is nothing more relevant and more revealing of the nature of political practice than bilateral, intimate conversations between leaders, and I was privileged to be very often the single testimony on our side of the table or at our end of the phone line.

My accumulated experience of these high-level interpersonal relations led me to two conclusions: first, that the individual personalities of leaders and the chemistry (or lack thereof) between them is more relevant and consequential for the course of history than most people think; and second, that leaders are, after all, people like us, not necessarily more perfect or immune to psychological fluctuations and outside pressure. Intuition, focused intelligence, perseverance, physical and mental stamina, an acute understanding of the dynamics of power – and the pleasure they obtain from using it to attain political goals – are what distinguishes them from the rest of us.

I could add a third remark: I realised that the EU is, by and large, one of the most open and accessible international partners, one that basically talks to everyone and is listened to by everyone, regardless of the degree of proximity regarding interests and values. This is an ability that should not be underestimated and certainly not ignored in times of global fragmentation and potential divorce, times when dialogue is absolutely crucial to overcome differences.

Retrospectively, two achievements of Barroso's first term, among many, illustrate the overall scope of his task and also the EU's international dimension: the Treaty of Lisbon, which was signed in December 2007 under Portuguese presidency and entered into force two years later, providing the EU with a new level of ambition and more efficient tools, including as a global actor, reversing the painful rejection of the Constitution in 2005; and the first ever energy and climate action strategy, which equipped the Union to lead the world on the existential fight against climate change. Both accomplishments set the foundations for further progress in European integration and for more effective EU action at global level.

In his second mandate, which I followed from Washington, Barroso would see the storms of the financial crisis come to shore. Resilient as a true *transmontano*, faithful to his family roots in the rough and remote Trás-os-Montes mountains of north-east Portugal, he successfully led the Commission in its efforts to preserve and even enlarge the euro area and the EU itself, and to contribute to decisive action at the level of the G20. The EU stayed alive and relevant enough to deserve the Nobel Peace Prize, which Barroso received on its behalf in 2012.

THE 'MUTTI' CHANCELLOR, THE CAPTIVATING PRIME MINISTER AND THE EFFERVESCENT PRESIDENT

The EU's public image is a complex puzzle of relatively abstract concepts, most of the time difficult to apprehend, and a rollout of recognisable political actors who somehow personify and embody the EU. In the absence of a real Europe-wide common public space, confronted with multiple languages, cultures, media environments and domestic political debates, it is hard for the EU to convey, on its own, a clear and understandable message. It needs voices and faces that are easier to relate to and recognisable by a maximum number of EU citizens.

The most obvious representative 'messengers' are the leaders of the Brussels-based institutions, and particularly the President of the Commission, its executive body, empowered by a wide scope of policy and legal competences, a sizeable budget and a five-year-long mandate, and also the presidents of the European Parliament and of the European Council. Additionally, the leader of the country holding the six-month rotating presidency of the Council of Ministers can also be considered as part of that inner core of institutional representatives, although this role has been considerably diminished since the entry into force of the Treaty of Lisbon. The rotating presidency involves virtually no external representation of the Union at head of government level, even if some prime ministers tend to forget it and one recently even attempted to usurp it.

There are, however, limits to what Brussels-based institutional leaders, seen as foreigners in each of the nations beyond their home country, can do to bring the EU's image and message to almost half a billion people throughout the EU. This is also true of the projection of the EU's 'brand' to the wider world, where national leaders are normally more visible and identifiable. That is why one should not underestimate the relevance – and the associated co-responsibility – of heads of state or government of individual EU member states in shaping the internal and external image of the Union.

Looking back at the first quarter of the century and considering the relative importance of national leaders' contribution to forging the EU's internal and external profile and its visibility and credibility, three such individuals stand out in my view: Angela Merkel, Tony Blair and Emmanuel Macron.

Merkel was Chancellor of Germany for an astonishing sixteen years, from 2005 to 2021, and Blair held for ten years the position of Prime Minister of the United Kingdom, between 1997 and 2007. Macron has been in power since 2017. Whereas the German chancellor's career covered almost the entire quarter century, the UK prime minister left Downing Street early in the period but had an impact on it well beyond his departure, while the French president has uniquely influenced the EU in the almost eight years since he became the tenant of the Elysée.

Angela Merkel

I distinctly remember Angela Merkel's performance in European Council meetings. I was one of the few officials allowed into the room, seated at a second row desk right behind the President of the Commission, an ideal observation point. I tried always to keep an eye on her, her look, her body language, her reactions, when she would stand up or leave the room, whom she would go talk to. And I am sure I was not the only one ...

Merkel was a kind of mother figure. Respected, warm and friendly to everyone, 'Mutti', as she was affectionately called by her supporters in Germany, was nevertheless also feared. She was a hands-on organiser by nature, a doer, but a very thoughtful one. Before the chair's call for order, she would stand up and go around the big oval table, saluting everyone, whispering here, shaking hands or kissing cheeks there. During formal sessions, she would listen and listen, and when she either was tired of too much talk or thought that things were mature enough for her to play her cards, she would take to the floor and most of the time set the scene for a final decision. With one rule: she would only make concessions when she really had to, as late as possible. She was a supreme tactician and a subtle manager of her enormous influence and power. There was definitely 'a Merkel method'. Some wonder, however, whether there was a long-term 'Merkel vision'.

In private meetings, she would never appear as pretentious or a *prima donna*, never be dismissive of officials accompanying her fellow leaders, and she could laugh at a good joke and enjoy good wine. But she was results-oriented. Driven by her scientific background as a chemist, she would have read the file, she would ask clinical questions and would begin to get nervous and bored if there was too much small talk and no conclusion on the horizon.

During her long time in office, she was tremendously influential in the running of EU affairs. Too influential for some who feared an excessive German influence, but also not influential enough for others, who thought that she was often too reluctant, too cautious or not courageous enough in making use of her own personal charisma and of her country's might. In 2011, Radek Sikorski, then and now the Polish foreign minister, famously stated in Berlin (and this is not a small thing coming from a Pole): 'I fear German power less than I fear German inaction.'[3]

No one was able to stay indifferent to Angela Merkel. She embodied the whole set of contradictory patterns of behaviour of post-Second World War and post-reunification Germany, and triggered the whole set of reactions to the central position, and indisputable role, of her country. Merkel is inseparable from the history of the Union during the first quarter of this century, in both its good and its not-so-good moments.

She was focused and determined in pursuing her goals. While already CDU leader but not yet German Chancellor, Merkel, working closely with other centre-right leaders and Tony Blair, was instrumental in moving the balance of the European Council in favour of her favourite candidate – José Manuel Barroso – to the detriment of Guy Verhofstadt, the Belgian Prime Minister, who was supported by the French and German leaders, Chirac and Schröder.

I must say that I was, and still am, a great fan. But I am also critical of some of her options. I question the way Frau Merkel handled Putin, Russia and Russian gas in particular, how quickly, too quickly in my view, she decided to drop nuclear energy as part of the German energy mix, following the Fukushima disaster in Japan, and how she resisted, for too long, creating the conditions for a way out of the EU sovereign debt crisis. In retrospect, the over-reliance of Germany on trade with China can be questioned – but I can guarantee that at the time it was rather a source of envy, not criticism, from other countries' leaders ...

More personally, besides having learned a lot from her about the exercise of power and the critical importance of the emotional intelligence of leaders, I will always recall that neither she nor her close collaborators (Uwe Corsepius, EU adviser, and Christoph Heusgen, foreign policy czar, my main interlocutors) ever let Barroso or myself down. With Angela Merkel, a deal was always a deal. The same could not be said, I am afraid, of all EU leaders.

Tony Blair

A series of words were suggested when I tried to find one that could encapsulate how Tony Blair was perceived as a national and European leader during his time in office. 'Moderniser' was suggested by someone who knew him well and admired him for what he has achieved, in spite of his contradictions. Another chose 'enchanting'. I could have opted for pragmatic, brilliant, controversial or simply charismatic. Listening to people critical of Blair's personality and performance, 'shallow' or 'a bluff' came up as more radical options. I could have underlined that he was meticulous and detailed in his grasp of files, but at the same time more intuitive than strategic when decisions had to be taken – 'more feel than reason', as a close aide described Blair's 'driving factor'.

At the end of my search, 'captivating' came out as the least imperfect single word to describe a complex and multifaceted personality, to whom, as with Merkel, no one could possibly remain indifferent and many were attracted.

Among all the global leaders I came across, he joins Bill Clinton in the category of 'political animals' who are capable of immediately dominating a room without instilling any perception of intellectual or social arrogance, and also of designing a compelling and often irresistible political narrative. Moreover, Clinton and Blair could connect not only with the crowds but also with each individual, as if every single voter counted more than any other.

The first lines of *Primary Colors* – a famous book by the American columnist Joe Klein (who signed it as Anonymous),[4] which allegorically describes Bill Clinton's presidential campaign of 1992 and was adapted to cinema, starring John Travolta as the candidate – say it all about a natural leader's connectivity potential:

> We shook hands. My inability to recall that particular moment more precisely is disappointing: the handshake is the threshold act, the beginning of politics. I've seen him do it two million times now, but I couldn't tell you how he does it, the right-handed part of it – the strength, quality, duration of it, the rudiments of pressing the flesh. I can, however, tell you a whole lot about what he

does with his other hand. He is a genius with it. He might put it on your elbow, or up by your biceps: these are basic, reflexive moves. He is interested in you. He is honored to meet you. If he gets any higher up your shoulder – if he, say, drapes his left arm over your back, it is somehow less intimate, more casual. He'll share a laugh or a secret then – a light secret, not a real one – flattering you with the illusion of conspiracy. If he doesn't know you all that well and you've just told him something 'important', something earnest or emotional, he will lock in and honor you with a two-hander, his left hand overwhelming your wrist and forearm. He'll flash that famous misty look of his. And he will mean it.

Blair came into office as a 'Kennedyesque figure', mirroring another iconic American leader, promising to shift the UK to a new generation and to build a modern, forward-looking country – and he significantly contributed to that. He was very keen – some even say too keen – to align with the USA 'no matter what', but he also clearly saw the EU as an important partner and wanted to see his country at the heart of it. Blair was the most committed pro-European among UK prime ministers of recent times and maybe even ever. He advocated a united Europe as a condition for the protection of the interests and values of its member states in the world. He allegedly even admitted supporting the UK joining the euro, but on this he was not followed by a majority in his party, let alone by his colleague Gordon Brown, then the Chancellor of the Exchequer.

Tony Blair was willing and ready to fight the EU's corner in the UK and in the world at large. Baroness Cathy Ashton, who was part of his government and later became European Commissioner for Trade and the first EU High Representative for Foreign Policy and Security Affairs, says of him:[5]

Blair was extraordinary and serving in his government was to feel a sense of progress and achievement. He put the UK back at the heart of Europe, was seen as a world leader, charismatic and clever, serious in his intent of making Britain a great nation.

Blair's rotating presidency of the European Council in the second half of 2005 was an important moment. It provided valuable impulse to several far-reaching policy files like energy, research and innovation, and new approaches to adapting to globalisation. It was a particularly well-timed presidency. This was the first full year of President Barroso's mandate at the helm of the Commission and a critical time for him and the EU, right after the two negative referenda in France and the Netherlands, which put an end to the draft Constitution. The positive boost provided by Blair was most welcome.

Blair's 'Third Way', conceived together with, among others, Anthony Giddens and Peter Mandelson, another leading 'New Labour', pro-European politician (who was also a commissioner in Barroso's first term), had a great impact on the evolution of the political thinking and action of the socialist and social-democratic centre-left family in Europe and helped forge a large degree of European consensus at the turn of the century. He could not, however, have achieved what he did on the British internal front without Gordon Brown, in spite of the difficult personal relationship between two such different personalities. Brown would later play, as Blair's successor, and as I witnessed firsthand, a critical international role in taming the global financial crisis that started in 2008.

Tony Blair was a driving force behind the 2004 (and then 2007) enlargement of the EU to include central and eastern European countries, most of them formerly behind the Iron Curtain. He may have overdone his support to the cause by voluntarily accepting from day one, without a transition period, the free movement to the UK of citizens from the countries that were joining in 2004. The UK was one of the very few member states that took that bold step (others were Sweden and Ireland). What was then seen by many as a clairvoyant decision, revealing total commitment to the success of enlargement and a gesture of solidarity towards the 'new member states', turned out to be one of the major sources of fuel for the populist and anti-European discourse in the UK.

Nigel Farage made very good use of it, and of David Cameron's carelessness in handling the whole referendum process, and created the conditions for a successful Brexit referendum. Tony

Blair identified Farage's threat early on and stood out as the first 'mainstream' top British politician who confronted him, ten years before the referendum.

A particular exchange in the Brussels hemicycle of the European Parliament, on 20 December 2005, became famous at the time and has since then become so 'viral' that from time to time you can still find it today in social media feeds. In some sites, it is presented as 'Tony Blair taking down Nigel Farage in 90 seconds'. Confronted with the display of the Union Jack on the seats of anti-EU and pro-Brexit MEPs from the UK Independence Party, and replying to a provocative speech by Farage, Blair did not mince his words: 'You sit with our country's flag but you do not represent our country's interests. This is the year 2005, not 1945. We are not fighting each other anymore, these are our partners, our future lies in Europe.' And he went on displaying his vision of Europe with the UK at its centre.

If you come across the video, you can check someone appearing just behind Blair, trying hard to keep a poker face, as an official should do. God knows how I wanted to applaud such a powerful dismantling of Farage's populist discourse ... but I managed to allow just a timid smile to betray my support. Barroso, seating to Blair's right, used his politician's freedom to allow himself a good laugh.

My direct contact with Blair's leadership qualities and personal abilities as a politician included also his role as the chairperson of G8 and host of the group's Gleneagles summit, in July 2005, the first one I helped prepare and attended. There he was confronted with a unique challenge, which he managed to statesman-like perfection, of hosting the most important gathering of world leaders at the same time as being confronted with a terrorist attack in London (of which more detail later in this chapter). He decided to fly to London but not suspend the G8 summit as a sign of solidarity with his people and a rejection of terrorists' ability to disrupt the normal functioning of global governance.

Tony Blair returned to Gleneagles in the evening of that dreadful Thursday. He was exhausted but he had made the right decision: he needed to be with his people in London that day. 'He showed on his return a quality that I have noticed on other occasions,' says Sir

Michael Jay, now a member of the House of Lords and Blair's sherpa at the time.[6] 'An ability that few people have to focus entirely on the issue at hand and not be distracted by other things. Despite the horrors of the day, he focused now on what had happened at Gleneagles in his absence and on the challenges of the following day.'

The Gleneagles final press conference put an end to an amazingly heavy week for Blair. He had flown to Singapore and back in time to open the G8 Summit when he got the good news, back from the Olympic gathering in Singapore, that London had defeated Paris in their race to host the Olympics. His decision to present London's candidacy had not been consensual, but now he was fully vindicated. The same could not be said of Chirac, who had also been to Singapore but came back with less good news ...

Another bold and even more consequential decision by the PM was less consensual and will remain as part of his legacy, albeit on the negative side: seen as an expression of full solidarity with the UK's biggest ally – but also revealing a certain degree of hubris and his lack of government experience, according to some of his friends – Blair's solid support for the invasion of Iraq had a serious impact on the UK, obviously, but also on the EU and on the UK's bilateral relations with some of its member states.

The invasion divided the Union member states, with several of them, including my own country, supporting the war initiative, but also some, not least France and Germany, opposing it. Its aftermath hindered the capacity of the West, including the EU, to pursue an agenda of engagement with those around the world who challenged the wisdom of the Iraq adventure.

For all his positive contributions, but also for the less fortunate ones, Blair contributed to the shaping of the EU's profile in the first decades of the twenty-first century. In the UK, notwithstanding his flaws, 'Blair remains the bar against which all future Labour leaders are measured', as Cathy Ashton puts it.

Emmanuel Macron

Emmanuel Macron entered the European stage from the lower ranks of top officialdom as an international economics adviser to

President François Hollande in 2012 and ended up succeeding him in the Elysée five years later, at the age of 39. This promising young rising star of French technocracy, with a diploma from the prestigious École nationale d'administration and a successful career at Rothschild's bank, ended up as one of the most visionary political leaders of the EU in the first quarter of this century.

In contrast to his two predecessors François Hollande and Nicolas Sarkozy, he was re-elected and is now serving a second five-year term as President of the Republic. The fact that he lost his majority in Parliament right after his second victory, in 2022, and that he had to endure an even bigger defeat two years later, at the European elections – followed by a big surge in far-right support in an extraordinary general election in the summer of 2024 – did not limit his determination always to put new ideas forward, even if some would argue that their rate of implementation is ultimately relatively low.

I have most likely been with him at a couple of venues and events, but I never really met him while I worked as Chief of Staff in Brussels as he was more in touch with members of my team at the time. From them I got very clear feedback, from day one: 'There is a very good new young guy working for Hollande,' were the words of António Cabral soon after his first meeting with his counterpart Emmanuel Macron. Cabral is a good friend and was an excellent colleague as Barroso's economic adviser, and eventually succeeded me as G20 sherpa. Since then I have been following Macron's *parcours* from a distance, with interest and curiosity, as I recognise in him the inventiveness and creativity that has often been lacking in Europe's political class.

Paul Adamson, from *Encompass*, an acute observer of the EU scene for many years, summarised well what many think of Macron: 'I think the key to understanding Macron is to see him as a kind of political entrepreneur – "le goût du risque", sure, but coupled with optimism and self-belief,' Paul wrote on 'X' soon after the president dissolved the National Assembly following the far-right landslide in European elections. 'No guarantee of success (as with any real entrepreneur) but at least you try,' added Adamson.

Europe needs the qualities Macron has deployed, and the reality is that, since his arrival at the Elysée, he has had a significant impact on the EU agenda. With several grandiose speeches, for sure, but also with numerous initiatives, some better thought through than others, albeit all innovative, Macron has occupied the centre of the EU stage. His Sorbonne master classes on EU affairs, his surprise gatherings at the Elysée of unpredictable groups of leaders, the different processes he has started, including the European Political Community, all reveal an effervescent personality, fully committed to European integration. He has been the EU's agitator-in-chief.

Before that, he had agitated the French political scene like no one else in recent times. Macron revolutionised the French political landscape. In his first years at the Elysée, he alone reduced the Socialist Party and its centre-right former main contender, Les Républicains, almost to fringe parties and imposed himself and his centrist movement as an election winner. However, in his second term, the situation deteriorated considerably. The far right and the far left recovered their positions and the political movement he had inspired lost its momentum and electoral base. The anticipated legislative elections he called in the summer of 2024, following a disastrous performance at the European elections, resulted in a very unstable political landscape and he was accused of political recklessness for allowing the far right and the far left to come too close to power.

All in all, one wonders: how much did Macron's creativity and inventiveness produce that can be counted as real and positive results for his country and for Europe? What is the real impact of effervescence? Is it destined sooner or later to fall flat?

On the French internal front, he has not managed to create a solid and deep-rooted political force to match his personal clout and occupy a moderate centre ground. His reform agenda is to be commended, but he has had trouble overcoming French people's well-known love of revolutions but apparent disdain for reforms. His merit is to persist, with acute awareness of how the huge potential of France might be hindered by its people's resistance to change.

In Europe, his agenda never really enthused Berlin, his lack of personal chemistry with both German chancellors Merkel and Scholz was detrimental to his goals and to the EU as a whole, and concrete results are still lacking. However, who else in Europe has had the courage and the creativity to address upfront, from a truly pro-European perspective, such complex issues as strategic autonomy, immigration and security, the combined urgency of economic and technological competitiveness and protection of our markets from unfair competition, the need for reform to enable enlargement, the concept of concentric circles and different speeds of integration and ambition? Even if one can challenge some of his premises and proposals, it is hard to deny Macron's energy and commitment.

More globally, he tried to become good friends with Trump and an interlocutor for Putin, but mainly not because of him, both goals failed. Recently, he has courageously changed his approach regarding Ukraine, Russia and NATO and has not spared efforts to find a way to connect with Xi. That is part of his constant search for solutions, alternatives and new ways forward, which is difficult to condemn but does not in itself guarantee success.

I would dare to say that the judgement of history on Macron will most likely happen only when we know who will succeed him. If, having decimated most of the French moderate political forces and not managed to consolidate a centrist movement, he ends up handing over power to the far-right and Putin-soft Marine Le Pen as his successor on the steps of the Palais de l'Elysée, we might be tempted to compare him with the equally brilliant Barack Obama, who had painfully to endure Donald Trump's populist inaugural speech on the Capitol's West Terrace. More often than not, the real success of political leaders is mercilessly measured by who succeeds them.

THE STRANGE ANIMAL

On the international stage, when considering global governance, and contrary to nations and states, the EU is not intuitively perceived as a natural actor.

That is understandable, even if not justified. The multilateral system is based on the role of nations and states, on the primacy of national sovereignty, on the intergovernmental nature of decision-making procedures and on the personal visibility of national leaders. There is no immediate perception of a place and role for a 'strange animal' like the EU, or its leaders, in global governance. And yet, given the contribution the EU makes, the influence it projects and the power all this entails, such a role does exist.

That should not come as a surprise because multilateralism is part of the EU's DNA. The EU is the embodiment of multilateralism at regional level and the best expression of its principles and values, through the promotion of co-operative and peaceful solutions to common problems. It possesses international legal existence and its economic, regulatory and political weight is beyond challenge. Even after Brexit, the EU is part of the trio of global economic powerhouses, the second biggest global importer and exporter, the top foreign investment source and the largest provider of humanitarian and development aid, apart from being the biggest financial contributor to the UN system. It is the primary trading partner of more than eighty countries around the world.

In all honesty, the EU is also partly to blame for the lack of adequate recognition of its global role. In spite of the scope of its action and the depth of its influence in world affairs, the way the EU deploys its representation in global governance bodies has never been exempt from contradictions and challenges – and has even sometimes been part of the problem. I was often confronted with situations that represented a waste of energy and resources because of shortsighted views from some member states' capitals and some leaders. I witnessed many missed opportunities to use our weight to influence the course of events, simply because unanimity required an alignment at a low level of ambition, or because of misplaced rivalries between EU institutions, or between them and member states, and among the latter.

This notwithstanding, clear progress was made throughout the first quarter of the twenty-first century in projecting a more effective EU global role.

The Treaty of Lisbon contributed extensively to that, via the creation of the post of a permanent President of the European Council, as opposed to the six-monthly rotating presidency that diminished the weight and influence of the position. Establishing a High Representative for Foreign Affairs and Security Policy, who is also a vice-president of the Commission, supported by a new foreign service (EEAS) equipped with a network of more than 140 diplomatic missions and newly empowered EU ambassadors around the world, was another major contribution. The first HRVP (which is how the function became known), Catherine Ashton, played a critical role in launching the EEAS, in what was not an obvious task because it involved a redistribution of competences, roles and power to which the EU system is always averse. In her book *And Then What?*[7] she accurately and entertainingly describes the uniqueness of the new EU role, as well as her personal contribution to important files like Iran and the western Balkans.

Already before 'Lisbon' and even more so after it, thanks to the institutional clarification it brought, a unique role in the external representation of the Union is allocated to the President of the European Commission. José Manuel Barroso was the first holder of the position to invest substantially in it during his two mandates. His successor, Jean-Claude Juncker, focused more on the internal management of the Union and did not have, as he confessed several times, including to me, a great personal interest in travelling around the world and sitting in long multilateral gatherings. Things changed again, as we know, with Ursula von der Leyen and her 'geopolitical Commission', which prolonged Barroso's efforts and investment, as described above.

Personal inclinations of leaders matter as well. Barroso had a personal interest in international relations, as a former foreign minister and prime minister, and ever since his early days in politics as a very young junior minister in the Foreign Affairs ministry of Portugal.[8] As President of the Commission, he was keen to use fully his treaty powers on the external front in order to enhance the EU's global influence and clout – beginning with areas of 'exclusive competence' of the Commission, such as trade policy, completed by the external dimension of internal Community policies (energy, environment, climate action and many more) but also covering foreign policy issues, in co-ordination with the other relevant players. Von der Leyen had been minister of defence in Germany before becoming President of the Commission and her interest – and that of her influential chief of staff, Björn Seibert – in security and foreign policy issues played a key role in the shaping of her mandate.

Challenging exogenous factors, paradoxically, also helped project the EU globally. They forced EU member states and institutions to close ranks, converge rather than diverge, and make an effort to be more effective than in the past on the external front. The way the EU reacted to both Covid and the Russian war in Ukraine, and before that the leadership it showed as regards the international deal to constrain Iran's nuclear development (JCPOA) and the invasion of Georgia by Russia, and its intense diplomatic efforts in the Balkans and in the Caucasus, are good recent examples of progress, even if the EU was often confronted with insurmountable obstacles to its action.

The same could be said of the efforts being deployed to develop a more focused development policy, capable of countering the growing influence of other actors, particularly in Africa, and to address major challenges such as demographic pressure and related migration flows. Hopefully, in the nascent political cycle the Union will be capable of investing in a higher-quality dialogue with developing countries on how the next phase of economic globalisation and global governance should be managed.

As regards the Middle East, and particularly Israeli–Palestinian relations and even more so the Israel–Hamas conflict, things are always more complex to handle and division within the EU is hard to deny, even if there is coherence and convergence around the ultimate two-state solution and a collective determination to pursue that goal.

The EU is today a more committed and respected global actor than at the beginning of the century, even if I believe it is still punching below its weight and is underestimated by too many.

Some basically still see the EU more as a global 'payer' than as a global 'player'. Some still take the EU for granted as a development or humanitarian aid provider, and don't take our conditionality too seriously, or underestimate our potential to be a security provider. Some are still too tempted, and may even find it not too difficult, to divide the EU to the benefit of their agendas.

The EU can do more and better to maximise its weight and its capacity to act, as well as to convey the right messages regarding its specific role within a system of governance founded on the primacy of national sovereignty. For that, Europeans need to be both less naive and less arrogant, both more realistic and better focused on the pursuit of our interests and more understanding and adaptable in promoting or projecting our values on other partners. In parallel, and as a matter of obvious urgency, the EU must invest more in hardware capabilities (defence, security, foreign policy) to complement our enviable software assets.

The need for unanimity in foreign policy and security issues is often seen as the worst of all evils and abolishing it the miraculous solution to all our problems. I beg to disagree. First, because differences in policy can never be dismissed and put aside by institutional and legal expediency. Second, because there are ways of mitigating the impact of the recourse to unanimity through transparent and co-operative solutions. One thing is clear for me: the EU should always pursue united positions but should never be paralysed by its obsession with unity.

One aspect often underestimated is the wealth that diversity brings, the relevance of the diversified expertise the EU can deploy. I experienced that in real time in my posts as EU ambassador and particularly in New York as I realised that, on every geographic area or thematic discussion on the very wide UN agenda, I could call on a member state ambassador who would provide detailed knowledge based on their country's specific experience and network of relationships around the world. That is obviously even more relevant at leaders' level. It is an asset no single country can claim to possess and one that the EU and each and every one of its member states can benefit from.

A creative search for enhanced effectiveness in foreign policy and security issues is definitely a priority if the EU wants to maximise its clout in a volatile world. It is the new frontier of European integration. And maybe even a condition for its survival. The EU cannot satisfy its existence by guaranteeing peace only within its borders. If it wants to be a true peace project, it also has to guarantee peace in its neighbourhood and contribute to conflict prevention around the world.

Provided there is a clear awareness of the magnitude of the risks of not doing so and of the leverage it can provide, I am sure that, once again, the EU will be able to swim against the tide. And be a strong counter-divorce factor in our region and around the globe.

It can certainly build on the fact that, for a few years now, the EU has been present in each and every instance of informal global governance. The 'strange animal' has become almost like any other member of the global fauna.

G8/20: THE HIGH TABLE

I witnessed the potential and the shortcomings of the EU's role as a global actor during my twenty years of activity on the external relations front, and nowhere more evidently than at the top echelons of global governance: the G8, G20 and UN.

Even some well-informed media often ignore it, but the leaders meeting as G8 were in fact not eight but ten. In addition to the heads of state or government of the USA, Canada, Germany, France, Italy, the UK, Russia and Japan, the presidents of the European Council and of the European Commission were also full members (as they are of the current G7, which counts nine members, not seven). That was not easy to explain and understand and, for some, even difficult to accept because it meant that, within the G8 for instance, no fewer than six out of ten were Europeans.

The G8, like much as the G7 today (Russia was suspended from the G8 after the invasion of Crimea in 2014 and definitively expelled a few years later), was the most influential – and powerful – informal group of countries, with a key role in global governance. Five years of attendance at dozens of 'sherpa' meetings and eight summits gave me enough confirmation of its relevance but also of the added value, for the G8 and for the EU, of the Union's direct representation in it. The summit agendas gradually widened to cover a wide spectrum of policies and domains, from foreign policy, security and geostrategic issues to economic, trade, regulatory and environmental ones. Seen from the EU, this typically encompasses areas of exclusive national competence but equally domains of shared competence and even files that fall squarely into exclusive Union competence. Hence the need to have such a double representation of member states and EU institutions. Additionally, the presence of EU leaders – and the EU sherpa – in complementing those of four member states (or three now, within the G7) guarantees the representation and protection of the interests of the absent twenty-four.

The G8 annual summit was prepared months in advance in several meetings of the so-called 'sherpas', high officials closely connected to their respective leaders, who were entitled to speak on their behalf in defining the agenda and drafting the final declaration. Apart from the leaders, they were the only persons allowed in the room when the summit finally took place, usually in June or July, on a rotating basis in the territory of each of the G8 member countries. These kinds of summit are especially designed to guarantee maximum intimacy and informality in order to foster personal chemistry among leaders. That is true also of the sherpas network.

My presence side by side with colleagues from four EU member states – France, Germany, the UK and Italy – made the job particularly interesting. We had inside the G8 what the French call a *force de frappe*, a critical mass, which, if well managed, could have considerable influence on the final positions of the group. However, a condition for success, as in any instance of external representation of the EU, was that we had a common or at least a convergent position on the issues under discussion. When that was not the case, we counted considerably less and I had to be more discreet or even just keep quiet. Alternatively, as sometimes happened, I would try *in loco* to forge a common line. For the most experienced of my American, Japanese, Canadian and Russian colleagues, it had long been understood why the EU presence, instead of evidence of European overrepresentation, was in fact useful and contributed to the effectiveness of the implementation of the summit's output. But this did not mean that, if given a chance, they would not try to find gaps in our unity. We had to stay on our toes.

I had high expectations, and a certain degree of anxiety, ahead of my first G8 sherpa meeting, to prepare the Gleneagles summit, under British presidency, in 2005. This was, after all, a gathering of the highest-level officials and closest advisers of the leaders of the most powerful countries in the world, discussing key issues on the international agenda and charged with preparing the summit debates and drafting its final declaration. Thanks to the warm welcome of Michael Jay and other colleagues, my integration was sweet and short. I quickly became, and still am to this day, a loyal and proud member of the 'sherpas mafia', a benign one, I hasten to reassure.

As mentioned earlier when referring to Tony Blair, the Gleneagles G8 summit was a peculiar one as it coincided with serious terrorist attacks in London. It provided me with front-row access to the intimacy of international co-operation and govern-ance at the highest level and to the personal role that leaders – and their sherpas – play in it. It is worth looking briefly behind the Gleneagles scene.

Summit days start early as all leaders try to optimise their free time for the sake of personal preparation and bilateral meetings, before being overtaken by the whole 'show'. Thursday, 7 July 2005, the first day of the Gleneagles G8 summit, was no different (at least, that's what I thought as I woke up in the middle of a beauti-ful Scottish landscape).

Together with a couple of colleagues, I joined José Manuel Barroso in his suite for a short early morning briefing and review of overnight events in the EU. Being President of the Commission means you are never allowed to disconnect from Brussels and the

EU's internal affairs, even if you are otherwise focused on global issues. We reviewed the forthcoming working sessions, checked the speaking points and I added an account of the sherpas' work the previous evening, shaping up the final communiqué. This was also when we became aware of violent incidents happening in London.

Elsewhere in the Gleneagles Hotel, Tony Blair was having breakfast with George W. Bush. The two then went for a friendly walk in the garden and had a short bilateral press conference. Blair then saw President Hu. As expected, Hu was formal, well briefed, speaking firmly and without notes, though 'no real rapport could be seen with the PM – whose informal, more spontaneous style didn't really gel with Hu's,' recalls Michael Jay. As his boss was seeing Hu, news started coming through to the prime minister's chief of staff, Jonathan Powell, of explosions in London. 'Not clear to start with if they were terrorist attacks,' recalls Jay – 'but that had become pretty obvious by the time the PM went to greet the other G8 leaders formally before the summit itself started.'

Shortly before the morning plenary session was due to begin at 9 a.m., Jonathan Powell in fact received the first indications of a terrorist attack in London. The first news of the incidents, still vague, had broken on television earlier and it was with a degree of concern that all the leaders and sherpas headed towards the grand room at the Gleneagles Hotel. The details and the severity of the attack were still uncertain, and Tony Blair decided that the plenary session should go ahead as planned. The first topic was the global economy.

The ten leaders of the G8 sat around a large circular table (in 2005, Putin was still a member of the G8, and he would, indeed, chair it in St Petersburg the following year, as described above). Apart from the sherpas, no one else was present in the room. Communication was from each sherpa by notes scribbled on an electronic pad, which were sent automatically to each delegation in their rooms elsewhere in the hotel.

About ten minutes into the session, a note was sent to Tony Blair that the terrorist attack was really serious, that there was more than one and that victims were being counted.[9] We watched

Blair's advisers whisper the latest information to him. There was tension and concern in the room. I saw Blair's face becoming grimmer by the minute, before he decided to raise the issue directly with his fellow leaders. The normal work of the G8 was suspended, and the leaders discussed instead how to respond to the terror attacks.

Michael Jay recalls the occasion, which also had a direct consequence for him: 'This was unique,' he says:

> The leaders of the G8 discussing in real time, without the benefit of advice or notes from their staff, how to respond to a serious but still evolving emergency. Three leaders, Blair, Bush and Chirac, led the discussion. Blair explained the situation as he understood it. Chirac and Bush were clear that Blair must go to London. 'Tony, you must be with your people', said Chirac. They also agreed, as did all the G8 leaders, that the summit should go on. To interrupt it would be seen to be giving in to the terrorists.[10]

As was often the case at G8 summits, other world leaders had been invited to a working session and a lunch that day. They included Hu Jintao from China, Manmohan Singh from India, Thabo Mbeki from South Africa, Lula da Silva from Brazil and the Secretary-General of the United Nations, Kofi Annan. 'The earliest the PM could get a helicopter and plane was 1 p.m., so we resumed for the 12.15 session of the G8 + 5 + Kofi Annan and others,' Michael Jay notes. 'There was a mixture of solidarity with London, condemnation of terrorism and a discussion of the global economy and climate change.'

Tony Blair proposed, and the other G8 leaders agreed, that at the end of the morning's plenary session, all the world leaders present at Gleneagles should be photographed together in a unanimous stand against terrorism while Blair spoke on their behalf. Which they did, providing a powerful image of anti-terror unity. Immediately afterwards, Blair would fly to London.

There was one other decision that had to be taken: who should chair the G8 in Tony Blair's absence? That is when Michael Jay's brilliant diplomatic career reached new heights:

Chirac proposed that I, as Blair's sherpa, should chair the lunch. He knew me from my time as ambassador in Paris and said: 'The British sherpa can chair and we will treat his authority as your own.' This was agreed, and the session ended a few minutes early, around 11.20.

Blair then left. Michael Jay recalls the sequence thereafter:

There was a short break for drinks during which Lula da Silva asked me to pass on to Tony Blair his acceptance of an invitation to a state visit, I mingled with heads on the lawn, introducing myself to Putin, Schröder, Koizumi, Martin, Fox and others. I invited them all into lunch, in the conservatory overlooking the Gleneagles grounds. I took Blair's seat and spoke to Manmohan Singh on my right – reminding him of our meetings in Delhi twenty-five years ago when he was financial secretary – and to Mbeki on my left, who said that he had been at Sussex University with my twin cousins. Hu was opposite. Bush had come up to me earlier and said, 'I only have one thing to say: keep them to time.'

Michael Jay chaired the discussion that followed, well aware that his G8 sherpa colleagues were listening in to the conversation from their own lunch table (we warmly congratulated him after-wards for his performance, enhancing the reputation of the sherpa corporation). Lula da Silva spoke first, followed by Manmohan Singh, Mbeki, Chirac, Kofi Annan, Barroso, Rato, head of the IMF, Bush, Supachai, Koizumi and Martin. 'Aware of Bush's advice,' says Michael Jay, 'I called things to a halt just before 3 and – having debated with myself whether or not to do so – summed up, pref-acing it with "if the prime minister were here, I know there are two or three threads that he would want to draw from the discus-sion …" and focusing mainly on the clear political commitment to work for a good Doha trade round outcome' (which unfortu-nately never happened, as one of the first signs that a consensus about globalisation and the WTO's role in it was not as obvious as previously expected).

The afternoon session of the G8 was chaired by Jack Straw, the foreign secretary, who was rushed in from London. 'I was in King Charles Street that morning,' the former minister recalls:[11]

The first explosion happened about 8.50 a.m. It was clear by about 9.15–9.25 that we were facing a major terrorist outrage. Not long after that I got a message to say that Tony had decided to come back to London, and I would need to travel to Gleneagles to chair the remainder of the sessions that day.

A helicopter was rustled up from somewhere, very quickly. 'What I do remember is that it was a glorious day, especially over the Pennines, which seemed oddly incongruous given the carnage which had been caused by the terrorists,' Jack Straw adds.

The foreign secretary arrived around 4 p.m., and chaired the G8 session at 5 p.m. with the head of the World Bank, Jim Wolfensohn, focused on Gaza and the Middle East, and the G8 dinner on other foreign policy issues, dominated by 'an eccentric, rambling speech by Chirac on Lebanon and a sharp disagreement between Putin and Chirac on Syria'. The prime minister returned at the end of dinner, and leaders met in the glamorous, Scotch whisky-dominated Gleneagles bar, joined by spouses. It had been a long and eventful G8 day. In a separate room, sherpas were putting the last touches to the final communiqué. Their day was not over yet.

G8 sherpas extended their 'territory' with the advent of the G20, forced upon the international community by the 2008 financial crisis (discussed in Chapter 2). It brought together the members of the G8 and the other major economies of the world, starting with China and India, and including a geographical mix of emerging and middle powers. At the beginning of its existence, the G20's agenda was more 'economic' than political or strategic, although at the time of the crisis nothing could have been more political and strategic than avoiding a financial meltdown and a global depression, which was the group's main purpose.

Like other colleagues, I initially felt the need to be supported by economists and financial specialists, but with time the G20 agenda became less centred on economics. The G20 summits are today basically a global forum that has lost some of its initial results-oriented economic and financial focus, without gaining diplomatic and political clout because of the current divisions in the international community – the G20 was instrumental in fighting back global economic and financial risks but has been unable to overcome geopolitical polarisation.

The main difference between the G8 and G20, however, was not in the nature of their agenda but rather in their make-up: the G8 countries were more like-minded and found it easier to work together, unlike the large, diverse G20. This became even more obvious when, after the expulsion of Russia, the G8 became the G7 and gradually enlarged the scope of its agenda, reinforcing its status as the co-ordination hub of liberal, democratic and industrialised countries, and regularly admitting countries like Australia and Korea to participate in some of their discussions. Even if the G7 is keen to reach out to some developing countries, particularly from Africa, it has rightly become the inner core of 'Western' co-ordination in times of unpredictability and volatility.

The G20 is the main platform for the G7 to engage collectively with China, Russia and India and a host of middle and emerging powers on all continents, which do not necessarily share G7 values or strategic interests. I believe it has still an untapped potential, but the truth is that it can only deliver what its members are ready to contribute to. As it currently stands, there is not much on offer, unfortunately.

THE UN: THE SKY-BLUE CHAIRS

At the United Nations, the EU faced serious issues of representation and recognition exactly for the reasons mentioned above, linked to the primacy of national sovereignty. When I arrived in New York in 2015, after four years in Washington, the EU had already successfully overcome some of the biggest institutional and administrative limitations to our operations at the UN. We had obtained the status of enhanced permanent observer, which entitled us basically to perform as a member but without the right to vote or to be elected (this was the domain of our member states) and with a few other, relatively minor constraints.

What remained to be done in New York was further to enhance our visibility, credibility and diplomatic clout. Elsewhere, inside UN entities based in other cities around the world, such as Vienna and particularly in Rome, where the EU as such is hardly recognised, a lot more was required, and still is, to enhance the EU's capacity to act in conformity with its ambitions.

As in the G8 or G7, we were also still somehow seen as an oddity within the UN community. My purpose was to make us feel and be perceived as more 'normal' and more 'central'. Two axes quickly became obvious priorities if we wanted the 'EUatUN' (as in our Twitter handle) to move up the ladder of recognition and influence: the Security Council and the secretary-general.

The Security Council – or 'the Council', as it is known in UN corridors – meets in a beautiful hall deep inside the UN headquarters, by the East River, in midtown Manhattan. Around an almost closed circle, elegant sky-blue chairs (not necessarily the most comfortable, though) provide seats for its fifteen members and a few occasional guests. Within the Council, there are two sorts of members: the permanent and the elected. The permanent ones are the USA, Russia, China, France and the UK, the so-called P5, allowed to veto any resolution. The ten elected members vary and stay in the Council for a mandate of two years, without veto power. They are voted by the General Assembly after arbitration among the geographic groupings of the UN membership.[12] Within the Council, the EU counted two members as part of the P5 and a variable number within the elected ones.

The dynamics of the candidatures to the Security Council are quite peculiar (and not always totally transparent). Seating in the Council is a major priority of national diplomacy, I would say almost an obsession, leading countries to deploy important financial resources and use different methods, starting long before the actual slot is available, to guarantee the votes of their fellow members. I always watched with great curiosity the creativity deployed to charm and convince, but also to trade off the required votes.

On the EU side, things were not always straightforward as to elections to the Council. This was in fact an area where I had to be extremely cautious, so as not to hurt national sensitivities. This was a *chasse gardée*, or private hunting ground, of the member states. Every EU member state, like any other country at the UN, wanted to get 'in' and the last thing they wanted to hear was that they would have to deviate from their Council-bound trajectory and make concessions for the sake of another member of the EU. This is maybe the only area where I never detected any openness or desire for ex-ante co-ordination in New York.[13]

More often than one should expect, this can create situations of direct competition between EU member states for a given slot. The most visible and potentially very harmful situation during my term in New York was the direct competition between the Netherlands and Italy in 2016 (of all years).

Both countries were candidates as representatives of the 'Western European and others' geographic group, but only one could get in. After five rounds of voting on 28 June, which I witnessed with consternation and even despair from the EU seats in the upper rows of the elegant general assembly hall, our two member states were tied at ninety-five votes each. One might say that both had conducted a great campaign, as they were capable of collecting a solid number of votes from the UN's membership, but neither reached the two-thirds majority required to be elected. We felt an impasse was impossible to overcome locally, following hectic attempts. The issue required the leaders to intervene.

My main concern was not the individual position of Italy or the Netherlands, as I had to be impartial. I was worried by the reputational damage of this highly visible competition between two members of the same EU that had, just the week before, been damaged by the results of the Brexit referendum. So 2016 was definitely not looking like a great year.

Then something remarkably positive happened: back in Brussels, where they were meeting in the European Council at the same time as New York voted, the Dutch and the Italian prime ministers agreed a Solomonic solution, relayed to their representatives in New York: they would share the two-year slot between them. It was a brilliant, reputation-saving move. This solution had been adopted many years ago, in 1960, when after fifty-two rounds of voting, Poland and Turkey also decided to split their term, but the idea had been lost in the memory of UN members. Everybody greeted this with enthusiasm as an innovative solution and a great show of maturity, except some of our lesser friends who would have loved to prolong this fratricidal display of EU internal competition. I made a point of saying, afterwards, that the solution found showed the high degree of convergence and solidarity among EU member states, although I would have preferred to avoid an excruciating five rounds of voting, exposing our lack of co-ordination.

Reflecting the selection system described above, EU geometry in the Security Council changed each year according to the results of elections. During my four years in New York, I was lucky enough to have a relatively favourable sequence of groups of EU countries elected to the Council, which facilitated my plan of organising their work in a more efficient way. At one point, altogether the EU members of the Council counted five, one-third of the overall composition.

We created an 'EU caucus' comprising the two permanent members and whichever member states were sitting as elected ones. I would invite them for regular ambassadorial lunches to discuss the Council's agenda and our priorities, and whenever the High Representative was in town (I served in New York under Federica Mogherini), she would invite the respective foreign ministers for lunch or dinner at my residence with the same purpose. This trickled down to our colleagues, created a spirit of co-operation inside the Council and resulted in real qualitative progress for EU co-ordination and visibility.

EU Security Council co-ordination came on top of another tool we used quite frequently: the possibility given to the EU ambassador to intervene in the Council proceedings as an invited speaker, alongside individual member states of the UN. I did this several times a year on different topics whenever we thought it necessary to express a common EU position. Iran was a mandatory topic for me and the Middle East peace process or anything related to it was the most complex one. The former reflected the EU's role as co-ordinator of the negotiations for a nuclear deal with Tehran – I would be asked on behalf of the HRVP to take stock of the process – and the latter illustrated how difficult it had become to rally our member states around common language on the Israel–Palestine issue.

All in all, in spite of all the difficulties and as a result of common efforts from the whole European family, the EU increasingly became a regular customer at the Council table, either through a physical presence or as a remote operator, impacting the individual, co-ordinated positions of our member states (data shows that, in the General Assembly of the UN, EU Member States vote consistently and overwhelmingly in unison, with the exception of some ethical/moral issues and a very few items of foreign policy and security).

THE SECRETARY-GENERAL: THREE IN ONE

The Secretary-General of the United Nations was my other target area. I presented my credentials to Ban Ki-Moon during the last segment of his mandate as secretary-general, in the autumn of 2015 (his term would come to an end a year later), but the UN system was already beginning to focus on the election of his successor. I had to do the same.

There was a good chance of having a European as the successor to Ban Ki-Moon, but it was far from a given. It could be accommodated within the informal geographic groups rotating principle, although Latin American and Caribbean candidates had some good arguments in their favour. If we had a good candidate, I thought we had a fair chance of getting the position and I was motivated by the challenge.

That being said, 'European' does not necessarily mean 'EU' and because of that I saw in the election cycle a double challenge: first, to have a European; and second, to make sure that that person was a citizen of one of our member states. Little did I know at the time that there could be a third, very attractive, additional challenge and opportunity: that the EU citizen would come from my home country, Portugal. I couldn't think then of a more appealing cherry on the cake. Or rather three in one.

António Guterres was confirmed as the new Secretary-General of the United Nations on October 2016, after a faultless journey including six consecutive successful straw polls since July. The long procedure was concluded by a unanimous endorsement of the Security Council. I could not have been happier with the result.

What a week it was! For the record, it was an EU double act: first, an EU citizen became the next secretary-general, as António Guterres brought together for the first time in many years all fifteen UN Security Council ambassadors in person to announce in front of the press pack their decision by acclamation; and second, when I and seven other EU ambassadors handed over our respective ratification documents and the UN reached the required minimum number of ratifications, it meant that it was the EU that formally triggered the entry into force of the Paris agreement on climate change, less than one year after Paris.

Ahead of Guterres's historic election as the first ever EU citizen to take that position,[14] I had had to engage with half a dozen candidates originating from EU member states and offer my support to all of them in full impartiality and equality of treatment. I provided them with platforms at EU ambassadors' meetings and offered whatever help they requested, although their main source of assistance was their own national permanent mission to the UN. At the end of the day, to the surprise of no one, I had trouble hiding how happy I was with Guterres's appointment. That evening, sipping port wine (of course) at my residence overlooking the UN building, I couldn't resist a smile at having a compatriot at the helm of the UN, of speaking Portuguese with the UN's secretary-general, just a year after my arrival in the job. As in Brussels, I would coexist in a major international organisation with a Portuguese national at the helm. I thought briefly of Luis de Camões' sixteenth-century epic poem, 'Os Lusíadas', celebrating Portuguese global endeavours.

When Guterres was confirmed, we were just a few weeks away from the election of the new President of the United States. That was indeed the only election talked about in the American media and on the streets of New York. Inside the UN, apart from the natural focus on the newly elected Guterres, many of us were wondering whom he would have as an interlocutor in the White House at the beginning of his mandate, in January 2017, and how relevant that would be for his role and for the UN.

I cannot speak for him, but it would surprise me if Guterres was not already in touch with Hillary Clinton's team. So was I, at my level, not only because she was our favoured candidate and I knew some people in her team from my time in Washington, but also because her election was the largely shared expectation of the UN universe. As described elsewhere in the book, our disappointment was immense the day after the 8 November 2016 election and I personally regretted that Guterres would have to start his mandate by engaging with a US president so distant from his own views about global governance.

Two parallel transitions started to dominate diplomatic conversations in New York as 2016 entered its last month: from Ban to Guterres, and from Obama to Trump. Everybody was wondering how the different personalities of the new tenants of the thirty-eighth floor and of the Oval Office would manage to build a constructive working relationship, and how their simultaneous arrival on the international scene would affect global governance. In fact, these two ongoing power transitions were part of a much wider and fast-changing landscape that would see the arrival of new political actors at the top of relevant countries around the world. Moreover, the emergence of new political leaders could lead to a shift in relations between them and their main counterparts, particularly in Russia and China, where the leadership was, however, not likely to change.

As soon as the confirmation of Guterres became relatively irreversible, I became the object of unusual attention. My fellow ambassadors wanted to be briefed about the person, the politician, trying to collect maximum input for their cables to capitals about the new strongman. My good friend and colleague Álvaro Mendonça e Moura, the very competent Portuguese ambassador and Permanent Representative, had even more calls and invitations to all sorts of events, as he had had a critical role in getting Guterres to the finish line. One of the first tasks I imposed on myself was to teach people to pronounce his name correctly. Not an easy task, though. The way we Portuguese speak our language does not make the life of foreigners easy, and in the case of the new secretary-general the 'es' at the end of his name was difficult to incorporate, as in fact it comes out as 'êsh'. There is also a similar family name in Spanish, Gutierrez, and the last thing I wanted was for the first ever Portuguese secretary-general's name to sound Spanish (with all due respect to our Spanish neighbours and friends).

The most linguistically capable ambassadors were able to absorb my teaching and correctly pronounce António Guterres, but some never did. Fair enough. What was really important is that we had from then on, and for the first time ever, an EU citizen, and a very capable one, at the top of the UN.

Like Barroso in his time in Brussels and the EU itself on many occasions in its long trajectory, Guterres would soon be confronted with tough challenges and would be called upon to swim against the tide. Fortunately, the Portuguese are historically used to navigating in rough waters.

7

And Now What? The EU, the West and the Divorce of Nations

As we enter the second quarter of the century, how can the world resist and reverse the trend towards a global divorce? What is the degree of danger and how should the global community act? What should we expect – and demand – from 'the West', from the United States, from the EU and the UK, from China and Russia and from 'the South'? I refuse to fall into despair: I believe we are not condemned to fragmentation and confrontation. In the next twenty-five years we should be able to do better than in the first quarter. But for that to happen, the world needs to have a serious conversation.

A CLEAR AND PRESENT DANGER

The end of the 'end of history' period, from 9/11 to the Russian invasion of Ukraine and beyond, has triggered new global tensions and a fierce debate between systems of values and norms. It is no longer 'capitalism versus communism', no longer the dispute between the 'big ideologies' of the past century. The twenty-first century confronts us with a new paradigm.

One might be tempted to say that there is a new divide between representative liberal democracies on one side, and plainly authoritarian and outright dictatorial regimes on the other, with, in between, illiberal half-democracies playing a double game. This is not, however, the sole and maybe even not the most relevant dividing line, as today's picture of international relations is more complex than that.

Regardless of how we classify their formal political systems, the fact is that virtually all relevant countries have adopted capitalism as their economic operating system, even if they apply it in diverse formats. They are all part of a globalised economy and benefit, at different degrees of intensity, from sophisticated networks of interconnection and interdependence, and from trade and technological exchanges. However, they are not aligned in their views of how nations and the world should be governed. They are, in fact, much less aligned than they were at the beginning of the century.

For many countries, for instance, the values and rules of global governance, which have been collectively agreed in the past, should no longer in any way subvert the primacy of national sovereignty as interpreted by national authorities, regardless of how they gained power and exercise it. National interests increasingly trump international law and values-based principles. The most obvious case in point is the concept of human rights. Its universal nature – an indispensable pillar of the UN system for us in the West – is being challenged head on by 'national' interpretations, and its predominance is being relegated to lower levels of priority, to the benefit of the non-values-based concept of 'development rights'.

The global order as we knew it is under growing existential stress and multilateral governance is being tested to the limit.

In spite of some remarkable successes in 2015 on climate action, SDGs and Iranian nuclear proliferation, or, more recently, the High Seas biodiversity protection treaty (Biodiversity Beyond National Jurisdictions), and despite honest steps towards internal reform of the UN taken by its secretary-general, the sad fact is that the multilateral system is today paralysed at its very top as a result of violations of the UN Charter by some of its main stakeholders and the lack of commitment to uphold its principles by many others.

Moreover, the UN runs the serious risk of being engulfed by the rising waters of great-power rivalry and sidelined by the loss of trust among those who depend on it for their survival. The UN's impotence as a guarantor of peace and security will generate additional frustration, which will further dent its credibility and usefulness in a range of other roles it plays, from conflict prevention to humanitarian action, from the protection of women and children to the support of minorities and victims. A vicious circle of multilateralist decline is looming.

Is it too far reaching to conceive that in the future, mirroring similar behaviour by permanent Council members, sufficiently self-confident emerging powers will simply choose systematically to ignore, if not reject, Security Council resolutions that threaten their national interests? Or organise collective resistance and deploy efforts to subvert and replace the UN framework by an alternative one? This could well determine the fall of the multilateral system as we know it, like a collapsing 'house of cards'.

Antonio Patriota, the Brazilian Ambassador to London and former foreign minister under President Lula da Silva, who knows the multilateral system well, believes that 'it may be near a tipping point' and 'for it to remain relevant and operative, a credible reform process will be necessary'.[1] Having in mind Barbara Tuchman's book *The March of Folly*, a Pulitzer prize-winning essay about war from Troy to Vietnam, Patriota calls for 'a march of reason'. In the same vein, he rejects any accusation that Brazilian President Lula is leaning towards China and away from the USA. 'We don't want to replace American unilateralism by Chinese unilateralism. We want co-operative multipolarity. We need to manage multipolarity to avoid unilateralism.'

If we consider that the UN is facing an existential crisis, in all honesty, what is today's alternative to it? If we want to avoid a state of near anarchy in global governance, we should think twice about the alternatives to our inheritance from the past century. Before we throw the baby out with the bathwater, we should ask a very simple question: if we had to create the UN again, would we be able to do it today? Or would we be able to build something better?

This existential doubt triggers a set of urgent questions that the international community needs to put on the table. First, are the initial shapers of the international governance system – to be clear, those who won the Second World War – ready and willing to redesign the system they put together, even if it means a loss of relative power and influence? Are they willing to reform the Security Council or the Bretton Woods institutions better to reflect the new global reality? Or will any of them (the USA?) prefer to use their power and influence unilaterally, to the detriment of collective efforts? On the other hand, are initial shapers-turned-challengers like China and Russia and a few rising middle powers ready to assume their responsibilities fully as co-guarantors of global governance, on the basis of the commonly agreed set of principles, values and norms? Are they ready to swear by them and help manage them, or do they want to reform them totally? Do they feel strong and united enough to build a separate, de-coupled system of governance? If so, would they really benefit from that?

After four years as Permanent Representative of the EU at the United Nations, my conclusion was clear: everyone in the corridors of the UN, in New York, or Geneva, says they are in favour of multilateralism, but they do not all necessarily mean the same. Hardly anyone dares to oppose it, but the reality is that among those who claim to defend multilateralism we see fundamentally different concepts. Some of the major stakeholders and most vocal supporters of multilateralism seem, in fact, less keen on preserving the essence of it than on arranging the building blocks of their own alternative version of multilateralism. One that preserves their narrower vision of the scope and intensity of international norms and procedures, and the universal nature of the values that uphold them, offering variable ways of safeguarding the primacy of national sovereignty and national interests as interpreted by those in power at a given moment.

Let's take some distance to understand better where we stand today: current divisions reflect a recent profound reconfiguration of power relations and of what some have called the revenge of geography and history. On balance and with hindsight, we may realise that the first quarter of the new century has indeed failed to deliver on the twentieth century's romantic expectations about how the world should evolve.

After an initial surge of interventionism, the 'unipolar hegemon' lost relative weight and willingness to patrol, the 'new kid on the block' grew rapidly, abandoned its shyness and became more assertive, and the 'eastern bear' went too far – and recklessly – in its reconquering stride.

For its part, the 'old continent' realised that economic power is only half of what its nations need to be able to determine their own destiny. Having acquired a continental dimension and deepened its political relevance, the EU, the world's most sophisticated expression of regional globalisation and economic and political integration among nations, lost one of its most prominent members and is now confronted with the triple challenge of security, enlargement and reform, not to mention competitiveness and prosperity.

The EU's only 'runaway member' is struggling to find a new balance, having growing doubts about the wisdom of Brexit, whose implementers are leaving politics ingloriously and whose initiators are returning to front-line politics, all unapologetically refusing any degree of responsibility for what they generated.

The self-titled 'Global South' countries are mostly engaged in hedging their bets between the two new axes, refusing to align too soon or too closely with either of them in the hope of getting the best deal possible. Some middle powers are realising their bargaining potential and see the chance of gaining specific weight in the new balance of power, refusing all sorts of unilateralism, whether American or Chinese. We are promised a dynamic evolution of these relationships in the years to come.

Democracy is in retreat worldwide and authoritarian models – and strongmen – are exerting a fascination among developing countries and even within developed ones. A gap is widening among different regions of the world, reflecting distinct concepts of global order and values, and contrary to our expectations and hopes, Western views are not winning the debate. Samuel Huntington's concept of a 'clash of civilisations', initially presented in 1992 as a response to his former student Francis Fukuyama's *End of History*, was derided by many when published as a book.[2] However, it has recently resurfaced in some debates because of the growing relevance of cultural and religious differences in international relations.

And then there is the spectre of war, impossible to ignore as we witness not only the current conflicts but what could be triggered by the looming arms race around new technologies (artificial intelligence, robotics and space-based weaponry, to name just a few areas of potential groundbreaking military developments).

Domestically, populist leaders of right and left inclinations are either forcing mainstream politicians to change their discourse or gradually imposing their own. The resulting polarisation is further feeding their agenda, in which nationalism and protectionism are gaining an advantage over the previously assumed model of international openness and co-operation. Today, among nations, the hopes of a consensually managed and progressively implemented new multipolarity are quickly vanishing. The twentieth century's laboriously managed 'marriage of nations' is now on the brink of collapse.

The 'end of history' was a temporary illusion. The end has ended. A global Age of Divorce is looming, with potentially disastrous consequences: there is a clear and present danger.

THE EU'S 'BERMUDA TRIANGLES'

In normal circumstances, volatile and disrupted international contexts are both a challenge and an opportunity for a political construction like the EU. They represent a challenge because it is hard for a union of countries, founded on the pillars of voluntarily shared sovereignty, common values and principles, and sincere co-operation, enshrined in a solid legal framework, to accommodate the rise of nationalism and hard geopolitics within and beyond its borders. They represent an opportunity because the EU's successful model of 'regional multilateralism' can inspire a way forward for the international community and provide Europeans with the opportunity to influence the course of events.

We are not, however, living in 'normal circumstances', either in the wider world or in the EU. At the dawn of the second quarter of this century, the EU is facing a crossroads that many are tempted to classify as 'existential'.

This is not the first time such a term has been used to qualify a particular EU historical context. During my career I have lived through several such moments, of which the most relevant were the 'euro-sclerosis' of the 1970s and '80s, the rejection of a European Constitution in 2005, the Great Recession and the sovereign debt crisis of 2008–12. Defeating the worst prognosis, the EU has always managed to navigate successfully through these dire straits. The question today is simple, even if the answer is undoubtedly complex: will it be different this time?

What distinguishes the current crossroads for the EU, apart from the complex global challenges that necessarily impact it and that we have covered above, is the magnitude and interaction of several simultaneous factors and the fact that, either individually or in combination, they might have dramatic consequences. If we group them into interrelated sets of issues and problems, we find a number of triangulations that will ultimately determine the EU's future trajectory. The risk this time for the EU is that if they are not handled properly, they have the potential to sink the boat. They could become the EU's 'Bermuda triangles'.[3]

I can think of five critical 'triangles' and have identified a particular area of tension at each of their fifteen vertices.

The EU's Five 'Bermuda Triangles'

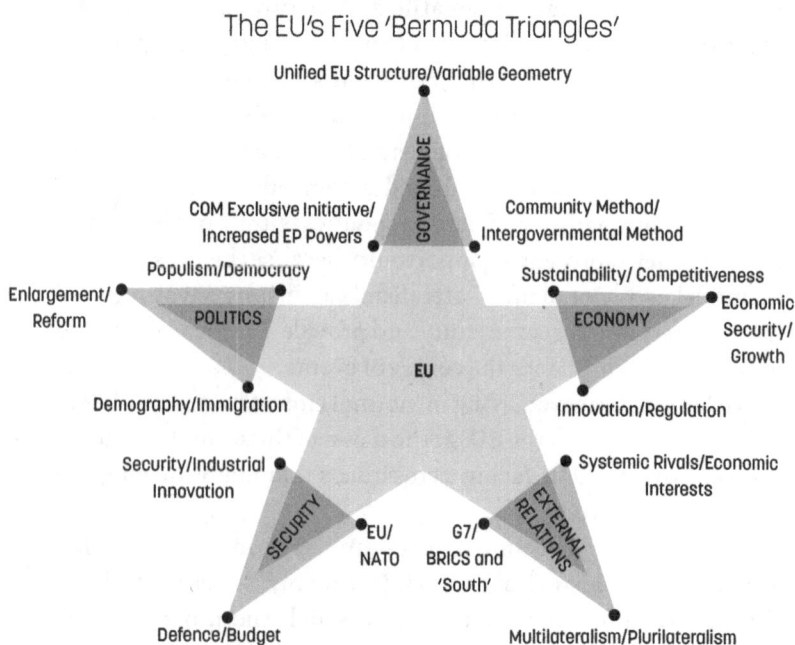

Unified EU Structure/Variable Geometry

GOVERNANCE

COM Exclusive Initiative/
Increased EP Powers

Community Method/
Intergovernmental Method

Populism/Democracy

Enlargement/
Reform

Sustainability/ Competitiveness

Economic
Security/
Growth

POLITICS

ECONOMY

EU

Demography/Immigration

Innovation/Regulation

Security/Industrial
Innovation

Systemic Rivals/Economic
Interests

SECURITY

EXTERNAL
RELATIONS

EU/
NATO

G7/
BRICS and
'South'

Defence/Budget

Multilateralism/Plurilateralism

Politics

Starting with the politics triangle, the points of tension at its vertices would be: democracy versus populism, demography versus immigration, and enlargement versus reform.

The fallout of the European Parliament elections of June 2024 – including what they revealed about the political landscape in EU member states and what they eventually triggered as domestic political consequences in some of them, and particularly in France – confirmed the complex challenges facing representative democracy in times of populism and insecurity. The 'centre' was able to hold, only just, and extreme political forces, particularly on the right, made considerable progress, but overall slightly less than feared. More important than the actual EU-wide numbers, what really matters are the underlying trends and tensions in European societies, in each of the EU countries and beyond.

Domestically, a 'demographic winter' and the resistance by locals to lower pay and lower-quality jobs became a pull factor for labour immigration, which when not accompanied by effective integration policies resulted in fertile ground for extreme parties. War in Ukraine, with its impact on the cost of living, and the feeling of insecurity it added to the perception of uncertainty and impotence, affected national incumbents and increased challengers' clout.

At the EU level, solidarity with Ukraine and resistance to Russian aggression – and the potential threat to its own security and interests – led to a relaunch of enlargement proposals and questions about absorption capacity and inherent costs. This in turn reinforced the call for institutional reform and potential treaty changes, with associated political concerns.

This 'politics' triangle will require in the coming years a very careful balancing. The 'Bermuda' risk is a major surge in anti-EU feelings and an associated deterioration in the political consensus around the way forward for the EU.

Economy

The economy triangle raises the issues of economic security versus growth, sustainability versus competitiveness and innovation versus regulation as the vertices' points of tension.

Prolonging and building on the points made in the previous paragraphs, the recent pandemic and the growing economic and political assertiveness of China, combined with increased tension between the USA and China and a flare of nationalist protectionism in America, have made the EU more aware and sometimes quite focused on the links between economy and security. How are we to continue to focus on trade and external exchanges of all kinds as a source of economic growth and at the same time guarantee the necessary security of supply and strategic autonomy of our economies?

As if this equation were not complex enough, tensions around the implementation of the Net Zero agenda and its impact on certain economic sectors (such as agriculture) and on consumers (costs are immediate, benefits are longer term) have translated into pressure to slow the rate of progress and have introduced political uncertainty about the way forward to ensure green economic competitiveness.

Regarding another source of growth – technology – a degree of anxiety has grown, as Europe has trouble in competing with the USA and China, while having to cope with their tech giants in its own single market. Regulation, competition policy and sectorial legislation are being used to ensure fair market conditions, but there are limits to their capacity to address what is at heart a lack of innovation competitiveness, a gap that requires urgent action.

Governance

The governance triangle has at its vertices the community method versus the intergovernmental method, a unified EU structure versus variable geometry, and exclusive Commission initiative versus increased powers for the European Parliament.

Tensions between Union and intergovernmental methods are an integral part of the EU's DNA and they will continue to be. It has always been a question of balance, historically more favourable to the former. In times of insecurity and war, and in the face of major external challenges, the tendency is to reinforce the latter, even if rationally the opposite should happen.

Prospects of a new wave of enlargement raise, again, the issue of the EU's architecture, and ideas around concentric circles, variable geometry and multiple speeds come back to the floor. The debate is still in its early stages and the resistance to treaty changes is considerable for political reasons, as some countries are obliged to hold referenda with no guarantee of success. What is clear is that further enlargements, particularly to include Ukraine, will raise very serious issues of a budgetary, institutional and policy nature.

Last but not least, a somewhat contradictory trend will have to be managed as the European Parliament will, as in the past, seek to strengthen its inter-institutional position, this time by insisting on acquiring its own right of initiative, up to now an exclusive Commission prerogative.

Security

The security triangle may include the following vertices: defence capabilities versus budget, security versus industrial innovation, and the EU versus NATO.

The most immediate point of tension, once the need for further progress on security is agreed, will concern the increase in financial means needed to boost EU member states' defence capabilities. The starting point must be the convergence of what I would call the Putin and Trump factors or the combined threats of Russian aggressiveness and American disengagement.

Security in Europe cannot be separated from its industrial dimension. It requires exploiting the full potential of the single market in defence to reduce costs and increase effectiveness, efficiency and co-operation, and should represent a stimulus to technological innovation with obvious collateral civilian advantages.

With twenty-three out of twenty-seven EU member states now also belonging to NATO, there is an obvious avenue for co-operation and synergy between the two entities. This should be pursued while respecting respective idiosyncrasies and aiming at complementarity and cross-fertilisation, without ignoring some potentially difficult issues of interaction between the two organisations, specifically those linked to strained relations among members (for instance, between Greece/Cyprus and Turkey) and to the status of non-NATO EU members (Austria, Cyprus, Ireland and Malta).

External relations

The external relations triangle would give rise to the following points of tension: systemic rivals versus economic interests, multilateralism versus plurilateralism, and the G7 versus BRICS and the 'South'.

Here, the relationships with China and Russia are obviously of critical importance and permeate all three tension points. Bilateral and multilateral dimensions should come together in the pursuit of balanced and responsible terms of engagement. Regarding the concept of BRICS, which brings together both systemic rivals and more like-minded countries, the central issue is whether what unites them – which is not very much – is capable of surviving what divides them – which is a lot, but we should also measure the extent to which a China-led BRICS might affect the G20's usefulness. On Russia, everything will depend on the outcome of the war in Ukraine, which has totally hijacked the relationship. Things could get worse before, hopefully, they get better in the relationship with Moscow and we will at last be able to agree jointly on the terms of peaceful coexistence on our common continent. For the time being, the EU's focus has to be on protecting Ukraine's territorial sovereignty and integrating it further into the European–Atlantic space, which would involve making sure the USA is fully on the same wavelength.

The EU is and must continue to be the main supporter and defender of multilateralism, but it needs to be creative and flexible in contributing to the evolution of multilateralism as the main pillar of international relations, while at the same time showing a willingness to engage in bilateral, minilateral or plurilateral forms of co-operation.* The USA is a changing reality, a moving target, but one that remains essential and even existential for the EU's security and prosperity. It is unavoidable to widen and deepen our relationship, to avoid de-coupling of any kind, but also to be firm in the defence of our interests. Friends often require more investment than adversaries if we want to preserve the quality of the relationship, and that is certainly the case with the USA.

Finally, the EU must reject the rigid and artificial concept of 'Global South' and rather identify in the developing world different constellations of partners with whom to engage in a sincere and open dialogue, in the pursuit of common interests and agendas, while deploying mutual respect.

This brief and non-exhaustive listing of the challenges and potential pitfalls with which the EU is and will be confronted reveals the magnitude of the tasks facing this group of countries in the second quarter of the century. My hope, I would even say my conviction, is that the member states of the Union will understand that they have a better chance of overcoming the challenges and avoiding the 'Bermuda' pitfalls if they work together, not separately. Equally, I believe they will understand that the Union cannot survive as an island of peace and prosperity in an ocean of conflicts and poverty, and that consequently the EU must continue to be a beacon of international co-operation and solidarity, and become an even stronger and more effective global actor.

THE WEST AND THE NEW DISORDER

Having to deal with extreme complexity is not exclusive to the EU, obviously. The present global context is so volatile and challenging

---

* In the face of the crisis of multilateralism, more creative ways of organising co-operation among countries are flourishing, on the basis of specific common interests or agendas. In this context, minilateral is a minimalist concept and plurilateral encompasses a greater number of countries, short of a multilateral dimension.

that it leads many to evoke examples of the past and to create parallels with previous events in order to explain it. This is a risky approach. We should rather focus on what is distinctive about the present global situation if we want to address its consequences.

It is, for instance, wrong and misleading to talk about a new Cold War (between the USA and China) and quite unhelpful to refer to the likelihood of a Third World War. Both concepts, apart from being based on false similarities, can easily become dangerous self-fulfilling prophecies. We should reject the laziness of trying to find past events to serve as models of behaviour and instead try harder to be creative.

In the case of the Cold War, I detect a certain degree of nostalgia for a context we used to manage and that provided a certain degree of predictability, a black and white world with few shades of grey, to which some seem to attach an aura of glamour. The reality is quite different: first, there is little glamour, I believe, in living under the permanent threat of mutual annihilation and the proliferation of regional proxy wars; and secondly, not much in today's relationship between the USA and China bears comparison with the one between Americans and Russians at the height of the Cold War. Pursuing this parallel road would not lead us to the right conclusions and could be highly risky because, as the former American diplomat and Jean Monnet's assistant George W. Ball once said, 'nostalgia is a seductive liar'.[4]

As a former journalist and diplomat and the holder of a history degree, I can assert that in this particular field of historical comparisons, historians are indeed more credible than journalists and diplomats. They recognise the value of critical distance and the fact that history seldom – or never – repeats itself.

That is one of the reasons why, for lack of a better formula, I prefer 'divorce' as a driving concept for what we need to worry about and prevent. And as in any divorce, most of the time the real victims are the children. The central questions we should ask ourselves are: What can we do to stop this separation trajectory and prevent a deeper divorce? How can we best safeguard its victims, its 'children' – the peoples of the world, aspiring to peace, security and prosperity, and the planet itself, risking climate and environmental disaster – or in any case limit its negative consequences for them? And in doing all this, how can we best defend our values, protect our interests and promote an international order that caters for both?

I approach the issue from an assumed Western-centric and European–Atlantic perspective. These are my roots and this is where I have been observing the world from. This is the part of the world that best practises and protects the values I stand for. The question tormenting me is thus: how can the West handle the new disorder?

My preliminary consideration is that we in the West must have clear-sighted awareness of our own values and interests as democrats, believers in the universality of human rights, guardians of individual freedoms and of the primacy of law, supporters of open economies and open societies, and recognise that these values and these interests are being seriously challenged.

With this in mind, and considering that the extreme complexity briefly described in this book demands extreme modesty when proposing solutions, here is my personal fourteen-point task list for the Western world:

1.   Don't de-couple. Either between the USA and China or between the EU and China – or between the USA and the EU – there has been a lot of talk recently about de-coupling. We must avoid it. Even if the concept remains vague in its formulation, we need to be cautious and realistic about it. And push it back because, as Martin Wolf put it, 'there is no painless way of de-coupling'.

Why? Because:

• The degree of interconnection and interdependence accumulated in the recent decades of deep globalisation is of such magnitude that any serious de-coupling would have huge costs for all sides, beginning with China and including the USA and certainly the EU and the developing world. Decoupling would hurt our competitiveness, would close markets for countries whose growth is export-driven, would reduce efficiency, would slow global growth and stimulate inflation, and would not create more jobs – or, for that matter, more security.

• By diminishing interconnection, interdependence and even personal interaction, we would enhance the chances of increasing global tensions, which would negatively affect our countries. De-coupling would promote divorce, not prevent it. In an upward scale of dangerousness, de-risking is better than de-coupling and de-coupling is better than divorce. But we should be aware that de-coupling risks exponentially increasing the likelihood of divorce, and de-risking needs to be well managed so as not to lead to de-coupling.

• As regards the EU, the last thing Europeans want is to be faced with a binary option: to choose between the USA and China. The choice would be simultaneously very obvious (in favour of the USA, I hope) but very costly economically because of the relevance of our economic links with China.

• The 'last but one' thing Europeans want is to see our adversaries cashing in on a transatlantic de-coupling as a side effect of the prospect of another, bigger de-coupling, or as a protectionist anticipation of it. This would be a self-inflicted wound of major proportions.

2. <u>Don't be complacent.</u> The alternative to divorce – or to de-coupling – is not inaction. We cannot afford to sit idly by, watching China, Russia or Iran challenge our values, principles and interests, while actively seducing a group of 'new non-aligned' countries that they expect would objectively support their agenda. We should not allow ourselves to be paralysed by fear or by the complexity of the task. We cannot afford to allow the world to sleepwalk towards the cliff edge.

3. <u>Ask the right questions.</u> A rational and pragmatic approach to life and politics implies asking the right questions and avoiding the wrong ones, which can seriously mislead us in our choice of options.

One of the wrong questions being asked too often today is whether we want China to win or to fail, to become stronger or weaker. In fact, in all honesty, a failed or a weaker China might entail as profound consequences for our countries and the world as a stronger China. In any case, it is not in our capacity, even if we wanted it, to prevent China from fulfilling its immense potential. So, the right question to ask is: how do we manage the rise of China? In other words: how do we manage the 'relative rise' of China and the simultaneous 'relative decline' of the USA? And if, in doing so, we are capable of avoiding Professor Graham Allison's 'Thucydides trap' that whenever a rising power threatens to displace a ruling one, a violent clash is likely to occur, so much the better.[5]

4. <u>Raise our levels of self-confidence.</u> Europeans and Americans, and all those who support liberal democracies, in spite of their weaknesses, should believe in the beauty of our system of values and principles, in the capacity of open societies, open economies and open markets to find the most efficient and sustainable solutions, and to move forward in an inclusive and balanced way. And we should spell it out more often. We cannot be strong abroad if we are not confident at home.

5. <u>Be less naive and more realistic and 'realist'.</u> We should be more realistic than we have often been, particularly in the EU, regarding the rest of the world. Not all actors performing on the global stage are as loyal as we believe we are to the original 'script'. Some are twisting the 'director's guidance', even changing the lines to their convenience. We should do more to call them to their responsibilities. Those who reach the 'high table', to invoke my recent experiences in the magnificent dining halls of the University of Cambridge, need to behave accordingly. It is not enough to claim cynically one's adherence to multilateralism, in the abstract, and then systematically to violate its principles and its rules on a daily basis. At the same time, the West cannot afford to be exclusively principled in its external relationships – a balanced dose of foreign policy 'realism' needs to be factored in.

6. <u>Be less arrogant and more pragmatic and tolerant.</u> We should be more pragmatic in the pursuit of our goals, particularly with developing countries belonging to different cultural contexts, if we want to win them back to our cause. Some of my most heated discussions at the UN were about human rights and ethical issues, particularly with ambassadors from developing nations who complained about our insensitivity and our lack of self-criticism. One told me:

> Some Western countries have only recently promoted legislation on ethical issues which they had refused for many centuries and now they want to impose on us, developing countries, to introduce the same fundamental changes after just a few decades of transition from tribal structures to organised states. That's not fair.

We need a convincing, non-patronising answer to arguments like this, without abandoning our principles and values.

7. <u>Use our comparative advantage toolbox.</u> We should draw on our immense inventiveness and entrepreneurship, on our policy, financial, technological and regulatory expertise and sophistication – and on our power. The borders between domestic and foreign policies are today totally blurred, as discussed previously. We need across-the-board, coherent responses, combining different tools. Even if one should not underestimate the fact that hard defensive capabilities are still the ultimate instrument of power projection, security today is as much about economic and cyber security as it is about military means, let alone conventional armies. Policy areas interact and cross-fertilise – or cross-undermine – and none is immune from geostrategic and geo-economic considerations. We should not be afraid of being transactional and using the power tools at our disposal.

8. <u>Remain careful to prevent pernicious downsides.</u> While using the full toolbox, we should be attentive to collateral damage.

Trade is a good example of a previously largely technocratic tool that became a highly sensitive political domain. It has lost its innocence. Governments today look at trade increasingly through the angle of security, or strategic autonomy and sovereignty if you prefer. A high risk of protectionism is looming, as countries move increasingly towards restrictions on imports and exports. Both could lead to the closing of markets. This is worrying for economies like those of the EU and its allies, counting on free trade and free markets for their sustained growth. We should rather look at more sustainable alternatives. We should concentrate on competition in the markets, not on competition at the borders.

A three-track approach could be envisaged: first, to combine defensive instruments, which are totally legitimate and required, with a focus on raising our own productivity and competitiveness (for instance, in the case of the EU, by completing its single market, achieving a Capital Markets and Savings Union and, among other areas, liberating 'fin-tech' and 'blockchain' potential); second, to leverage our capacity to have emerging countries create more jobs in our societies, through investment, and to destroy fewer jobs, by managing their exports of cheaper products produced in their home countries, often thanks to state support and with disregard of human rights; and finally, to make sure market access and market conditions guarantee reciprocity. The right balance is needed to avoid negative consequences for our economies.

9. <u>Prioritise technological leadership.</u> Today more than ever, technology is, together with trade, where geo-economics meets geostrategy, where markets meet politics. Technology is power. What is already happening or about to happen at the forefront of technological developments is enormously powerful and absolutely fascinating, even if it is not without serious concerns. New developments (in AI, quantum computing, 3D printing and biotechnology) will have an immense impact on our industrial base, maybe more than previous waves of tech revolution. This is a new frontier. If it is combined with a balanced, non-protectionist but also non-naive, industrial policy – and sound regulation,

particularly of AI – technology could potentially offset some of the negative consequences for our competitiveness of onshoring and de-risking, and allow for an ambitious rebuilding of our industrial and manufacturing strengths. Think of us being able to produce efficiently in relatively poor areas of our countries the goods that were previously assembled in China or India, with the benefit of technology and the comfort and security of our own consumer and social protection systems. And while still being competitive.

Last but not least, our oceans provide a vast opportunity for a climate-friendly source of sustainable economic growth and 'blue-bio' technological advancement.

10. Focus on regulatory co-operation among allies and friends. We should aim to align our regulatory tools and frameworks in order to create enough critical mass to counter our competitors' advantage, instead of being obsessed with regulatory competition among Western economies. Why not have a solid triangular regulatory dialogue and co-operation among the EU, the USA and the UK? And if it works, it could well be expanded to all G7 members and the like-minded. Perhaps we could create a 'G7 effect', prolonging and enhancing the 'Brussels effect'?[6]

11. Be better organised and more focused. Building on EU and NATO, which should remain pillars of political and economic integration in Europe and of security and defence co-operation in the Atlantic area and beyond. There is no doubt in my mind that the G7 is indispensable as a representation of the interests of 'the West' and would benefit from further strengthening of its capabilities. But the G7 is not enough. The body itself understood this long ago and regularly extends invitations to other like-minded countries for thematic exchanges. That outreach still has an untapped potential that needs to be explored in implementing the agenda outlined above. Having variable G7+ formats and variable agendas with different parts of the world (think of democratic countries in Latin America and Indo-Pacific, for instance), focusing on different issues of common interest, is the way forward. The

G20 should remain as a forum of collective dialogue and action where we can rally also the non-like-minded. Proactive presence and investment in a reformed UN system should continue to be a priority, even if taken forward in a more focused way.

12. <u>Have an open and effective interaction with the developing world.</u> We need to interact effectively with countries in Africa and beyond if we want to project our influence globally, as we should. The starting point should be that developing countries are being courted by others, that they feel both tempted to accept seductive offers and sceptical about what lies behind them and what that implies for their future autonomy. We should do our best to overcome the main constraint in our relationship – the weight of our common history and the resentment linked to it – by proposing joint initiatives to reform global governance and to address financial imbalances (being aware of the mounting debt timebomb), in order better to reflect their specific interests and liberate their growth and environmental potential. A constructive, open, non-paternalistic approach, calling for a less defensive and accusatory response from our interlocutors, while reminding them of the continuous need for better national governance, coupled with a meaningful offer of a debt deal, could be the launching pad for a frank and transparent dialogue.

13. <u>Start building a new Cold Peace …</u> All of the 'to-do list' above reflects the potential of the 'old world' assets and the magnitude of the challenges we are facing. But it also reveals the distinctive features of today's context, very different from the one prevailing during the Cold War era. As I have said, we should stop talking about a new Cold War but rather start building a new Cold Peace – rational, less ideological and sufficiently transactional and co-operative, with each actor assuming its part of collective responsibility.

14. <u>… But keep a certain degree of strategic ambiguity.</u> There is, however, one concession we should make to the Cold War comparison. As we try to manage the various stages of the deterioration of global

relationships and build solid foundations for the future, we should also remind ourselves of some of the useful features of the 'good old' Cold War. And one of them is a certain degree of strategic ambiguity. We don't need always to seek a black and white characterisation of situations or positions. Diplomacy must be about clarity when clarity is absolutely necessary, but it often has to be about ambiguity – or at least some degree of fogginess – if it can help us avoid worst-case scenarios of confrontation. Don't break it if you can't fix it. Going back to the source of my analogy in this book, ambiguity and compromise is often the solution for a marriage in crisis ...

WE WILL ALWAYS HAVE GLORIA

As we conclude this journey into the divorce of nations, we must honestly admit that it is not irrational, in 2025, to be pessimistic about the future of our planet and the way we govern it.

As underlined above, the global community could potentially be faced with:

- The deepening of cleavages between two main camps entrenched in their respective systems of values and co-operation, or even a more anarchic and potentially ungovernable fragmentation, including with serious tension within each camp.
- The disruption – and even actual rupture – of global economic, trade and financial flows and supply chains.
- The collapse of multilateral institutions and mechanisms of concertation and dialogue.
- And, in the worst-case scenario, an outright great-power confrontation and/or a multitude of regional conflicts.

My realistic assumption, if the context does not fundamentally change, is the deepening of a 'divorce of nations' among the global community and the widening of the gap in our own national communities, a sort of 'divorce within nations'.

My genuine concern is that even if an open confrontation between great powers or opposing camps is avoided in the short and medium term, the escalation of the current climate would be enough to lead the international community into a period of non-cooperation from which it would be increasingly difficult to extract itself. This could then create the bedrock for an open conflict.

However, even in dire times such as ours, hope and belief in humankind should drive us. Not pessimism.

I sincerely hope and believe that the international community – and particularly its main players and all those who cherish the preservation of peace and the conditions of global progress we have enjoyed in recent decades – will be capable of repairing the damage already done and reassessing the terms of engagement among nations.

I remain convinced that people of good will, sensible and moderate politicians and opinion leaders alike, in different corners of the world, can still avoid a worst-case scenario and learn from past historical evidence of the consequences of sleepwalking, complacency, self-centred power play or even delusion. I still hope this young century can evolve into a mature adult, as most teenagers do. An adult with a cause and no longer a rebel without one.

Back in the 1970s, in her iconic disco song about finding personal strength after a devastating break-up, Gloria Gaynor cried out loud: 'I will survive!' And so did many of us, teenagers or young adults as old as this new century, dancing to her hit.

I believe that, contrary to Gloria's break-up, but inspired by her message, we will salvage the marriage of nations and avoid divorce. However, for that to happen, as with dysfunctional couples, the world needs to have a serious conversation. How and where that will happen remains to be seen, but if in the process we ever lose hope or get discouraged, we will always have Gloria to motivate us to try again, harder.

Afterword

The 'Grand Finale'

If the first quarter of this century were an opera, it could not have hoped for a more impactful 'grand finale' than the one Putin and Trump have been providing.

In a matter of a few days between October and November 2024 and then in mid-January 2025, apart from definitely confirming that there are no calendar coincidences, a string of events fully vindicated this book's narrative and the trends it describes: from 9/11 to war in Europe, from the Great Recession to a global pandemic, from globalisation to populism, from order to disorder, from Obama and Biden to Trump, from Putin to ... Putin.

In Kazan, the capital of Tatarstan, in October, the leader of the Russian Federation gathered forty national leaders representing more than half of the world's population to prove to the West that it had not been capable of isolating his country after he unlawfully invaded and declared war on Ukraine.

In the Kursk region, a thousand kilometres west of Kazan, North Korean soldiers were being deployed on the battlefield to help Russians fight the Ukrainian army, adding boots on the ground to Chinese and Iranian military supplies and technological support. A new axis – the CRINKs – was born and, with it, a potential globalisation of the conflict.

In Mar-a-Lago, Florida, in early November, Donald Trump rejoiced at the support of more than half of the American voters for a populist and protectionist agenda that guaranteed his return to the White House with full control of Congress and a loyal conservative majority in the Supreme Court. The greatest comeback in modern US politics had just materialised, but its impact will resonate well beyond the country's borders. His second inauguration speech on 20 January, and the flurry of executive actions he signed a few hours after taking office, left no doubts that Trump's re-election will affect America's traditional allies and disrupt the international liberal order. Trump will continue to change the United States and seduce many around the world receptive to the appeal of strongmen.

At the dawn of 2025, as the century prepares to wrap up its first quarter, the divorce among and within nations is less and less a distant threat.

TRUMP'S 'BLOWOUT'

Donald Trump embodies the most extraordinary political and electoral phenomenon of this century, so far. By winning back power after a first successful attempt and a second failed one, building this time on an even more divisive, aggressive rhetoric, Trump has set new (low) standards of decency in politics. Now with almost unchallenged power, his resurgence has consolidated a global populist trend.

He left his opponent and the whole Washington establishment, including traditional media and pollsters, wondering how and why the American people could have elected a candidate who had been convicted of crimes and labelled by many as misogynistic, racist and even fascist. Instead of correcting the 'mistake' of 2016, they concluded, voters had 'doubled down' on Trumpism.

The astonishment grew when it became clear that Trump had penetrated fringes of the electorate that traditionally supported the Democrats, like Hispanic and African American voters – not to mention white blue-collar males who had abandoned the Democratic Party some elections ago and had only temporarily been brought back by Biden in 2020. Many were shocked when data revealed that, in several states, via separate votes, women had made a distinction between protecting abortion rights and supporting a candidate who was not known to be a champion of those rights, but who was seen as better than his opponent at fixing the economy and controlling immigration.

The summer of 2024 had not prepared Democrats and commentators in the US and around the world for this autumnal outcome, hence the surprise of many (contrary to 2016, this time my prediction had always been that Trump would win). President Biden's 7 July 'debate debacle' had opened the door for his Vice President's nomination as the Democratic Party candidate for the White House. Kamala Harris seized the opportunity and turned the table two months later, crushing Donald Trump in their only pre-election debate, surprising many as she resurrected her former prosecutor instincts and adopted a more centrist discourse.

As summer ended, and with President Biden kept off centre stage, the last mile on the way to the November election looked unexpectedly promising for a reunited and re-energised Democratic family, stimulated by the wishful thinking of many opinion makers. Kamala Harris could soon become the first female American President, as well as the first Asian tenant of the White House.

It was not to be, at least not yet. And the defeat announced in the early hours of 6 November was painful.

Blame games started off immediately among the Democrats, pointing alternatively to Kamala Harris's weaknesses and Joe Biden's too-late withdrawal, and sometimes to both, as the main causes of Trump's victory. What became rapidly obvious, however, was that Americans had voted more with their wallet than with their moral compass, that they were more worried by inflation than by the character of the next President or the risks he presented for democracy, that many of them conceived their identity more as working- or middle-class citizens struggling to pay their bills than as members of ethnic or sexual minorities or supporters of 'niche' causes. Moreover, less privileged Americans, with many Hispanics among them, were also worried by the arrival to their neighbourhoods of illegal immigrants whom they felt were given preferential treatment, pressured down their own salaries and negatively impacted the reputation of their well-established communities.

Initial depression gave way, in some centrist and centre-left quarters in the US and Europe, to a temptation to minimise the meaning of the defeat. After all, Trump's difference to Harris was narrower than Ronald Reagan's to Walter Mondale in 1984 or George H.W. Bush's to Michael Dukakis in 1988. He had not really significantly increased in absolute terms the number of votes nationally, compared to 2020. It was, as many said, simply another illustration of the demise of incumbents, which had been happening everywhere in the Western world – as if this was not in itself already a very worrying political reality. One commentator labelled 2024 as the 'graveyard of incumbents' to underline that Harris's defeat was to be expected, regardless of her merits.

And yet the worst thing moderates could do, in America or elsewhere in the world, is bury their heads in the sand after Trump's victory.

In fact, more granular analyses of the results soon led to the conclusion that Kamala Harris and Democrats around the country were perceived as distant and not connected by the very electorate that had been their *raison d'être*. They were seen by many as elitists, urban and somehow patronising. Their main causes did not echo the daily concerns of voters struggling with high inflation – the price of a Big Mac went up 21.1 per cent between 2019 and 2024. Their proposals did not address the anxiety of voters feeling insecure in their neighbourhoods. Young voters were more energised by Trump's discourse. Democrats had lost touch. The endorsement of Hollywood and Grammy grandees, billionaires and East and West Coast party stalwarts only added to the elite syndrome. The excesses of 'woke' culture did the rest. Divorce happened.

Trump's victory was not technically an electoral landslide, even if it was not far from it, but was definitely a political 'blowout', as Francis Fukuyama (him again ...) wrote in the *Financial Times*. Trump's second and more explosive eruption benefitted from those who abandoned the Democrats by not voting, including those disillusioned with Biden's approach to the Gaza war, and those who switched camps. Most importantly, and surprisingly, he made important inroads into younger generations and ethnic minorities, and stole the Democrats' most precious jewel: the trust of many working people, transversely across the country.

On the domestic American front, one can expect Trump's populist and protectionist agenda to be deployed with greater zeal and professionalism as compared to the largely improvised first mandate – experience, preparedness and Cabinet and staff loyalty will be key factors in implementing his programme (add a dose of personal revenge as well). There will be few moderate adults in the room, none of the 'conservatives that progressives like', to constrain him. Given the depth and width of Trump's victory, his new complicity with big tech and his control of the Supreme Court, it is also legitimate to wonder whether the famous US checks and balances will be fully operational.

In spite of this, I remain stubbornly confident in America's democracy and civil society. I am confident that both will be strong enough to prevent inadmissible excesses. I also count on federalism, and the often underestimated capacity of states to resist the federal government's agenda, to play a stabiliser role. Last but not least, the jury is still very much out as far as the real impact of Trump's 'tariffs and deportation' playbook on the American economy and the way voters will perceive its effects. There is always a mid-term election around the corner for each elected American President.

I am more concerned by the external repercussions of Trump's success. His triumph reflects and reveals a political and sociological reality existent elsewhere, and particularly in Europe, and confirms trends of the last couple of decades, as discussed in this book.

It will reverberate globally in two main ways: by sending an encouraging message to illiberal and authoritarian leaders, and by challenging US allies in Europe and Asia. The former will feel empowered by the example and inspired by the success of a populist agenda and discourse. The latter will struggle to accommodate an unpredictable but indispensable partner and to define their own autonomous path.

Trump's victory will stress test the capacity of Europeans, EU and UK alike, to decide exclusively on their own how to prioritise their policy and budgetary options. Their military dependence on America in the face of a Russian threat exposes their vulnerability towards a President who will not hesitate to politically weaponise defence spending. America's economic might will weigh heavily when discussing the re-balancing of trade relations, either across the Atlantic or with China. Haunted by Trump's transactional agenda, allies will be faced with hard choices – some that should have been dealt with a long time ago, others that could turn out to be almost existential.

Trump 2.0 should in any case be a wake-up call for moderate political leaders around the world, on both the left and right. They need to think seriously about their engagement with voters and their policy agendas, not to mention their political discourse. The priority cannot be other than to avoid the consolidation of extreme political forces; protect the quality and the decency of democratic processes; and prevent further polarisation within and among nations.

THE KAZAN REUNION

The pretext was a BRICS summit, bringing together old and recently added members. The location was Kazan – not an innocent choice of venue. I visited it as part of the G8 Sherpas' preparations for the St Petersburg summit (see Chapter 2). It impressed me not only for its central Asian features, but also, importantly, because it brings together, on one single hill, the local Kremlin, built by Ivan the Terrible, orthodox religious buildings and a Muslim mosque. Ecumenic and symbolic of several worlds coming together: a global crossroads. Vladimir Putin wanted to use it as the backdrop for a moment of global recognition, support and clout.

In Kazan, Putin welcomed not only the leaders of BRICS, but also several leaders from the 'global south' or 'global majority', as some like to call a differentiated group of countries that are not part of the West or the North, and even NATO member Turkey. Surrounded by forty-two heads of state and government, Putin trumpeted a new world order in the making. As leaders were meeting, the first North Korean soldiers were being deployed on Russian soil to fight the Ukrainian army: the first physical expression of a far-reaching bilateral agreement and a concrete illustration of the new CRINKs axis (China, Russia, Iran and North Korea).

In Kazan, Putin defeated the West's intent of marginalising him, China pursued its effective exercise of leadership of the anti-West movement, India enjoyed its role as the fastest-growing big economy and upcoming 'leader of the South' and several middle powers remained loyal to their 'sitting on the fence' and 'hedging their bets' strategic playbook. Most importantly for him, Putin rallied his guests around the mantra of a new, multipolar international order not commanded by the USA and the West, which was the unifying goal of many invited to Kazan.

It is true that Putin fell short of some of his key goals, such as gaining unconditional support for his actions in Ukraine or attaining an agreement for a payments system capable of circumventing the US dollar and related Western sanctions (ironically, according to good sources, the conference fees were paid in US dollars). Additionally, signs are accumulating that reflect serious economic and financial difficulties inside Russia as a result of the war effort and international sanctions, and some of Putin's initiatives, like the North Korean deal, reveal weakness rather than strength. In the medium term we could witness a serious deterioration in Putin's capabilities on the internal and external fronts, but we are not yet there.

For now, overall, the Kazan/CRINKs operation, combined with advances on the war theatre in Ukraine, have provided Putin with sufficient gains to allow him to engage with the post-Biden, Trump 2.0 cycle in a stronger tactical position.

BOILING POINT

Overall, the transition from 2024 to 2025 failed to provide reasons for optimism. For the first time, Israel and Iran engaged in open and consecutive military attacks, expanding and deepening the conflict in the region, adding to the Hamas and Hezbollah fronts. The Middle East found itself led further down a dangerous path of confrontation, while America and Europe managed their delicate political transitions. The German coalition fell the day after Trump's victory, confirming the weakness of executives in the Western world. The French government followed suit a few weeks later, leaving the EU's two top economies and most influential countries in vulnerable positions. In the Ukrainian theatre of war, Zelenskyy was allowed to use longer-range Western missiles, capable of reaching hundreds of kilometres into Russian territory. In reaction, Putin revised its nuclear doctrine to make Ukraine's allies with nuclear-striking capability legitimate targets and tested new threatening missiles. The only good news was the sudden fall of the Assad regime in Syria. However, it remains unclear exactly what it reveals of the relative power of Russia, Turkey and Iran, as well as USA and Israel, in the region. Most importantly, what the future will bring for martyrised Syrians is still very much in the balance. The ceasefire agreement between Israel and Hamas is certainly a welcome development but doubts remain about its sustainability.

What is clear today, as discussed, is that we are entering a more unpredictable, more anarchic and multifaceted global order that breaks away from established patterns. There will be more room and better acceptance, if not support, for strongmen with simplistic discourses. There will be a more transactional and less norms- and rules-based way of handling international relations, impacted by great powers' rivalry but not necessarily organised around stable blocs, although G7 and BRICS could consolidate even further as antagonising entities. What we are likely to witness is rather a dynamic system of allegiances and alignments fuelled by interests, flexible to a point of appearing inconsistent and incoherent, but ultimately serving short- and medium-term goals of each country or groups of countries, but void of an operating system founded on common values and principles. An operating system that would be capable of preventing and managing conflicts, and addressing existential needs of the planet and humankind.

The historical trends of the first quarter of the century have recently accelerated. The temperature has been rising steadily and could soon be close to boiling point.

Troubling coincidence: in Tatar language, *Kazan* means boiler.

Brussels
January 2025

Notes

Chapter 1

1. Francis Fukuyama, *The End of History and the Last Man* (Free Press, 1992).
2. 'Joint Comprehensive Plan of Action', signed in 2015 between Iran, Germany, the EU and the five permanent members of the UN Security Council (China, France, the Russian Federation, the UK and the USA).
3. Tribute to Thomas L. Friedman, *The World Is Flat: A Brief History of the Twenty-First Century* (Farrar, Strauss and Giroux, 2005).
4. There are multiple definitions of populism. All of them stress the fact that populism considers society as divided into two groups: 'the pure people' and 'the corrupt elite', as Professor Cas Mudde, a renowned specialist, has framed it. Populism proposes simple, if not simplistic, solutions to complex problems and feeds on antagonism, intolerance, aggressive language and dramatisation. It strives to appeal to ordinary people who feel their concerns are disregarded by established elite groups. Populists mistrust representative democracy and are fascinated by strongmen. Relevant authors on populism include, apart from Mudde, Jan-Werner Müller, Benjamin Moffit and John Judis, among others.

Chapter 2

1. Quotes as per my personal notes of the meeting.
2. Russia was the only country in the world given that 'double summit per year' treatment by the EU at the time.
3. In 2001, after meeting with President Putin for the first time, in Slovenia, US President George W. Bush said: 'I looked the man in the eye. I found him to be very straightforward and trustworthy. I was able to get a sense of his soul.' He obviously changed his mind later.
4. Mary Esther Sorotte, *Not One Inch: America, Russia, and the Making of Post-Cold War Stalemate* (Yale University Press, 2021).
5. Leonard Cohen's song 'Anthem', 1992.
6. Mario Draghi, then President of the European Central Bank, speaking at the Global Investment Conference, London, 26 July 2012.

7. Remarks by President Obama to the White House Press Corps, 20 August 2012.
8. Article by Ben Rhodes in *The Atlantic* magazine, 3 June 2018.
9. In conversation with the author, spring 2024.
10. In conversation with the author, spring 2024.
11. In conversation with the author, spring 2024.
12. In conversation with the author, spring 2024.
13 In conversation with the author, spring 2024.
14. The Mercosur/Mercosul group is composed of the following South American countries: Brazil, Argentina, Uruguay and Paraguay.
15. Jake Sullivan's speech at the Brookings Institution, 'A Foreign Policy for the Middle Class', Washington DC, April 2023.
16. GAVI is The Vaccine Alliance. According to its official website, gavi.org, it has helped vaccinate more than 1 billion children in seventy-eight lower-income countries, preventing more than 17.3 million future deaths. Its core partners are the World Health Organization, UNICEF, the World Bank and the Bill and Melinda Gates Foundation, and it works with a large group of donors and vaccine manufacturers. More at gavi.org.

Chapter 3

1. This calendar coincidence allegedly did not please China. Curiously enough, years later, Western intelligence services claimed that the Chinese authorities had agreed with their Russian counterparts that the invasion of Ukraine should be delayed in order to happen only after the closing ceremony of the Winter Olympic Games held in China, in 2022. Conspiracy theories aside, the facts are that the games finished on 20 February and the invasion started on the 24th.
2 In conversation with the author, spring 2024.
3. Speech by President Bill Clinton at the Paul H. Nitze School of Advanced International Studies (SAIS) of the Johns Hopkins University, in Washington DC, on 9 March 2000.

Chapter 4

1. Exactly 1,020 days or 2 years, 9 months and 16 days.
2. In the aftermath of the British decision to leave the EU, two international treaties were negotiated, signed and ratified by the UK and the EU: the Withdrawal Agreement and the Trade and Co-operation Agreement (TCA).
3. Dominic Cummings on 'Twitter' (now 'X'), on 10 October 2021: reacting to another comment saying that David Frost had stated that the government intended to implement the protocol as agreed, he writes:

'He has to say that! It was never my intention, I always intended an IMBill [Internal Market Bill] after we won a majority to tidy things up.'
4. A period during which, while formally outside the Union, the UK would still be treated like a member state of the EU regarding trade and economic matters until the new treaty, the future TCA, came into force.

Chapter 5
1. In conversation with the author, spring 2024.
2 All Stefanie Bolzen quotes from conversation with the author, spring 2024.
3. Peter Ricketts, *Hard Choices: The Making and Unmaking of Global Britain* (Atlantic Books, 2021).
4. In conversation with the author, spring 2024.
5. In conversation with the author, spring 2024.
6. In conversation with the author, 2024.
7. In conversation with the author, 2024.

Chapter 6
1. 'Eurobarometer' public opinion surveys, produced by the European Commission for many decades, show a remarkable increase in support for the EU during the first quarter of this century. In 2000, 49 per cent of EU citizens found that EU membership had been positive. In 2024, that number was 71 per cent.
2. Interview with the BBC in June 2004: 'about as difficult a job as there is in the Western world'.
3. Speech by Radoslaw Sikorski, Polish foreign minister, 28 November 2011, in Berlin.
4. *Anonymous, Primary Colors: A Novel of Politics* (Random House, 1996).
5. In conversation with the author, spring 2024.
6. In conversation with the author, spring 2024.
7. Catherine Ashton, *And Then What? Inside Stories of 21st Century Diplomacy* (Elliot and Thompson, 2023).
8. As Secretary of State and Minister of Foreign Affairs of Portugal, José Manuel Barroso played key roles in the processes that led to the peace accords in Angola and the independence of Timor-Leste.
9. The '7/7' London terrorist attacks of 7 July 2005 caused fifty-six deaths (including the four terrorists) and 784 injured.
10 In conversation with the author, spring 2024.
11. In conversation with the author, spring 2024.
12. UN geographic groups: Western European and others; Eastern European; Latin-American and Caribbean; African; Asia-Pacific.
13. The first stage of a candidature to the Security Council would run

inside each geographic group, where countries organise the calendar and the sequence of their applications. Some countries announce their candidature ten years or more before the actual slot is available and start campaigning several years ahead of the start of their mandate. The existence of anachronic geographic groups, established long ago in the early days of the UN and reflecting the Cold War reality, resulted into the odd situation of having our twenty-eight EU member states scattered around three different groups: the 'Western European and others' group, the 'Eastern European' group and even the 'Asia-Pacific' group. This had the advantage of increasing the likelihood of having EU countries elected to the Council and to other bodies of the UN, and provided us with access to information and intelligence about discussions in those groups. However, it had one major downside: it was odd to have our central and eastern European members siding with Russia, and Cyprus siding with China, in their respective groups.

14. Kurt Waldheim, from Austria, had been secretary-general, but at the time his country was not yet part of the EU.

Chapter 7

1   All Antonio Patriota quotes from conversation with the author, spring 2024.

2. Samuel P. Huntington, *The Clash of Civilisations and the Remaking of the World Order* (Simon and Schuster, 1996).

3. The Bermuda Triangle is, according to the *Encyclopaedia Britannica*, 'a section of the North Atlantic Ocean off North America in which more than 50 ships and 20 airplanes are said to have mysteriously disappeared. The area, whose boundaries are not universally agreed upon, has a triangular shape that reaches approximately from the Atlantic coast of Florida to Bermuda to the islands known as the Greater Antilles.' However, according to the US National Oceanic and Atmospheric Administration, 'there is no evidence that mysterious disappearances occur with any greater frequency in the Bermuda triangle than in any other large, well-travelled area of the ocean'. The Bermuda Triangle has become an urban legend used to refer to potentially doomed situations and projects.

4. George W. Ball (1909–94) was an American diplomat and banker. He served in the State Department and was known for his opposition to the escalation of the American effort in the Vietnam War. He held the positions of Under-Secretary of State and Ambassador to the United Nations. He worked with Jean Monnet in the early days of European integration, helping consolidate American support, specifically via the

Marshall Plan.

5. Graham Allison, *Destined for War: Can America and China Escape Thucydides' Trap?* (Scribe, 2017).

6. The 'Brussels effect' is an expression coined by Professor Anu Bradford, from Columbia Law School, and refers to the capacity of the EU to influence global regulation, norms and standards.

Acknowledgements

Like all relevant things in my adult life, this book would not have been possible without the love, support, encouragement and critical views of my wife, Maria Ana Jara de Carvalho. I wholeheartedly thank Miana for that. It would not have made much sense either without my concern about the world that our beloved sons, João Maria and Lourenço, and our grandchildren, Júlia, Félix and George, will live in. For all these reasons, this book is dedicated to them. To my late father and to my mother, a word of gratitude for their love and for allowing me to spread my wings already as a teenager.

As with a village for the education of a child, it takes many people's contributions to shape one's professional life. I could count on great professionals in school and academia – particularly in Liceu Pedro Nunes and Faculdade de Letras, in Lisbon – as well as in journalism and diplomacy. All helped in improving my skills and enlarging my horizons.

Starting with my seven-year stint as a journalist in the 1970s and '80s, my gratitude goes to Luis de Barros, Mário Mesquita, Mário Bettencourt Resendes, Fernando Pires, Mário Zambujal and many other distinguished journalists who shaped me as a very young reporter at *Diário de Notícias*, in Lisbon. In regard to my EU career, I wish to recognise all those who trusted me as direct or indirect bosses, among whom are Robert Pendville, António de Menezes, Claus-Dieter Ehlermann, Bruno Dethomas, Nikolaus van der Pas, Commissioners António Cardoso e Cunha, Abel Matutes, João de Deus Pinheiro and Benita Ferrero-Waldner, Presidents Jacques Santer, Romano Prodi, Jean-Claude Juncker, Ursula von der Leyen, Herman van Rompuy, Donald Tusk and Charles Michel, and High Representatives Cathy Ashton, Federica Mogherini and Josep Borrel. A word of respect for Jacques Delors, Emile Noël and Pascal Lamy, who influenced me in my early days at the European Commission, and Karl-Heinz Höller, who first hired me at the EC Delegation in Lisbon, in 1982.

A special word of gratitude goes to my friend and former boss, José Manuel Durão Barroso, whose trust back in 2004 allowed me to widen my professional perspectives on politics, geopolitics and power, the main subjects of this book. We share a lot about all these issues, even if an insuperable difference remains on football club preferences.

Regarding this book, a number of friends have, in different ways, helped me to move this project forward since my early days of retirement from the EU, at the beginning of 2023. Some contributed with ideas for the concept – even if they were not aware of the book plan – others with drafting suggestions and pictures, some even with quotes in the text. In alphabetical order, the list includes (with the exception of those who preferred not to be named) Paul Adamson, James Arroyo, Cathy Ashton, José Manuel Barroso, Gavin Barwell, Miguel Berger, Catherine Barnard, Federico Bianchi, Stefanie Bolzen, Ricardo Borges de Castro, António Cabral, Carlos Costa, the late José Cutileiro, Kim Darroch, Martin Fraser, Fernando Frutuoso de Melo, Joana Gonçalves, Charles Grant, Jean-Marie Guéhenno, António Guterres, Jonathan Hill, Maria Ana Jara de Carvalho, Michael Jay, Nuno Jonet, Michael Kenny, Julian King, the Earl of Kinnoull, Charles Kupchan, Dominic Lawson, David Liddington, Peter Mandelson, Nicole Mannion, João Marques de Almeida, Antonio Patriota, Marc Pierini, Jonathan Powell, David Rennie, Ivan Rogers, Stefano Sannino, Brendan Simms, Julian Smith, Hugo Sobral, Jack Straw, Lourenço Vale de Almeida, Pierre Vimont, Bart Vodderie, Fabien Zuleeg and my good old friend João Paulo Velez, who was never too far away. I apologise in advance to those I may have missed in this list, but I am sure they will find their points of view somehow reflected in these pages – or not.

I wish to thank those in the academic community in the USA and the UK who gave me the opportunity to teach and lecture in their respective universities – or simply enjoy the exchange of views with faculty and students around the campuses – and thus allowed me to focus for more than a year on the subjects covered in the book: from the University of Columbia, in New York, former and current deans of the School of International and Public Affairs (SIPA), Merit Janow and Keren Yarhi-Milo, as well as Senior Associate Dean Hazel May, for inviting me as the '2023 George W. Ball Professor' and helping me teach my course on 'Divorce of Nations and Role of Diplomacy'; from the University of Cambridge, at Trinity College, Master Dame Sally Davies and particularly Professor Catherine Barnard and, at Peterhouse, Master Andy Parker and particularly Professor Brendan Simms.

Last but not least, I thank my agents at NorthBank, Diane Banks and Matthew Cole, and my editors at Flint Books, Claire Hartley and Chrissy McMorris, for their precious help in making this book come into being.

Index

Note: *italicised* page references indicate illustrations.